POOR LAW UN RECORDS

4. Gazetteer of England and Wales

Jeremy Gibson and Frederic A. Youngs Jr.

SECOND EDITION

Federation of Family History Societies

First published 1993 by the
Federation of Family History Societies.

Second edition, 1997, published by
Federation of Family History Societies (Publications) Ltd., c/o The Benson Room,
Birmingham and Midland Institute, Margaret Street, Birmingham B3 3BS, England
in association with the
Royal Historical Society.

ISBN 1 86006 062 5

Cover graphics by Linda Haywood.
Cover illustration: from George Cruickshank's 'Oliver asks for more', in Charles Dickens'
Oliver Twist.

Printed by Parchment (Oxford) Limited.

Acknowledgments
Sixty pages of this Gazetteer are directly photocopied from the Royal Historical Society's
monumental two-part *Guide to the Local Administrative Units of England*. Volume One,
Southern England, appeared in 1980, with a corrected reprint in 1981. A fortunate outcome
of the long gestation period of the Guide to *Poor Law Union Records* is that Volume Two,
Northern England, eventually published in 1991, was thus available too. The sections on the
Poor Law Unions of each English county immeasurably helped the compilation of the Guide.
The Royal Historical Society's generosity in allowing these sections to be reprinted here will
I believe encourage the historical research which is the avowed aim of both that Society and
the Federation of Family History Societies. I should like to mention specifically the friendly
help of Mrs J. McCarthy, the Society's executive secretary, and the provision of a copy of the
1981 reprint, from which the relevant pages have been copied.
The fact that these two volumes were compiled by Frederic A. Youngs, jr., of Louisanna
State University, once again shows the debt that British historians owe to the 'special
relationship', and, though he has had no direct hand in the actual preparation of this
publication, it would be entirely inappropriate for his name not to appear on the title page
together with mine. His was the research which has provided this authoritative information
on the composition of English Poor Law Unions between 1834 and 1930. The copious superior
figures denoting references have been left in this photographic reprint, though of course for the
sources to which they refer it is necessary to consult the Royal Historical Society volumes.
There is no recently published source for the composition of Poor Law Unions in Wales. I
was advised by the National Library of Wales to consult the *1851 Census Population Tables,
XI, Welsh Division*, and the Welsh section (pp. 63 on) is based on that. However, in this second
edition, these pages have been freshly typeset. I am most grateful to Catherine Camfield for
undertaking this arduous task, and to her mother, Sheila Rowlands, for proof reading.
J.S.W.G.

Federation of Family History Societies (Publications) Ltd. is a wholly owned subsidiary of the
Federation of Family History Societies, Registered Charity No. 1038721.

BEDFORDSHIRE

In Bedfordshire Poor Law County:[14]
AMPTHILL PLU[15]
Ampthill, Aspley Guise (1899–1930), Aspley Heath (1899–1930), Battlesden (1899–1930), Clophill, Cranfield, Eversholt (1899–1930), Flitton, Flitwick, Gravenhurst (1888–1930), Lower Gravenhurst (1835–88), Upper Gravenhurst (1835–88), Harlington (1899–1930), Haynes, Higham Gobion, Holcot (1899–1930), Houghton Conquest, Husborne Crawley (1899–1930), Lidlington, Marston Moretaine, Maulden, Millbrook, Milton Bryan (1899–1930), Potsgrove (1899–1930), Pulloxhill, Ridgmont (1899–1930), Salford (1899–1930), Shillington, Silsoe, Steppingley, Tingrith (1899–1930), Toddington (1899–1930), Westoning, Woburn (1899–1930)
BEDFORD PLU
Great Barford, Bedford St Cuthbert, Bedford St John, Bedford St Mary, Bedford St Paul, Bedford St Peter, Biddenham, Bletsoe, Bolnhurst, Bromham, Cardington, Carlton, Chellington, Clapham, Colmworth, Colworth Farm (1858–95), Cople, Eastcotts, Elstow, Felmersham, Goldington, Harrold, Kempston, Kempston Rural (1896–1930), Keysoe, Knotting, Melchbourne, Milton Ernest, Oakley, Odell, Pavenham, Ravensden, Renhold, Riseley, Roxton, Sharnbrook, Souldrop, Stagsden, Stevington, Thurleigh, Turvey, Wilden, Willington, Wilshamstead, Wootton, Yelden
BIGGLESWADE PLU
Arlesey, Astwick, Biggleswade, Blunham, Campton, Chicksands (1858–1930), Clifton, Dunton, Edworth, Everton, Eyeworth, Cockayne Hatley, Henlow, Langford, Meppershall, Moggerhanger, Northill, Potton, Sandy, Shefford, Shefford Hardwick, Southill, Upper Stondon, Stotfold, Sutton, Tempsford, Old Warden, Wrestlingworth
LEIGHTON BUZZARD PLU[15]
Billington, Chalgrave (1899–1930), Eaton Bray (1840s–1930), Eggington, Heath and Reach, Hockliffe (1899–1930), Leighton Buzzard, Stanbridge, Tilsworth (1899–1930)
LUTON PLU
Barton in the Clay, Caddington, Dunstable, Eaton Bray (1835–40s), Houghton Regis, Humbershoe (1835–97), Hyde (1896–1930), Kensworth, Leagrave (1896–1928), Limbury (1896–1928), Luton (1835–94), Luton (1896–1930), Luton Rural (1894–96), Luton Urban (1894–96), Streatley, Stopsley (1896–1930), Studham, Sundon, Totternhoe, Whipsnade
WOBURN PLU[15]
Aspley Guise, Aspley Heath (1883–99), Battlesden, Chalgrave, Eversholt, Harlington, Hockliffe, Holcot, Husborne Crawley, Milton Bryan, Potsgrove, Ridgmont, Salford, Tilsworth, Tingrith, Toddington, Woburn

In Other Poor Law Counties:
HITCHIN PLU[16] (Herts)
Holwell
ST NEOTS PLU[17] (Hunts)
Little Barford, Dean, Eaton Socon, Pertenhall, Shelton, Little Staughton, Tilbrook
WELLINGBOROUGH PLU (Northants)
Farndish (1835–84), Podington, Wymington

BERKSHIRE

In Berkshire Poor Law County:[12]
ABINGDON PLU (Berks, Oxon)
Abingdon (1894–1930), Abingdon St Helen (1835–94), Abingdon St Helen Without (1894–1930), Abingdon St Nicholas (1835–94), Appleford, Appleton with Eaton, Bagley Wood (1835–1900), Besselsleigh, Chandlings Farm (1835–1900), Culham, Cumnor, Draycot Moor, Drayton, Frilford, Fyfield, Garford, North Hinksey, South Hinksey, Kingston Bagpuize, Lyford, Marcham, Milton, Radley, Seacourt, Steventon, Sunningwell, Sutton Courtenay, Sutton Wick, Tubney, Wootton, Wytham
BRADFIELD PLU (Berks, Oxon)
Aldermaston, Ashampstead, Basildon, Beech Hill, Beenham, Bradfield, Bucklebury, Burghfield, Englefield, Frilsham, Grazeley, Padworth, Pangbourne, Purley, Stanford Dingley, Stratfield Mortimer, Streatley, Sulham, Sulhamstead Abbots, Sulhamstead Bannister Lower End, Sulhamstead Bannister Upper End, Theale (1894–1930), Tidmarsh, Tilehurst, Ufton Nervet, Whitchurch, Wokefield, Yattendon
COOKHAM PLU (renamed 1899 'MAIDENHEAD')
Bisham, Bray, Cookham, Hurley, Maidenhead (1894–1930), Shottesbrooke, White Waltham, Waltham St Lawrence
EASTHAMPSTEAD PLU
Binfield, Crowthorne (1894–1930), Easthampstead, Sandhurst, Warfield, Winkfield
FARINGDON PLU (Berks, Oxon, Glos)
Ashbury, Baulking, Bourton, Buckland, Buscot, Charney Bassett, Coleshill, Compton Beauchamp, Great Coxwell, Little Coxwell, Eaton Hastings, Great Faringdon, Fernham, Hatford, Hinton Waldrist, Kingston Lisle, Longcott, Longworth, Pusey, Shellingford, Shrivenham, Stanford in the Vale, Uffington, Watchfield, Woolstone

3

HUNGERFORD PLU (Berks, Wilts, renamed 1896
'HUNGERFORD AND RAMSBURY')
Avington, Chilton Foliat,[13] Combe,[14] East Garston, Hungerford, Inkpen, Kintbury, Lambourn,
Shalbourn, East Shefford, West Shefford, West
Woodhay

MAIDENHEAD PLU–renaming 1899 of COOKHAM PLU, qv

NEWBURY PLU
Boxford, Brimpton, Chieveley, Cold Ash (1894–
1930), Enborne, Greenham, Hamstead Marshall,
Leckhampstead, Midgham, Newbury, Sandleford,
Shaw cum Donnington, Speen, Thatcham, Wasing,
Welford, Winterbourne, Woolhampton

READING PLU
Reading (1905–30), Reading St Giles (1835–
1905), Reading St Lawrence (1835–1905), Reading
St Mary (1835–1905)

WALLINGFORD PLU
Aston Tirrold, Aston Upthorpe, Brightwell, Cholsey, Clapcot (1894–1930), Didcot, East Hagbourne, West Hagbourne, North Moreton, South
Moreton, Moulsford, Sotwell, Wallingford (1919–
30), Wallingford All Hallows (1835–1919), Wallingford Castle Precincts (1858–94), Wallingford
St Leonard (1835–1919), Wallingford St Mary le
More (1835–1919), Wallingford St Peter (1835–
1919), Little Wittenham, Long Wittenham

WANTAGE PLU
Aldworth, Ardington, Beedon, Blewbury, Brightwalton, Catmore, Chaddleworth, East Challow,
West Challow, Charlton, Childrey, Chilton, Compton, Denchworth, Farnborough, Fawley, Goosey,
Grove, Hampstead Norris, East Hanney, West Hanney, Harwell, East Hendred, West Hendred, East
Ilsley, West Ilsley, Letcombe Bassett, Letcombe
Regis, East Lockinge, West Lockinge, Peasemore,
Sparsholt, Upton, Wantage

WINDSOR PLU
Clewer (1835–94), Clewer Within (1894–1930),
Clewer Without (1894–1930), Sunningdale
(1894–1930), Sunninghill, New Windsor, Old
Windsor, pt Windsor Castle (1866–1930)

WOKINGHAM PLU
Arborfield, Barkham, Earley, Finchampstead, Broad
Hinton, Hurst St Nicholas (1894–1930), Newland,
Remenham (1894–1930), Ruscombe, Shinfield,
Sonning, Swallowfield (1894–1930), East Swallowfield (1866–94), West Swallowfield (1866–
94), Twyford (1894–1930), Wargrave, Whistley
(1835–94), Winnersh, Wokingham (1835–94),
Wokingham Within (1894–1930), Wokingham
Without (1894–1930)

In Other Poor Law Counties:
HENLEY PLU (Oxon)
Remenham (1835–94)

BUCKINGHAMSHIRE

In Buckinghamshire Poor Law County:[9]
AMERSHAM PLU
Amersham, Ashley Green (1897–1930), Beaconsfield, Chalfont St Giles, Chalfont St Peter, Chartridge (1899–1930), Chenies, Chesham, Chesham
Bois, Coleshill, Latimer (1899–1930), Lee (1838–
1930), Great Missenden (1838–1930), Little Missenden (1901–30), Penn, Seer Green

AYLESBURY PLU
Ashendon, Aston Abbots, Aston Clinton, Aston
Sandford, Aylesbury, Bierton with Broughton,
Buckland, Chearsley, Cholesbury, Creslow, Cublington, Cuddington, Dinton-with-Ford and Upton,
Drayton Beauchamp, Grendon Underwood, Haddenham, Halton, Hardwick, Hartwell, Hawridge,
Hulcott, Kingswood, Ludgershall, Fleet Marston,
Oving, Pitchcott, Quainton, Quarrendon, Shipton
Lee (1835–86), Stone, Waddesdon, Weedon, Westcott, Weston Turville, Whitchurch, Lower Winchendon, Upper Winchendon, Wingrave with Rowsham,
Woodham, Wotton Underwood

BUCKINGHAM PLU
Addington, Adstock, Akeley, Barton Hartshorn,
Beachampton, Charndon, Chetwode, Middle Claydon, Steeple Claydon, Edgcott, Foscott, Hillesden,
Leckhampstead, Lillingstone Dayrell, Lillingstone
Lovell,[10] Luffield Abbey (1858–1930), Marsh Gibbon, Maids' Moreton, Padbury, Poundon, Preston
Bissett, Radclive-cum-Chackmore, Shalstone,
Stowe, Water Stratford, Thornborough, Thornton,
Tingewick, Twyford

ETON PLU
Boveney, Burnham, Datchet, Denham, Dorney,
Eton, Eton Wick (1894–1930), Farnham Royal,
Fulmer, Gerrard's Cross (1895–1930), Hedgerley,
Hedgerley Dean, Hitcham, Horton, Iver, Langley
Marish, Slough (1894-1930), Stoke in Slough
(1894–96), Stoke Poges, Taplow, Upton cum
Chalvey (1835–1901), Wexham, Wyrardisbury

NEWPORT PAGNELL PLU
Astwood, Bletchley, Bradwell, Bradwell Abbey
(1861-1930), New Bradwell (1919–30), Cold Brayfield, Bow Brickhill, Great Brickhill, Little Brickhill, Broughton, Castlethorpe, Chicheley, Clifton
Reynes, North Crawley, Emberton, Gayhurst, Hanslope, Hardmead, Haversham, Lathbury, Lavendon,
Great Linford, Little Linford, Loughton, Milton
Keynes, Moulsoe, Newport Pagnell, Newton Blossonville, Newton Longville, Olney, Olney Park
Farm (1861–1930), Petsoe Manor (1861–1930),
Ravenstone, Shenley Church End, Sherington,
Stantonbury, Stoke Goldington, Fenny Stratford,
Tyringham with Filgrave, Warrington, Water Eaton,
Wavendon, Weston Underwood, Woughton on the
Green

WINSLOW PLU
East Claydon, Drayton Parslow, Dunton, Granborough, Hoggeston, Hogshaw, Great Horwood, Little Horwood, North Marston, Mursley, Nash, Shenley Brook End, Stewkley, Swanbourne, Tattenhoe, Whaddon, Winslow

WYCOMBE PLU
Bledlow, Bradenham, Ellesborough, Fawley (1835–45), Fingest, Hambledon (1835–45), Great Hampden (1835–85), Great and Little Hampden (1885–1930), Little Hampden (1835–85), Hedsor, Horsenden, Hughenden, Ibstone, Ilmer, Great Kimble (1835–85), Great and Little Kimble (1885–1930), Little Kimble (1835–85), Lewknor Uphill (1866–85), Great Marlow, Little Marlow, Marlow Urban (1896–1930), Medmenham (1835–45), Little Missenden (1835–1901), Radnage, Monk's Risborough, Princes Risborough, Saunderton, Stoke Mandeville, Stokenchurch,[10] Turville, Wendover, Wooburn, Wycombe (1866–96), Chepping Wycombe (1835–94), Chepping Wycombe Rural (1894–1930), Chepping Wycombe Urban (1894–96), High Wycombe (1896–1930), West Wycombe

In Other Poor Law Counties:
BERKHAMPSTEAD PLU (Herts)
Marsworth, Nettleden,[11] Pitstone (1835–1923)
BICESTER PLU (Oxon)
Boarstall
BRACKLEY PLU[12] (Northants)
Biddlesdeon, Turweston, Westbury
HENLEY PLU[13] (Oxon)
Fawley, Hambleden, Medmenham
LEIGHTON BUZZARD PLU (Beds)
Cheddington, Edlesborough, Grove, Ivinghoe, Linslade, Mendmore, Pitstone (1923–30), Stapleton, Soulbury, Stoke Hammond, Wing
POTTERSPURY PLU[14] (Northants)
Calverton, Stony Stratford East, Stony Stratford West, Wolverton
THAME PLU (Oxon)
Brill, Chilton, Long Crendon, Dorton, Granborough, Ickford, Kingsey,[15] Oakley, Shabbington, Worminghall

CAMBRIDGESHIRE

In Cambridge Poor Law County[7]
CAMBRIDGE PLU
Cambridge (1900–30), Cambridge All Saints (until 1900), Cambridge Holy Sepulchre (until 1900), Cambridge Holy Trinity (until 1900), Cambridge St Andrew the Great (until 1900), Cambridge St Andrew the Less (until 1900), Cambridge St Benedict (until 1900), Cambridge St Botolph (until 1900), Cambridge St Clement (until 1900), Cambridge St Edward (until 1900), Cambridge St Giles (until 1900), Cambridge St Mary the Great (until 1900), Cambridge St Mary the Less (until 1900), Cambridge St Michael (until 1900), Cambridge St Peter (until 1886)

CAXTON PLU (Cambs, Hunts)
Arrington, Bourn, Caldecote, Caxton, Croxton, Croydon, Elsworth, Eltisley, Great Eversden, Little Eversden, Hardwick, East Hatley, Hatley St George, Kingston, Knapwell, Longstowe, Orwell, Papworth Everard, Papworth St Agnes, Tadlow, Toft, Wimpole

CHESTERTON PLU
Barton, Cambridge Without (1912–23), Cherry Hinton, Chesterton, Childerley, Comberton, Coton, Cottenham, Fen Ditton, Dry Drayton, Fulbourn, Girton, Grantchester, Harlton, Harston, Haslingfield, Hauxton, Histon, Horningsea, Impington, Landbeach, Madingley, Milton, Newton, Oakington, Rampton, Great Shelford, Little Shelford, Long Stanton All Saints, Long Stanton St Michael, Stapleford, Stow cum Quy, Teversham, Trumpington, Waterbeach, Westwick (1866[8]–1930), Great Wilbraham, Little Wilbraham, Willingham

ELY PLU (Cambs/IoE, Norfolk)
Coveney, Downham, Ely College (1858[8]–1930), Ely St Mary, Ely Trinity, Grunty Fen (1858[8]–1930), Haddenham, Littleport, Mepal, Redmere,[9] Stretham, Sutton, Thetford, Wentworth, Wilburton, Witcham, Witcham Gravel (1894–1930), Witchford

LINTON PLU (Cambs, Essex)
Great Abington, Little Abington, Babraham, Balsham, Bartlow, Castle Camps, Shudy Camps, Carlton, Duxford, Hildersham, Hinxton, Horseheath, Ickleton, Linton, Pampisford, Sawston, Weston Colville, Whittlesford, West Wickham, West Wratting

NEWMARKET PLU (Cambs, Suffolk/W Suffolk)
Ashley, Bottisham, Brinkley, Burrough Green, Burwell, Cheveley, Chippenham, Wood Ditton, Dullingham, Fordham, Isleham, Kennett, Kirtling, Landwade, Newmarket All Saints,[10] Snailwell, Soham, Stetchworth, Swaffham Bulbeck, Swaffham Prior, Westley Waterless, Wicken

WHITTLESEY PLU
Whittlesey (1926–30), Whittlesey Rural (1894–1926), Whittlesey St Andrew (1836–50), Whittlesey St Mary (1836–50), Whittlesey St Mary and St Andrew (1850–94), Whittlesey Urban (1894–1926)

Cambridgeshire *continued*

WISBECH PLU   (Cambs/IoE, Norfolk)
Elm, Leverington, Newton, Outwell,[11] Parson Drove, Tydd St Giles, Upwell,[11] Wisbech St Mary, Wisbech St Peter

NORTH WITCHFORD PLU
Benwick, Chatteris, Doddington, Manea, March, Welches Dam, Wimblington

In Other Poor Law Counties:
DOWNHAM PLU   (Norfolk)
Welney[11]

PETERBOROUGH PLU (Northants)
Stanground,[12] Stanground North (1905–30), Thorney

ROYSTON PLU   (Herts[13])
Abington Pigotts, Barrington, Bassingbourn, Great Chishill,[14] Little Chishill,[14] Fowlmere, Foxton, Heydon,[14] Kneesworth, Litlington, Melbourn, Meldreth, Guilden Morden, Steeple Morden, Royston,[15] Shepreth, Shingay, Thriplow, Wendy, Whaddon

ST IVES PLU   (Hunts)
Boxworth, Conington, Fen Drayton, Lolworth, Over, Swavesey

ST NEOTS PLU   (Hunts)
Graveley

CHESHIRE

In Ches Poor Law County:[32]
ALTRINCHAM PLU (1836–95[33])
Agden, Altrincham, Ashley, Ashton upon Mersey, Aston by Budworth, Baguley, Bexton, Bollington, Bollinfee, Bowdon, Carrington, Dunham Massey, Northern Etchells, Fulshaw (1836–94), Hale, Handforth cum Basen, Knutsford Nether, Knutsford Over, High Legh, Lymm, Marthall cum Warford, Mere, Millington, Mobberley, Northenden, Ollerton, Partington, Peover Inferior, Peover Superior, Pickmere, Plumley, Pownall Fee (1836–94), Rostherne, Sale, Styal (1894–95), Tabley Inferior, Tabley Superior, Tatton, Timperley, Toft, Unnamed (1894–95), Warburton, Wilmslow (1894–95)

BIRKENHEAD PLU (1891–1930)
Bidston cum Ford, Birkenhead, Claughton with Grange (1891–98), Liscard (1891–1912), Noctorum, Oxton (1891–98), Poulton cum Seacombe (1891–1912), Tranmere (1891–98), Wallasey

GREAT BOUGHTON PLU (1837–71) (Ches, Flints)
Aldersey, Aldford, Ashton, Bache, Backford (soon after 1837[34]–71), Barrow,[35] Barton, Blacon cum Crabwall (soon after 1837[34]–71), Great Boughton, Broxton, Buerton, Burton by Tarvin, Caldecott, Capenhurst, Carden, Caughall, Chorlton by Backford, Chowley, Christleton, Churton by Aldford, Churton by Farndon, Churton Heath, Clotton Hoofield, Clutton, Coddington, Cotton Abbotts, Cotton Edmunds, Crewe, Croughton, Dodleston[36] (1837–53), Duckington (1837–53), Duddon, Dunham on the Hill, Eaton (1837–53), Eccleston (1837–53), Edge (1837–53), Edgerley, Elton, Farndon, Golborne Bellow, Golborne David, Grafton, Handley, Hapsford, Harthill, Hatton, Hockenhull, Hoole, Horton, Horton cum Peel, Huntington, Huxley, Iddinshall, Ince, Kelsall, Kings Marsh, Lower Kinnerton (1837–53), Lea by Backford, Lea Newbold, Littleton, Marlston cum Lache (1837–53), Mollington Banastre, Mollington Tarrant, Moston, Mouldsworth, Newton by Chester, Newton by Tattenhall, Picton, Poulton (1837–53), Prior's Heys (1858–71), Pulford (1837–53), Rowton, Saighton, Great Saughall (1837–53), Little Saughall (1837–53), Shotwick (1837–53), Shotwick Park (1837–53), Stanlow, Great Stanney, Little Stanney, Bruen Stapleford, Foulk Stapleford, Stoke, Stretton, Guilden Sutton, Tarvin, Tattenhall, Thornton le Moors, Tilston, Bridge Trafford, Mickle Trafford, Wimbolds Trafford, Upton by Chester, Waverton, Wervin, Willington, Woodbank (1837–53)

BUCKLOW PLU (1895[33]–1930)
Agden, Altrincham, Ashley, Ashton upon Mersey, Aston by Budworth, Baguley, Bexton, Bollington, Bolinfee, Bowdon, Carrington, Dunham Massey, Northern Etchells, Hale, Knutsford, High Legh, Lymm, Marthall cum Warford, Mere, Millington, Mobberley, Northenden, Ollerton, Partington, Peover Inferior, Peover Superior, Pickmere, Plumley, Ringway (1900–30), Rostherne, Sale, Styal, Tabley Inferior, Tabley Superior, Tatton, Timperley, Toft, Unnamed, Warburton, Wilmslow

Cheshire *continued*

CHESTER INCORP FOR POOR (1762[37]—1869), PLU (1869—1930) [Ches, Flints (1871—1930)] Bache (1871—1930), Backford (1871—1930), Blacon cum Crabwall (1871—1930), Great Boughton (1871—1930), Capenhurst (1871—1930), Caughall (1871—1930), Chester (1884—1930), Chester Castle (1869—1930), Chester Holy Trinity (1762—1884), Chester St Bridget (1762—1884), Chester St John the Baptist (1762—1884), Chester St Martin (1762—1884), Chester St Mary on the Hill (1762—1884), Chester St Michael (1762—1884), Chester St Olave (1762—1884), Chester St Peter (1762—1884), Chorlton by Backford (1871—1930), Christleton (1871—1930), Claverton (1871—1930), Croughton (1871—1930), Dodleston (1871—1930), Dunham on the Hill (1871—1930), Eaton (1871—1930), Eccleston (1871—1930), Elton (1871—1930), Hapsford (1871—1930), Hoole (1871—1930), Hoole Village (1894—1930), Ince (1871—1930), Lower Kinnerton (1871—1930), Lea by Backford (1871—1930), Littleton (1871—1930), Marlstone cum Lache (1871—1930), Mollington (1901—30), Mollington Banastre (1871—1901), Mollington Tarrant (1871—1901), Moston (1871—1930), Newton by Chester (1871—1930), Picton (1871—1930), Great Saughall (1871—1930), Little Saughall (1871—1930), Shotwick (1871—1930), Shotwick Park (1871—1930), Stanlow (1871—1911), Great Stanney (1871—1930), Little Stanney (1871—1930), Stoke (1871—1930), Thornton le Moors (1871—1930), Bridge Trafford (1871—1930), Mickle Trafford (1871—1930), Wimbolds Trafford (1871—1930), Upton by Chester (1871—1930), Wervin (1871—1930), Woodbank (1871—1930)

CONGLETON PLU (Ches, Staffs) Alsager, Arclid, Betchton, Blackden, Bradwall, Brereton cum Smethwick, Buglawton, Congleton, Cotton, Cranage, Davenport, Elton, Goostrey cum Barnshaw, Hassall, Church Hulme, Hulme Walfield, Kermincham, Church Lawton, Leese, Moreton cum Alcumlow, Moston, Newbold Astbury, Odd Rode, Radnor (1837—95), Sandbach, Smallwood, Somerford, Somerford Booths, Somerford, Swettenham, Tetton, Twemlow, Wheelock

MACCLESFIELD PLU Adlington, Nether Alderley, Over Alderley, Alderley Edge (1894—1930), Birtles, Bollington, Bosley, Butley, Capesthorne, Chelford, Chorley, Eaton, Fallibroome, Gawsworth, Henbury cum Pexall, Hurdsfield, Kerridge (1894—1900), Kettleshulme, Lyme Handley, Macclesfield, Macclesfield Forest, Marton, Mottram St Andrew, Newton, Pott Shrigley, Poynton (1836—80), Poynton with Worth (1880—1930), Prestbury, Rainow, North Rode, Siddington, Snelson, Sutton, Taxal, Tytherington, Upton, Great Warford, Wildboarclough, Wincle, Lower Withington, Old Withington, Woodford, Worth (1836—80), Yeardsley cum Whaley

NANTWICH PLU Acton, Alpraham, Alvaston (1837—99), Aston juxta Mondrum, Audlem, Austerson, Baddiley, Baddington, Barthomley, Basford, Batherton, Beeston (1837—92), Bickerton, Bickley (1837—53), Blakenhall, Bridgemere, Brindley, Broomhall, Buerton, Bulkeley, Burland, Bunbury, Burwardsley (1837—92), Calveley, Checkley cum Wrinehill, Cholmondeley, Cholmondeston, Chorley, Chorlton, Coole Pilate, Church Coppenhall, Monks Coppenhall, Crewe, Dodcott cum Wilkesley, Doddington, Eaton (1837—94), Edleston, Egerton, Faddiley, Hampton (1837—53), Hankelow, Haslington, Hatherton, Haughton, Henhull, Hough, Hunsterson, Hurleston, Larkton (1837—53), Lea, Leighton, Macefen (1837—53), Marbury with Quoisley (1837—92), Church Minshull, Minshull Vernon, Nantwich, Newhall, Norbury (1837—53), Peckforton, Poole, Ridley, Rope, Rushton (1837—94), Shavington cum Gresty, Sound, Spurstow, Stapeley, Stoke, Tarporley (1837—94), Tiverton (1837—92), Tilstone Fearnall (1837—92), Tushingham cum Grindley (1837—53), Utkinton (1837—94), Walgherton, Wardle, Warmingham, Weston, Wettenhall, Willaston, Wirswall (1837—53), Wistaston, Woodcott, Woolstanwood, Worleston, Wrenbury cum Frith, Wybunbury

NORTHWICH PLU Acton, Allostock, Anderton, Barnton, Birches (1836—92), Bostock, Little Budworth, Byley, Clive, Cogshall, Comberbach, Crowton, Croxton (1836—92), Cuddington, Darnhall, Davenham, Delamere, Eaton, Eddisbury, Hartford, Hulse (1836—92), Kinderton (1894—1930), Kinderton cum Hulme (1836—94), Lach Dennis, Little Leigh, Leftwich, Lostock Gralam, Marbury, Marston, Marton, Middlewich, Minshull Vernon, Mooresbarrow cum Parme (1836—92), Moulton, Newhall (1836—92), Newton (1836—94), Northwich, Castle Northwich (1836—94), Oakmere, Occlestone (1836—92), Onston (1836—92), Low Oulton (1836—92), Over, Nether Peover, Ravenscroft (1836—92), Rudheath, Shipbrook (1836—92), Shurlach (1836—92), Sproston, Stanthorne, Stublach (1836—92), Sutton (1836—92), Unnamed (1894—1930), Unnamed (1894—1930), Wallerscoat (1836—92), Weaver (1836—92), Weavenham cum Milton, Wharton, Whatcroft, Wimboldsley, Wincham, Winnington, Witton cum Twambrooks (1836—94)

RUNCORN PLU Acton Grange, Alvanley, Antrobus, Appleton, Aston by Sutton, Aston Grange, Bartington, Great Budworth, Clifton, Crowley, Daresbury, Dutton, Frodsham, Frodsham Lordship, Grappenhall (1836—45), Halton, Hatton, Helsby, Keckwick, Kingsley, Kingswood, Latchford (1836—45), Latchford Without (1894—1930), Manley, Moore, Newton by Daresbury, Newton by Frodsham, Norley, Norton, Preston on the Hill, Runcorn, Seven Oaks, Stockham, Stockton Heath (1897—1930), Stretton, Sutton, Thelwall (1836—45), Walton Inferior, Walton Superior, Weston, Higher Whitley, Lower Whitley

7

Cheshire *continued*

STOCKPORT PLU (Ches, Lancs)
Bosden (1877—1930), Bramhall (1837—1900), Bredbury, Brinnington (1837—1920), Cheadle (1879—1930), Cheadle Bulkley (1837—79), Cheadle Moseley (1837—79), Compstall (1897—1930), Stockport Etchells, Handforth (1877—1930), Handforth cum Bosden (1837—77), Hazel Gro e and Bramhall (1900—30), Hyde, Marple, Norbury (1837—1900), Offerton (1837—1900), Reddish, Romiley, Stockport, Torkington (1837—1900), Werneth (1837—97)
TARVIN PLU (1871—1930)
Aldersey, Aldford, Ashton, Barrow, Barton, Beeston (1892—1930), Broxton, Buerton, Burton by Tarvin, Burwardsley (1892—1930), Caldecott, Carden, Chowley, Churton by Aldford, Churton by Farndon, Churton Heath, Clotton Hoofield, Clutton, Coddington, Cotton Abbotts, Cotton Edmunds, Crewe, Duddon, Eaton (1894—1930), Edgerley, Farndon, Golborne Bellow, Golborne David, Grafton, Handley, Harthill, Hatton, Hockenhull, Horton, Horton cum Peel, Huntington, Huxley, Iddinshall, Kelsall, Kings Marsh, Lea Newbold, Mouldsworth, Newton by Tattenhall, Prior's Heys, Rowton, Rushton (1894—1930), Saighton, Church Shocklach (1894—1930), Shocklach Oviatt (1894—1930). Bruen Stapleford, Foulk Stapleford, Stretton, Guilden Sutton, Tarporley (1894—1930), Tarvin, Tattenhall, Tilston, Tilstone Fearnall (1892—1930), Tiverton (1892—1930), Utkinton (1894—1930), Waverton, Willington
WIRRAL PLU
Arrowe, Barnston, Higher Bebington (1836—1922), Lower Bebington (1836—1922), Bebington and Bromborough (1922—30), Bidston cum Ford (1836—91), Birkenhead (1836—69), Brimstage, Bromborough (1894—1922), Burton, Caldy, Claughton with Grange (1836—91), Eastham, Ellesmere Port (1911—30), Frankby, Gayton, Grange, Greasby, Heswall cum Oldfield, Hoose (1836—94), Hooton, Hoylake cum West Kirby (1894—1930), Irby, West Kirby (1836—94), Landican, Ledsham, Leighton (1836—94), Liscard (1836—91), Great Melose (1836—94), Little Melose (1836—94), Moreton (1836—1928), Ness, Great Neston (1836—94), Little Neston (1836—94), Neston cum Parkgate (1894—1930), Netherpool (1836—1911), Newton with Larton (1836—89), Noctorum (1836—91), Overpool (1836—1911), Oxton (1836—91), Pensby, Poulton cum Seacombe (1836—91), Poulton cum Spital, Prenton, Puddington, Raby, Rock Ferry (1894—98), Saughall Massie, Storeton, Great Sutton, Little Sutton, Thingwall, Childer Thornton, Thornton Hough, Thurstaston, Tranmere (1836—91), Upton by Birkenhead, Wallasey (1836—91), Whitby, Willaston, Woodchurch

In Other Poor Law Counties:
ASHTON UNDER LYNE PLU (Lancs, Ches)
Dukinfield, Godley (1837—1923), Hattersley, Hollingworth, Matley, Newton (1837—1923), Mottram, Stalybridge (1894—1930), Stayley[27] (1837—94), Tintwistle
HAWARDEN PLU (1853—1930 [Flints, Ches (until 1871)])
Claverton, Dodleston, Eaton, Eccleston, Lower Kinnerton, Marlston cum Lache, Poulton, Pulford, Great Saughall, Little Saughall, Shotwick, Shotwick Park, Woodbank
HAYFIELD PLU (Derbys, Ches)
Disley[38]
MARKET DRAYTON PLU (orig 'Drayton') [Salop, Ches (1836—95)]
Tittenley[39]
WARRINGTON PLU (Lancs, Ches)
Grappenhall (1845—1930), Latchford[40] (1845—1930), Thelwall (1845—1930)
WEM PLU (Salop, Ches [1836—66])
Whitchurch[41]
WHITCHURCH PLU (Salop, Ches [1853—1930]) [all pars below in the PLU 1853—1930 unless o'wise noted])
Agden, Bickley, Bradley, Chidlow, Chorlton, Cuddington, Duckington, Edge, Hampton, Larkton, Macefen, Malpas, Marbury with Quoisley, Newton by Malpas, Norbury, Oldcastle, Overton, Stockton, Threapwood[42] (1894—1930), Tushingham cum Grindley, Wigland, Wirswall, Wychough
WREXHAM PLU (Denbigh, Ches [1837—94])
Agden (1837—53), Bradley (1837—53), Chidlow (1837—53), Chorlton (1837—53), Cuddington (1837—53), Malpas (1837—53), Newton by Malpas (1837—53), Oldcastle (1837—53), Overton (1837—53), Church Shocklach, Shocklach Oviatt, Stockton (1837—53), Threapwood[41] (1837—53), Wigland (1837—53), Wychough (1837—53)

8

CORNWALL

In Cornwall Poor Law County:[10]

BODMIN PLU
Blisland, Bodmin, Bodmin Borough, Cardinham, Egloshayle, Helland, Lanhydrock, Lanivet, Lanlivery (1837–94), Lanlivery Rural (1894–1930), Lanlivery Urban (1894–96), Lostwithiel, Luxulyan, St Endellion, St Kew, St Mabyn, St Minver Highlands, St Minver Lowlands, St Tudy, St Winnow, Temple, Wadebridge (1898–1930), Warleggan, Withiel

CAMELFORD PLU
Advent, Davidstow, Forrabury (1837–1919), Forrabury and Minster (1919–30), Lanteglos, Lesnewth, Michaelstow, Minster (1837–1919), Otterham, St Breward, St Clether, St Juliot, St Teath, Tintagel, Trevalga

FALMOUTH PLU
Budock (1837–94), Budock Rural (1894–1930), Budock Urban (1894–1920), Constantine, Falmouth, Falmouth Borough (1837–1920), Mabe, Mawnan, Mylor, Penryn, Perranarworthal, St Gluvias

HELSTON PLU
Breage, Crowan, Cury, Germoe, Gunwalloe, Grade, Helston, Landewednack, Manaccan, Mawgan in Meneage, Ruan Major, Ruan Minor, St Anthony in Meneage, St Keverne, St Martin in Meneage, Sithney, Wendron

LAUNCESTON PLU (Cornwall, Devon)
Altarnun, Boyton,[11] Egloskerry, North Hill, Laneast, Launceston (otherwise Dunheved)(1922–30), Lawhitton (1837–94), Lawhitton Rural (1894–1930), Lawhitton Urban (1894–1922), Lewannick, Lezant, South Petherwin, St Mary Magdalene (1837–1922), St Stephens (1837–94), St Stephens by Launceston Rural (1894–1930), St Stephens by Launceston Urban (1894–1922), St Thomas the Apostle (1837–94), St Thomas the Apostle Rural (1894–1930), St Thomas the Apostle Urban (1894–1930), St Thomas Street (1837–1922), Tremaine, Treneglos, Tresmeer, Trewen, Warbstow

LISKEARD PLU
Boconnoc, Broadoak, Callington (1894–1901), Duloe, South Hill, Lanreath, Lansallos, Lanteglos, Lanteglos, Linkinhorne, Liskeard, Liskeard Borough, East Looe (1894–1930), West Looe (1894–1930), Menheniot, Morval, Pelynt, St Cleer, St Dominick, St Ive, St Keyne, St Martin, St Neot, St Pinnock, St Veep, Talland

PENZANCE PLU
Gulval, Ludgvan, Madron, Madron in Penzance (1894–1930), Marazion, Morvah, Paul, Penzance, Penzance in Madron (1894–1930), Perranuthnoe, St Buryan, St Erth (1837–94), St Erth Rural (1894–1930), St Erth Urban (1894–1930), St Hilary, St Ives, St Just in Penwith, St Levan, St Michael's Mount (1858[12]–1930), Sancreed, Senned, Towednack, Uny Lelant, Wolfe Rock Lighthouse, Zennor

REDRUTH PLU
Camborne, Gwennap, Gwinear, Gwithian, Illogan, Phillack (1837–94), East Phillack (1894–1930), West Phillack (1894–1930), Redruth

ST AUSTELL PLU
Creed, Fowey (1894–1930), Gorran, Grampound, Mevagissey, Roche, St Austell (1837–94), St Austell Rural (1894–1930), St Austell Urban (1894–1930), St Blazey, St Dennis, St Ewe, St Mewan, St Michael Carhays, St Sampson, St Stephen in Brannel, Tywardreath

ST COLUMB MAJOR PLU
Colan, Crantock (1837–94), Crantock Rural (1894–1930), Crantock Urban (1894–1902), Cubert, Mawgan in Pyder, Newquay (1894–1930), Padstow (1837–94), Padstow Rural (1894–1930), Padstow Urban (1894–1930), Little Petherick, St Breock, St Columb Major, St Columb Minor (1837–94), St Columb Minor Rural (1894–1930), St Enoder, St Ervan, St Eval, St Issey, St Merryn, St Wenn

ST GERMANS PLU (Cornwall, Devon)
Antony, Botus Fleming, Landrake with St Erney, Landulph, Maker,[11] Millbrook (1896–1930), Pillaton, Quethiock, Rame, St Germans, St John,[11] St Mellion, St Stephens, Saltash, Sheviock, Torpoint (1904–30)

ISLES OF SCILLY PLU[13]
Bryher, St Agnes, St Martin's, St Mary's, Tresco

STRATTON PLU
Jacobstow, Kilkhampton, Launcells, Marhamchurch, Morwenstow, Poughill, Poundstock, St Gennys, Stratton, Stratton and Bude (1900–30), Week St Mary, Whitstone

TRURO PLU
Cornelly, Cuby, Feock, Gerrans, Kea, Kenwyn (1837–94), Kenwyn Rural (1894–1930), Kenwyn Urban (1894–1930), Ladock, Lamorran, Merther, Perranzabuloe, Philleigh, Probus, Ruan Lanihorne, St Agnes, St Allen, St Anthony in Roseland, St Clement (1837–94), St Clement Rural (1894–1930), St Clement Urban (1894–1930), St Erme, St Just in Roseland, St Michael Penkevil, Tregavethan, Tregony, Truro St Mary, Veryan

In Other Poor Law Counties:
HOLSWORTHY PLU (Devon)
North Tamerton[11]
PLYMPTON ST MARY (Devon)
St Budeaux[14]
TAVISTOCK PLU (Devon)
Calstock[15]

9

CUMBERLAND

In Cumb Poor Law County:[11]

ALSTON WITH GARRIGILL PLU
Alston with Garrigill

BOOTLE PLU
Birker and Austhwaite, Bootle, Corney, Drigg and Carleton, Eskdale and Wasdale, Irton, Millom, Millom Rural (1894—1930), Muncaster, Seascale (1901—30), Ulpha, Waberthwaite, Whicham, Whitbeck

BRAMPTON PLU
Askerton, Brampton, Burtholme, Carlatton (1861—1930), Castle Carrock, Cumrew, Cumwhitton, Nether Denton, Upper Denton, Farlam, Geltsdale (1861—1930), Irthington, Kingwater, Midgeholme (1861—1930), Walton, Waterhead

CARLISLE PLU
Beaumont, Belle Vue (1894—1912), Botchergate (1894—1904), Burgh by Sands, Caldewgate (1838—1904), Carlisle (1904—30), Crosby upon Eden, Cummersdale, Dalston, Eaglesfield Abbey (1862—1904), Grinsdale, Kingmoor, Kirkandrews upon Eden, Orton, Rickergate, Rockcliffe, St Cuthbert Within (1838—1904), St Cuthbert Without, St Mary Within (1838—1904), Stanwix, Warwick, Wetheral, Wreay

COCKERMOUTH PLU
Above Derwent (soon after 1838[12]—1930), ·Bassenthwaite, Bewaldeth and Snittlegarth, Blindbothel, Blindcrake Isel and Redmaine, Bothel and Threapland, Borrowdale, Brackenthwaite, Bridekirk, Briery Cottages (1858—1930), Brigham, Broughton (1898—1930), Great Broughton (1838—98), Little Broughton (1838—98), Broughton Moor (1898—1930), Buttermere, Camerton, Castlerigg St John's and Withyburn (soon after 1838[12]—1930), Great Clifton, Little Clifton, Cloffocks (1858—1930), Cockermouth, Crosscanonby (soon after 1838[12]—1930), Dean, Dearham, Dovenby, Eaglesfield, Ellenborough and Ewanrigg (1838—1928), Embleton, Flimby, Gilcrux, Greysouthern, Isel Old Park, Keswick, Lorton, Loweswater, Maryport (1928—30), Mosser, Netherall (1894—1928), Oughterside and Allenby, Papcastle, Plumbland, Ribton, Seaton, Setmurthy, Skiddaw (1862—1930), Stainburn, Sunderland, Tallentire, Underskiddaw, Whinfell, Winscales, Workington, Workington Rural (1894—1930), Wythop

LONGTOWN PLU
Arthuret, Bellbank, Bewcastle, Hethersgill, Kirkandrews Middle, Kirkandrews Moat, Kirkandrews Nether, Kirklington Middle, Nichol Forest, Scaleby, Solport, Stapleton, Trough, Westlinton

PENRITH PLU
Ainstable, Berrier and Murrah, Bowscale, Castle Sowerby, Catterlen, Croglin, Culgaith, Dacre, Edenhall, Gamblesby, Glassonby, Greystoke, Hesket in the Forest, Hunsonby and Winskill, Hutton in the Forest, Hutton John, Hutton Roof, Hutton Soil, Kirkland and Blencarn, Kirkoswald, Langwathby, Lazonby, Matterdale, Melmerby, Middlesceugh and Braithwaite, Mosedale, Mungrisdale, Newton Reigny, Ousby, Penrith, Plumpton Wall, Renwick, Great Salkeld, Little Salkeld, Skelton, Skirwith, Staffield, Threlkeld, Watermillock

WHITEHAVEN PLU
Arlecdon, Beckermet St Bridget, Beckermet St John, Cleator, Distington, Egremont, Ennerdale and Kinniside, Gosforth, Haile, Harrington, Hensingham, Low Keekle (1873—81), Lamplugh, Lowside Quarter, Moresby, Parton, Ponsonby, Preston Quarter (1838—96), Preston Quarter (1896—1930), Preston Quarter Rural (1894—96), Rottington, St Bees, Salter and Eskett (1861—1930), Sandwith, Seascale (1897—1901), Nether Wasdale, Weddicar, Whitehaven

WIGTON PLU
Aikton, Allhallows, Allonby (1894—1930), Aspatria and Brayton, Blencogo, Blennerhassett and Kirkland, Bolton High (1837—87), Bolton Low (1837—87), Boltons (1887—1930), Bowness (soon after 1837[12]—1930), Bromfield, Caldebeck, Dundraw, Hayton and Mealo, Holme Abbey, Holme East Waver, Holme Low, Holme St Cuthbert, High Ireby, Low Ireby, Kirkbampton (soon after 1837[12]—1930), Kirkbride, Langrigg and Mealrigg, West Newton and Allonby (1837—94), Oulton, Sebergham, Thursby, Torpenhow and Whitrigg, Uldale, Waverton, Westnewton (1894—1930), Westward, Wigton (1837—87), Wigton (1894—1930), Wigton cum Woodside (1887—94), Woodside (1894—1930), Woodside Quarter (1837—87)

DERBYSHIRE

In Derbys Poor Law County:[19]

ASHBOURNE PLU (Derbys, Staffs)
Alkmonton, Ashbourne, Atlow, Ballidon, Fenny Bentley, Hungry Bentley, Biggin, Bonsall, Bradbourne, Bradley, Brailsford, Brassington, Callow, Carsington, Clifton and Compton, Eaton and Alsop, Edlaston and Wyaston, Hartington Nether Quarter, Hartington Town Quarter, Hognaston, Hollington, Hopton and Griffe Grange (1858—1930), Hulland, Hullard Ward, Hulland Ward Intakes, Ible, Kirk Ireton, Kniveton, Lea Hall, Longford, Mapleton, Mercaston, Middleton by Wirksworth, Newton Grange, Offcote and Underwood, Osmaston, Parwich, Rodsley, Shirley, Snelston, Sturston, Stydd (1840—86), Thorpe, Tissington, Yeaveley, Yeldersley

BAKEWELL PLU
Abney and Abney Grange, Aldwark, Ashford, Bakewell, Baslow and Bubnell, Beeley, Birchover, Blackwell (soon after 1838[20]—1930), Bradwell (soon after 1838[20]—1930), Brushfield, Calver, Chatsworth (1861—1930), Chelmorton, Cromford, Curbar, Darley, Edensor, Elton (soon after 1838[20]—1930), Eyam, Eyam Woodlands, Flagg, Foolow, Froggatt, Gratton, Grindlow, Nether Haddon (1861—1930), Over Haddon, Harthill, Hartington Middle Quarter, Hassop, Hathersage, Hazlebadge, Highlow, Great

10

Derbyshire: Bakewell *continued*

Hucklow, Little Hucklow, Ivonbrook Grange, Litton, Great Longstone, Little Longstone, Matlock, Matlock Bath (1894—1930), Middleton and Smerrill, Monyash, Offerton (soon after 1838[20]—1930), Outseats (soon after 1838[20]—1930), Nether Padley, Pilsley, Rowland (soon after 1838[20]—1930), Great Rowsley, Sheldon, Stanton, Stoke, Stony Middleton, Taddington (soon after 1838[20]—1930), Tansley (soon after 1838[20]—1930), Tideswell, Wardlow, Wensley and Snitterton, Wheston, Winster, Youlgreave (soon after 1838[20]—1930)

BELPER PLU
Alderwasley, Alfreton, Allestree (soon after 1837[20]—1930), Ashleyhay, Belper, Crich, Denby, Dethick and Holloway (1897—1930), Dethick and Lea (1837—97), Duffield, Hazlewood, Heage, Holbrook, Horsley, Horsley Woodhouse, Idridgehay and Alton, Ireton Wood (1837—89), Kedleston, Kilburn, Kirk Langley, Mackworth, Mapperley, Markeaton, Milford (1897—1930), Morley, Muggington (soon after 1837[20]—86), Pentrich, Quarendon, Ravensdale Park (soon after 1837[20]—1930), Ripley, Rowditch (1890—98), Shottle and Postern, Smalley, Turnditch, Weston Underwood, Windley, South Wingfield, Wirksworth

CHAPEL EN LE FRITH PLU
Aston, Bamford, Brough and Shatton, Burbage (1894—1930), Buxton, Castleton, Chapel en le Frith; Chinley, Bugsworth and Brownside; Derwent, Edale, Fairfield, Green Fairfield (1917—30), Fernilee, Hartington Upper Quarter, Hope, Hope Woodlands, Kingsterndale (1894—1930), Peak Forest, Thornhill, Wormhill (soon after 1837[20]—1930)

CHESTERFIELD PLU
Ashover, Barlow (1871—1930), Great Barlow (1837—71), Little Barlow (1837—71), Bolsover, Brackenfield, Brampton, Brimington, Calow, Chesterfield, Clay Lane, Coal Aston, Dronfield, Dronfield Woodhouse (1894—1930), Eckington, Egstow (1894—1930), Hasland, Heath, Holmesfield, Killamarsh, Morton, Newbold and Dunston (1837—1920), Temple Normanton, Pilsley, Shirland and Higham, Staveley, Stretton, Sutton cum Duckmanton, Tapton (1837—1920), Tupton, Unstone, Walton, Wessington, Whittington (1837—1920), Wingerworth, North Wingfield, Woodthorpe

DERBY PLU
Little Chester (1837—98), Darley Abbey (1894—1930), Derby (1898—1930), Derby All Saints (1837—98), Derby St Alkmund (1837—98), Derby St Michael (1837—98), Derby St Peter (1837—98), Derby St Werburgh (1837—98), Litchurch (1837—98)

GLOSSOP PLU
Charlesworth (1894—1930), Chisworth (1896—1930), Glossop, Ludworth (1896—1930), Ludworth and Chisworth (1837—94)

HAYFIELD PLU (Derbys, Ches)
Beard, Thornsett, Ollersett and Whittle (1837—85); Disley,[21] Hayfield, Mellor, New Mills (1885—1930), Newtown (1894—1930)

SHARDLOW PLU[22] (Derbys, Leics, Notts)
Alvaston (1837—84), Alvaston and Boulton (1884—1930), Aston upon Trent, Barrow upon Trent, Boulton (1837—84), Breadsall, Breaston, Chaddesden, Chellaston, Dale Abbey, Derby Hills, Draycott and Church Wilne, Little Eaton, Long Eaton, Elvaston, Kirk Hallam, West Hallam, Hopwell, Littleover, Melbourne, Normanton (1837—1928), New Normanton (1890—98), Ockbrook, Osmaston (1837—1902), Osmaston (1894—1902), Risley, Sandiacre, Sawley and Wilsthorpe, Shardlow and Great Wilne, Sinfin and Arleston (soon after 1837[20]—1930), Sinfin Moor (1861—1930), Spondon, Stanley, Stanton by Bridge, Stanton by Dale, Swarkestone, Unnamed (1894—97), Weston upon Trent

In Other Poor Law Counties:

ASHBY DE LA ZOUCH PLU (Leics, Derbys)
Appleby[23] (1836—89), Appleby[23] (1889—97), The Boundary (1858—1930), Calke, Hartshorne, Measham, Netherseal[24] (1894—1930), Oakthorpe and Donisthorpe,[25] Overseal[26] (1894—1930), Packington,[27] Ravenstone[27] (1836—84), Smisby, Stretton en le Field, Ticknall, Willesley,[28] Woodville (1897—1930)

BASFORD PLU (Notts, Derbys)
Codnor and Loscoe, Codnor Park, Heanor, Ilkeston, Shipley

BURTON UPON TRENT PLU (Staffs, Derbys)
Ash (soon after 1837[20]—1930), Barton Blount (soon after 1837[20]—1930), Bearwardcote (soon after 1837[20]—1930), Bretby, Church Broughton, Burnaston, Caldwell, Catton (soon after 1837[20]—1930), Coton in the Elms, Dalbury Lees, Drakelow, Egginton, Etwall, Findern, Foremark, Foston and Scropton,[7] Castle Gresley, Church Gresley, Hargate Manor (1862—85), Hatton, Hilton, Hoon, Ingleby, Lullington, Marston on Dove, Mickleover, Newton Solney, Osleton and Thurvaston (soon after 1837[20]—1930), Radbourne, Repton, Rosliston, Stanton and Newhall, Stapenhill,[13] Sutton on the Hill, Swadlincote, Trusley, Twyford and Stenson, Walton upon Trent, Willington, Winshill[13]

ECCLESALL-BIERLOW PLU (Yorks W Riding, Derbys)
Beauchief, Dore, Norton, Totley

MANSFIELD PLU (Notts, Derbys)
Ault Hucknall, Blackwell, Glapwell (soon after 1836[20]—1930), Upper Langwith, South Normanton, Pinxton,[9] Pleasley, Scarcliffe, Shirebrook (1903—30), Tibshelf

ROTHERHAM PLU (Yorks W Riding, Derbys)
Beighton

TAMWORTH PLU (Staffs, Derbys [until 1895])
Chilcote,[29] Croxall[30]

UTTOXETER PLU (Staffs, Derbys)
Boyleston, Cubley (soon after 1837[20]—1930), Doveridge, Marston Montgomery (soon after 1837[20]—1930), Norbury and Roston (soon after 1837[20]—1930), Somersal Herbert, Sudbury

WORKSOP PLU (Notts, Derbys, Yorks W Riding)
Barlborough, Clowne, Elmton, Whitwell

DEVON

In Devon Poor Law County:[25]

AXMINSTER PLU (Devon, Dorset)
Axminster (1836–1915),[26] Axminster Hamlets (1915–30), Axminster Town (1915–30), Axmouth, Beer (1894–1930), Chardstock,[27] Colyton, Combpyne, Dalwood,[28] Hawkchurch,[27] Kilmington, Membury, Musbury, Rousdon, Seaton (1894–1930), Seaton and Beer (1836–94), Shute, Stockland,[28] Thorncombe[29] (1836–94), Uplyme

BARNSTAPLE PLU
Arlington, Ashford, Atherington, Barnstaple, Berrynarbor, Bittadon, Bratton Fleming, Braunton, High Bray, Brendon, Challacombe, Combe Martin, Countisbury, East Down, West Down, Fremington, Georgeham, Goodleigh, Heanton Punchardon, Horwood, Ilfracombe, Instow, Kentisbury, Landkey, Loxhore, Lynton, Martinhoe, Marwood, Mortehoe, Newton Tracey, Parracombe, Pilton (1835–94), East Pilton (1894–1930), West Pilton (1894–1930), Shirwell, Stoke Rivers, Swimbridge, Tawstock, Bishop's Tawton, Trentishoe, Westleigh

BIDEFORD PLU
Abbotsham, Alwington, Bideford, Bradworthy (1835–before 1850), Buckland Brewer, Bulkworthy, Clovelly, Hartland, Landcross, Littleham, Lundy Island, Monkleigh, Newton St Petrock, Northam, Parkham, East Putford, West Putford (1835–97), Welcombe, Woolfardisworthy

CREDITON PLU
Bow, Brushford, Chawleigh, Cheriton Bishop, Cheriton Fitzpaine, Clannaborough, Coldridge, Colebrooke, Crediton (1836–94), Crediton Hamlets (1894–1930), Crediton Town (1894–1930), Down St Mary, Eggesford, Hittisleigh, Kennerleigh, Lapford, Morchard Bishop, Newton St Cyres, Nymet Rowland, Poughill, Puddington, Sandford, Sherwood Villa (1858[30]–94), Shobrooke, Stockleigh English, Stockleigh Pomeroy, Thelbridge, Upton Hellions, Washford Pyne, Wembworthy, Woolfardisworthy, Zeal Monachorum

DEVONPORT PARISH (1898[31]–1930)
Devonport

EXETER INCORPORATION (1697–1930)
As for Exeter Bor/MB/CB (see listing above for BOROUGHS) less Devon Prison and Constabulary Barracks, St Leonard, St Thomas the Apostle

HOLSWORTHY PLU (Devon, Cornwall)
Ashwater, Abbots Bickington, Bradford, Bradworthy (before 1850–1930), Bridgerule East, Bridgerule West,[32] Broadwoodwidger (1837–52), Clawton, Cookbury, Halwill, Hollacombe, Holsworthy, Holsworthy Hamlets (1901–30), Luffincott, Milton Damerel, Northcott (1837–52), Pancrasweek, West Putford (1897–1930), Pyworthy, St Giles on the Heath (1837–52), Sutcombe, Tetcott, Thornbury, Black Torrington, Virginstow (1837–52)

HONITON PLU
Awliscombe, Branscombe, Broadhembury, Buckerell, Combe Raleigh, Cotleigh, Dunkeswell, Farway, Feniton, Gittisham, Harpford, Honiton, Luppitt, Monkton, Northleigh, Offwell, Ottery St Mary, Venn Ottery, Payhembury, Plymtree, Salcombe Regis, Sheldon, Sidbury, Sidmouth, Southleigh, Talaton, Upottery, Widworthy, Yarcombe (1894–1930)

KINGSBRIDGE PLU
East Allington, West Alvington, Aveton Gifford, Bigbury, Blackawton, Buckland Tout Saints, Charleton, Chivelstone, Churchstow, Dodbrooke (1836–93), South Huish, Kingsbridge (1836–93), Kingsbridge and Dodbrooke (1893–1930), Kingston, Loddiswell, Malborough, South Milton, Modbury, South Pool, East Portlemouth, Ringmore, Salcombe, Sherford, Slapton, Stoke Fleming, Stokenham, Thurlestone, Woodleigh

SOUTH MOLTON PLU (Devon, Somerset)
East Anstey, West Anstey, East Buckland, West Buckland, Burrington, Charles, Cheldon, Chittlehamholt (1866[30]–1930), Chittlehampton, Chumleigh, Creacombe, Exmoor,[33] Filleigh, Knowstone, Mariansleigh, Meshaw, Molland, North Molton, South Molton, Bishop's Nympton, George Nympton, King's Nympton, Queensnympton (1894–1930), Rackenford, Romansleigh, Rose Ash, Satterleigh (1835–94), Satterleigh and Warkleigh (1894–1930), Twitchen, Warkleigh (1835–94), Witheridge, East Worlington, West Worlington (1835–85)

NEWTON ABBOT PLU
Abbotskerswell, Ashburton, Bickington, Bishopsteignton, North Bovey, Bovey Tracey, Broadhempston, Buckland in the Moor, Chudleigh, Cockington (1836–1928), Coffinswell, Combe in Teignhead (1836–85), Dawlish (1836–94), East Dawlish (1894–1930), West Dawlish (1894–1930), Denbury (1836–94), Haccombe (1836–85), Haccombe with Combe (1885–1930), Hennock, Highweek, Ideford, Ilsington, Ipplepen, Kingskerswell, Kingsteignton, Lustleigh, Manaton, Milber (1901–30), Moretonhampstead, Ogwell (1894–1930), East Ogwell (1836–94), West Ogwell (1836–94), St Mary Church (1836–1924), St Nicholas, Stokeinteignhead, Teignmouth (1909–30), East Teignmouth (1836–1909), West Teignmouth (1836–1909), Teigngrace, Torbryan, Tormoham (1836–1924), Torquay (1924–30), Trusham, Widecombe in the Moor, Wolborough, Woodland

OKEHAMPTON PLU
Ashworthy, Beaworthy, Belstone, Bondleigh, Bratton Clovelly, Bridestowe, Broadwood Kelly, Chagford, Drewsteignton, Exbourne, Germansweek, Gidleigh, Hatherleigh, Highampton, Honeychurch, Iddesleigh, Inwardleigh, Jacobstow, Meeth, Northlew, Okehampton, Okehampton Hamlets (1894–1930), Monk Okehampton, Sampford Courtenay, Sourton, Spreyton, North Tawton, South Tawton, Throwleigh

12

Devon *continued*

PLYMOUTH INCORPORATION (1708-1930)
Plymouth (1898–1930), Plymouth Charles (1708–1898), Plymouth St Andrew (1708–1898)
PLYMPTON ST MARY PLU
Bickleigh, Brixton, Egg Buckland, Chelson Meadow (1858[30]–94), Compton Gifford, Cornwood, Ermington, Harford, Holbeton, Ivybridge (1894–1930), Laira Green (1858[30]–96), Newton Ferrers, Pennycross (1836–98), Plympton St Mary, Plympton St Maurice, Plymstock, Revelstoke, St Budeaux,[34] Shaugh Prior, Tamerton Foliot, Wembury, Weston Peverell (1899–1930), Yealmpton
ST THOMAS PLU
Alphington, Ashcombe, Ashton, Aylesbeare, Bicton, Brampford Speke, Bridford, East Budleigh, Budleigh Salterton (1894–1930), Christow, Broad Clyst, Clyst Honiton, Clyst Hydon, Clyst St George, Clyst St Lawrence, Clyst St Mary, Colaton Raleigh, Doddiscombsleigh, Dotton (1858[30]–94), Dunchideock, Dunsford, Nether Exe, Exminster, Farringdon, Heavitree, Holcombe Burnell, Huxham, Ide, Kenn, Kenton, Littleham, Lympstone, Mamhead, Newton Poppleford (1898–1930), Otterton, Pinhoe, Poltimore, Powderham, Rewe, Rockbeare, St Leonard, St Thomas the Apostle, Shillingford St George, Sowton, Stoke Canon, Tedburn St Mary, Topsham, Upton Pyne, Whimple, Whitestone, Withycombe Raleigh, Woodbury
STOKE DAMEREL INCORPORTATION (until 1898[31])
Stoke Damerel
EAST STONEHOUSE PLU
East Stonehouse
TAVISTOCK PLU (Devon, Cornwall)
Bere Ferrers, Bradstone, Brentor, Buckland Monachorum, Coryton, Dunterton, Kelly, Lamerton, Lewtrenchard, Lifton, Lydford, Marystow, Marytavy, Meavy, Milton Abbot, Petertavy, Sampford Spiney, Sheepstor, Stowford, Sydenham Damerel, Tavistock, Tavistock Hamlets (1898–1930), Thrushelton, Walkhampton, Whitchurch
TIVERTON PLU
Bampton, Bickleigh, Blackborough,[35] Bradninch (1835–1901), Butterleigh, Cadbury, Cadeleigh, Calverleigh (1835–85), Clayhanger, Cruwys Morchard, Cullompton, Halberton, Highley St Mary (1858[30]–94), Hockworthy, Holcombe Rogus (1835–before 1850), Huntsham, Kentisbeare, Loxbeare, Morebath (1835–56 and 1894–1930), Oakford, Sampford Peverell, Silverton, Stoodleigh, Templeton, Thorverton, Tiverton, Uffculme, Uplowman, Washfield, Willand
TORRINGTON PLU
Alverdiscott, Ashreigney, Beaford, High Bickington, Buckland Filleigh, Dolton, Dowland, Frithelstock, Huish, Huntshaw, Langtree, Merton, Peters Marland, Petrockstow, Roborough, St Giles in the Wood, Shebbear, Sheepwash, Great Torrington, Little Torrington, Weare Giffard, Winkleigh, Yarnscombe

TOTNES PLU
Ashprington, Berry Pomeroy, South Brent, Brixham, Buckfastleigh (1836–94), East Buckfastleigh (1894–1930), West Buckfastleigh (1894–1930), Churston Ferrers, Cornworthy, Dartington, Dartmouth (1891–1930), Dean Prior, Diptford, Dittisham, Halwell, Harberton, Little Hempston, Holne, North Huish, Kingswear, Marldon, Moreleigh, Paignton, Rattery, St Petrox (1836–91), St Saviour (1836–91), Staverton, Stoke Gabriel, Totnes, Townstall (1836–91), Ugborough

In Other Poor Law Counties:
CHARD PLU (Somerset)
  Yarcombe (1836–94)
DULVERTON PLU (Somerset)
  Morebath (1856–94)
LAUNCESTON PLU (Cornwall)
  Broadwoodwidger (1852–1930), Northcott (1852–1930), North Petherwin, St Giles on the Heath (1852–1930), Virginstow (1852–1930), Werrington
TAUNTON PLU (Somerset)
  Churchstanton[36]
WELLINGTON PLU (Somerset)
  Burlescombe, Clayhidon, Culmstock, Hemyock, Holcombe Rogus (before 1850–1930)

DORSET

In Dorset Poor Law County:[11]
BEAMINSTER PLU (Dorset, Somerset until 1896, ent Dorset thereafter)
Beaminster, Bettiscombe, Broadwinsor, Burstock, Chedington, East Chelborough, West Chelborough, Corscombe, Evershot, Halstock, Hooke, Mapperton, Marshwood, Melbury Osmund, Melbury Sampford, Mosterton, Netherbury, South Perrot, North Poorton, Pilsdon,[12] Powerstock, Rampisham, Seaborough, Stoke Abbot, Thorncombe[13] (1894–1930)
BLANDFORD PLU
Almer (1835–94), Anderson, Blandford Forum, Blandford St Mary, Bryanston, Charlton Marshall, Chettle (1894–1930), Durweston, Farnham (1894–1930), Hilton, Iwerne Courtney, Iwerne Steepleton, Langton Long Blandford, Milborne St Andrew, Milborne Stileham, Milton Abbas, Pimperne, Spetisbury, Stourpaine, Tarrant Crawford, Tarrant Gunville, Tarrant Hinton, Tarrant Keyneston, Tarrant Launceston, Tarrant Monkton, Tarrant Rawston, Tarrant Rushton, Turnworth, Winterborne Clenston, Winterborne Houghton, Winterborne Kingston, Winterborne Stickland, Winterborne Tomson, Winterborne Whitechurch, Winterborne Zelston

Dorset *continued*

BRIDPORT PLU
Allington, Askerswell, Bothenhampton, Bradpole, Bridport, Burton Bradstock, Catherston Leweston, Charmouth (1894–1930), Chideock, Chilcombe, Litton Cheney, Loders, Stratton St Gabriel, Swyre, Symondsbury, Walditch, Whitechurch Canonicorum, Wootton Fitzpaine

CERNE PLU
Alton Pancras, Batcombe, Buckland Newton, Cattistock, Nether Cerne, Up Cerne, Cerne Abbas, Cheselbourne, Frome St Quintin, Godmanston, Gorewood, Hermitage, Hillfield, Mappowder, Melbury Bubb, Melcombe Horsey, Minterne Magna, Piddletrenthide, Pulham, Sydling St Nicholas, Glanvilles Wootton

CRANBORNE PLU (Mar–Aug 1836, then incl in WIMBORNE PLU to cr WIMBORNE AND CRANBORNE PLU, qv where pars orig in this PLU are indicated)

DORCHESTER PLU
Athelhampton, Long Bredy, Bradford Peverell, Broadmayne, Burleston, Compton Abbas, Charminster, Chilfrome, Compton Valence, Dewlish, Dorchester (1927–30), Dorchester All Saints (1836–1927), Dorchester Holy Trinity (1836–1927), Dorchester St Peter (1836–1927), Fordington (1836–1900), Frampton, Frome Vauchurch, Kingston Russell, West Knighton, Littlebredy, Maiden Newton, Piddlehinton, Puddletown, West Stafford, Stinsford, Stratton, Tincleton, Toller Fratrum, Toller Porcorum, Tolpuddle, Warmwell, Watercombe, Whitcombe, Winterborne Came, Winterborne Herringston, Winterborne Monkton, Winterborne St Martin, Winterborne Steepleton, Winterbourne Abbas, Woodsford, Wynford Eagle

POOLE PLU
Branksome (1894–1905), Canford Magna, Hamworthy (1835–1905), Kinson, Longfleet (1835–1905), Lytchett Matravers, Lytchett Minster, Parkstone (1835–1905), Poole (1905–30), Poole St James (1835–1905)

PURBECK PLU (Mar–Sept 1836, then incl in WAREHAM PLU to cr WAREHAM AND PURBECK PLU, qv where pars orig in this PLU are indicated)

SHAFTESBURY INCORPORATION (until 1880s) See notes in following entry

SHAFTESBURY PLU
Alcester (1894–1921), Ashmore, Bourton (1894–1930), Buckhorn Weston (1894–1930), Cann, Compton Abbas, Fontmell Magna, Gillingham, Iwerne Minster, Kington Magna (1894–1930), Margaret Marsh, Melbury Abbas, Motcombe, East Orchard, West Orchard, Shaftesbury (1894–1930), Shaftesbury Holy Trinity,[14] Shaftesbury St James,[14] Shaftesbury St Peter,[14] Silton (1894–1930), East Stour, West Stour, Stour Provost, Sutton Waldron, Todber

SHERBORNE (Dorset, Somerset until 1896, ent Dorset thereafter)
Beer Hacket, Bradford Abbas, Castleton, Bishop's Caundle, Purse Caundle, Caundle Marsh, Chetnole, Clifton Maybank, Nether Compton, Over Compton, Folke. Goathill.[12] Haydon. Holnest. Holwell. Leigh, Leweston, Lillington, Longburton, Oborne, Poyntington,[12] Ryme Intrinseca, Sandford Orcas,[12] Sherborne, Stockwood, Thornford, Trent,[12] North Wootton, Yetminster

STURMINSTER PLU
Bellchalwell (1835–84), Stourton Caundle, Fifehead Magdalen, Fifehead Neville, Hammoon, Hanford (1858[15]–1930), Hazelbury Bryan, Hinton St Mary, Ibberton, Lydlinch, Manston, Marnhull, Childe Okeford, Okeford Fitzpaine, Shillingstone, Stalbridge, Stock Gaylard (1835–84), Stoke Wake, Sturminster Newton, Wooland

WAREHAM AND PURBECK PLU (pars in Purbeck PLU Mar–Sept 1836 only are indicated †)
Affpuddle, Arne, Bere Regis, Bloxworth, Chaldon Herring, Church Knowle†, Coombe Keynes, Corfe Castle†, East Holme, Kimmeridge†, East Lulworth, West Lulworth, Langton Matravers†, Moreton, Morden, St Martin (1894–1930), Steeple†, East Stoke, Studland†, Swanage†, Turners Puddle, Tyneham†, Wareham Holy Trinity, Wareham Lady St Mary, Wareham St Martin, Winfrith Newburgh, Wool, Worth Matravers†

WEYMOUTH PLU
Abbotsbury, Bincombe, Broadway, Buckland Ripers (1836–94), Chickerell, Fleet, Langton Herring, Melcombe Regis (1836–1920), Owermoigne, Portesham, Portland, Poxwell, Preston, Radipole, Upwey, Weymouth, Wyke Regis

WIMBORNE AND CRANBORNE PLU (pars in Cranborne PLU Mar–Aug 1836 only are indicated†)
Alderholt (1894–1930), Almer (1894–1930), Chalbury, Chettle†, Colehill (1896–1930), Corfe Mullen, Cranborne†, Long Crichel†, Moor Crichel†, Edmondsham†, Farnham† (1835–94), Gussage All Saints†, Gussage St Michael†, Hampreston, Sixpenny Handley†, Hinton Martell, Hinton Parva, Holt (1894–1930), Horton†, Pamphill (1894–1930), West Parley, Pentridge†, Shapwick, Sturminster Marshall, Verwood (1894–1930), Wimborne Minster, Wimborne St Giles†, Witchampton, Woodlands†, East Woodyates (1858[15]–1930), West Woodyates

In Other Poor Law Cos:
AXMINSTER PLU (Devon)
Chardstock,[16] Charmouth (1836–94), Hawkchurch,[16] Lyme Regis, Thorncombe (1836–94)

CHARD PLU (Somerset)
Wambrook[17]

MERE PLU (Wilts)
Bourton (1835–94), Silton (1835–94)

WINCANTON PLU (Somerset)
Buckhorn Weston (1835–94), Kington Magna (1835–94)

14

Co. DURHAM

In Durham Poor Law County:[61]

AUCKLAND PLU

Bishop Auckland (1837—86), Bishop Auckland (1894—1930), Bishop Auckland and Pollard's Lands (1886—94), West Auckland, Auckland St Andrew, Auckland St Helen, North Bedburn, South Bedburn, Binchester, Bolam, Byers Green, Coundon, Coundon Grange, Crook and Billy Row, Eldon, Escomb, Evenwood and Barony, Hamsterley, Helmington Row, Hunwick and Helmington, Lynesack and Softley, Merrington, Merrington Lane (1894—1930), Middlestone, Middridge, Middridge Grange, Newfield, Newton Cap, Old Park, Pollard's Lands (1837—86), Pollard's Lands (1894—1930), Shildon, East Thickley, Westerton, Whitworth, Whitworth Without (1894—1930), Windlestone, Witton le Wear

CHESTER LE STREET PLU

Barmston, South Biddick, Birtley, Burnmoor, Chester le Street, Cocken, Edmondsley, Harraton, Lambton, Lamesley, Great Lumley, Little Lumley, Ouston, Pelton, Plawsworth, Urpeth, Usworth, Waldridge, Washington, Witton Gilbert

DARLINGTON PLU (Durham, Yorks N Riding)

Archdeacon Newton, Great Aycliffe, School Aycliffe, Barmpton, Blackwell, Brafferton, Great Burdon, Coatham Mundeville, Coatsay Moor (1837—84), Cockerton (1837—1915), High Coniscliffe, Low Coniscliffe, Darlington, Denton, Low Dinsdale, Harrowgate Hill (1894—1907), Haughton le Skerne, Heighington, Houghton le Side, Hurworth, Killerby, Middleton St George, Morton Palms, Neasham, Piercebridge, Redworth, Sadberge, Sockburn, Summerhouse, Walworth, Whessoe

DURHAM PLU

Bearparck (1894—1930), Belmont (1894—1930), Brancepeth, Brandon and Byshottles, Broom, Cassop (1837—87), Cassop cum Quarrington (1887—1930), Coxhoe, Crossgate (1837—1916), Durham (1916—30), Durham Castle and Precincts (1862—1916), Durham College (1862—1916), Durham Magdalen Place (1862—1916), Durham St Mary le Bow [North Bailey] (1837—1916), Durham St Mary the Less [South Bailey] (1837—1916), Durham St Nicholas (1837—1916), Elvet (1837—1916), Framwellgate (1837—1916), Framwellgate Moor (1894—1930), Hett, Kimblesworth, Neville's Cross (1894—1930), Pittington, Quarrington (1837—87), St Giles (1837—1916), St Oswald's (1895—1930), Shadforth, Sherburn, Sherburn House, Shincliffe, Stockley, Sunderland Bridge, Tudhoe, Whitwell House (1862—1930), Willington

EASINGTON PLU

Burdon, Castle Eden, Cold Hesledon, Dalton le Dale, Dawdon, Easington, Haswell, Hawthorn, Hutton Henry, Kelloe, Monk Hesleden, East Murton, Nesbitt, Seaham, Seaton with Slingley, Sheraton with Hulam, Shotton, Thornley, Wingate

GATESHEAD PLU

Chopwell, Crawcrook (1836—1914), Gateshead, Heworth, Heworth Within (1894—1907), Ryton, Ryton Woodside (1836—1914), Stella, Whickham, Winlaton

HARTLEPOOL PLU (1859—1930)

Brierton, Claxton, Dalton Piercy, Elwick, Elwick Hall, Greatham, Hart, Hartlepool, West Hartlepool (1894—1930), Middleton (1894—1930), Seaton (1894—1930), Seaton Carew, Stranton, Thorpe Bulmer, Throston, Throston Rural (1894—1930)

HOUGHTON LE SPRING PLU

Great Eppleton, Little Eppleton, East and Middle Herrington, West Herrington, Hetton le Hole, Houghton le Spring, Moor House, Moorsley, Morton Grange, Newbottle, Offerton, Penshaw, East Rainton, West Rainton, Silksworth, Warden Law

LANCHESTER PLU

Benfieldside, Billingside (1837—87), Collierley, Consett (1894—1930), Conside and Knitsley (1837—94), Cornsay, South Cornsay (1894—1930), Craghead (1896—1930), Ebchester, Esh, Greencroft, Greencroft Within (1896—1930), Healeyfield, Hedleyhope, Iveston, Knitsley (1894—1930), Kyo, Lanchester, Langley, Medomsley, South Moor (1894—1916), Muggleswick, Oxhill (1894—1916), Satley, Stanley (1894—1930), Tanfield

SEDGEFIELD PLU

Bishop Middleham, Bishopton, Bradbury, Butterwick and Oldacres, Chilton, Cornforth, Elstob, Embleton, Ferryhill, Fishburn, Foxton and Shotton, Garmondsway Moor, Mainsforth, Mordon, East and West Newbiggin, Preston le Skerne, Sedgefield, Low Spennymoor (1894—1930), Great Stainton, Little Stainton, Stillington, Thrislington, Trimdon, Woodham

SOUTH SHIELDS PLU

Boldon, Boldon Colliery (1895—1930), Harton (1836—1921), Hebburn (1894—1930); Hedworth, Monkton and Jarrow (1836—94); Jarrow (1894—1930), Monkton (1894—1930), South Shields, Westoe (1836—97), Whitburn

STOCKTON PLU (Durham, Yorks N Riding)

Aislaby, Cowpen Bewley, Newton Bewley, Billingham, Brierton (1837—59), Carlton, Claxton (1837—59), Dalton Piercy (1837—59), Egglescliffe, Elton, Elwick (1837—59), Elwick Hall (1837—59), Greatham (1837—59), Grindon, Hart (1837—59), East Hartburn (1837—1913), Hartlepool (1837—59), Newsham, Long Newton, Norton, Preston on Tees, Redmarshall, Seaton Carew (1837—59), Stockton on Tees, Stranton (1837—59), Thorpe Bulmer (1837—59), Throston (1837—59), Whitton, Wolviston

SUNDERLAND PLU

Bishopwearmouth (1836—97), Bishopwearmouth Panns (1836—97), Bishopwearmouth Without (1894—1930), Ford, Fulwell (1836—1928), Hylton, Monkwearmouth (1836—97), Monkwearmouth Shore (1836—97), Monkwearmouth Without (1894—95), Ryhope, Ryhope Within (1894—97), Southwick (1836—1928), Sunderland, Tunstall

15

Co. Durham *continued*

TEESDALE PLU (Durham, Yorks N Riding)
Barnard Castle, Cleatlam, Cockfield, Eggleston, Forest and Frith, Gainford, Headlam, Hilton, Ingleton, Langleydale and Shotton, Langton, Marwood (1837— 84), Marwood (1894—1930), Middleton in Teesdale, Morton Tinmouth, Newbiggin, Raby with Keverstone, Staindrop, Streatlam and Stainton, Wackerfield, Westwick, Whorlton, Winston, Woodland

WEARDALE PLU
Edmondbyers, Hunstanworth, Stanhope, Stanhope Urban (1894—1930), Tow Law (1894—1930), Wolsingham

In Other Poor Law Counties:
BELFORD PLU[62] (Northumb, Durham until 1844, ent Northumb thereafter)
Elwick, Ross

BERWICK PLU (Northumb, Durham [until 1844])
Ancroft, Cornhill on Tweed, Duddo, Felkington, Grindon, Holy Island, Horncliffe, Kyloe, Loanend, Longridge, Norham, Normam Mains, Shoreswood, Thornton, Tweedmouth, Twizell

ESSEX

In Essex Poor Law County:[12]
BILLERICAY PLU
Basildon, North Benfleet, South Benfleet, Bowers Gifford, Brentwood, Great Burstead, Little Burstead, Childerditch, Downham, Dunton, East Horndon, West Horndon,Hutton, Ingrave, Laindon, Lee Chapel (1858[13]—1930), Mountnessing, Nevendon, Pitsea, Ramsden Bellhouse, Ramsden Crays, Shenfield, Thundersley (1835—), Vange, Great Warley, Little Warley, South Weald, Wickford

BRAINTREE PLU
Bocking, Bradwell, Braintree, Great Coggeshall (1883—1930), Little Coggeshall (1883—1930), Cressing, Fairstead (1883—1930), Faulkbourne (1883—1930), Feering (1883—1930), Finchingfield, Hatfield Peverel (1883—1930), Kelvedon (1883—1930), Markshall (1883—1930), Black Notley, White Notley, Panfield, Pattiswick, Rayne, Rivenhall (1883—1930), Great Saling, Shalford, Stisted, Terling (1883—1930), Wethersfield, Witham (1883—1930)

Essex *continued*

CHELMSFORD PLU
Great Baddow, Little Baddow, Boreham, Broomfield, Buttsbury, Chelmsford, Chignall (1888— 1930), Chignall St James (1835—88), Chignall Smealy (1835—88), Danbury, Good Easter, High Easter, Fryerning, East Hanningfield, South Hanningfield, West Hanningfield, Ingatestone, Great Leighs,[14] Little Leighs,[14] Margaretting, Mashbury, Pleshey, Rettendon,[14] Roxwell, Runwell,[14] Sandon, Springfield, Stock, Great Waltham, Little Waltham, Widford, Woodham Ferrers,[14] Writtle

COLCHESTER PLU
Berechurch (1835—97), Colchester (1897—1930), Colchester All Saints (1835—97), Colchester Holy Trinity (1835—97), Colchester St Botolph (1835— 97), Colchester St Giles (1835—97), Colchester St James (1835—97), Colchester St Leonard (1835— 97), Colchester St Martin (1835—97), Colchester St Mary at the Walls (1835—97), Colchester St Mary Magdalen (1835—97), Colchester St Nicholas (1835—97), Colchester St Peter (1835—97), Colchester St Runwald (1835—97),Greenstead (1835— 97), Lexden (1835—97), Mile End St Michael (1835—97)

DUNMOW PLU
Great Bardfield, Little Bardfield, Bardfield Saling, Barnston, Broxted, Great Canfield, Little Canfield, Chickney, Great Dunmow, Little Dunmow, High Easter, Great Easton, Little Easton, Felsted, Hatfield Broad Oak, Lindsell, Aythorpe Roding, High Roding, Leaden Roding, Margaret Roding, [Morrel Roding[15]], White Roding,[15] Stebbing, Takeley, Thaxted, Tilty

EPPING PLU
Buckhurst Hill (1894—1930), Chigwell, Chingford, Epping, Epping Upland (1896—1930), Harlow, Latton, Magdalen Laver, Loughton, Matching, Nazeing, Netteswell, Great Parndon, Little Parndon, Roydon,[16] Sheering, Theydon Bois, Theydon Garnon, North Weald Bassett

HALSTEAD PLU
Earls Colne, White Colne, Colne Engaine, Gosfield, Halstead (1835—94), Halstead Rural (1894—1930), Halstead Urban (1894—1930), Castle Hedingham, Sible Hedingham, Great Maplestead, Little Maplestead, Pebmarsh, Ridgewell, Stambourne, Tilbury juxta Clare, Toppesfield, Great Yeldham, Little Yeldham

WEST HAM PLU
Cann Hall (1894—1930), East Ham, West Ham, Little Ilford (1836—1900), Leyton, Walthamstow, Wanstead, Woodford

16

Essex *continued*

LEXDEN AND WINSTREE PLU
Abberton, Aldham, West Bergholt, Birch, Boxted, Brightlingsea (1836–80), Mount Bures, Chappel, Wakes Colne, Copford, Dedham, East Donyland, Easthorpe, Fingringhoe, Fordham, Great Horkesley, Little Horkesley, Inworth (1883–1930), Langenhoe, Langham, Layer Breton, Layer de la Haye, Layer Marney, East Mersea, West Mersea, Messing (1883–1930), Peldon, Salcot, Stanway, Great Tey, Little Tey, Marks Tey, Virley, Great Wigborough, Little Wigborough, Wivenhoe, Wormingford

MALDON PLU
Althorne, Asheldham, Bradwell on Sea, Great Braxted (1883–1930), Little Braxted (1883–1930), Burnham, Creeksea, Dengie, North Fambridge, Goldhanger, Hazeleigh, Heybridge, Langford, Latchingdon, Maldon All Saints, Maldon St Mary, Maldon St Peter, Mayland, Mundon, Cold Norton, Purleigh, St Lawrence, Southminster, Steeple, Stow Maries, Tillingham, Tollesbury, Tolleshunt d'Arcy, Tolleshunt Knights, Tolleshunt Major, Great Totham, Little Totham, Ulting (1883–1930), Wickham Bishops (1883–1930), Woodham Mortimer, Woodham Walter

ONGAR PLU
Blackmore, Bobbingworth, Doddinghurst, Fyfield, Greenstead, Kelvedon Hatch, Lambourne, High Laver, Little Laver, Moreton, Navestock, Norton Mandeville, Chipping Ongar, High Ongar, Abbess Roding, Beauchamp Roding, Berners Roding, Shelley, Shellow Bowells, Stanford Rivers, Stapleford Abbotts, Stapleford Tawney, Stondon Massey, Theydon Mount, Willingale Doe, Willingale Spain

ORSETT PLU
Aveley, Bulphan, Chadwell St Mary, Corringham, Fobbing, Horndon on the Hill, Langdon Hills, Mucking, North Ockendon, South Ockendon, Orsett, Stanford le Hope, Stifford, Grays Thurrock, Little Thurrock, West Thurrock, East Tilbury, West Tilbury

ROCHFORD PLU (Essex, Suffolk)
Ashingdon, Barling, South Benfleet (1847–1930), Canewdon, Canvey Island (1880[13]–1930), Eastwood, South Fambridge, Foulness,[14] Hadleigh, Havengore (1858[13]–1930), Hawkwell, Hockley, Leigh (1885–1913), Paglesham, Prittlewell (1835–1913), Rawreth, Rayleigh, Rochford, North Shoebury, South Shoebury, Shopland, Southchurch (1835–1913), Southend on Sea (1913–30), Great Stambridge, Little Stambridge, Sutton, Thundersley (1847–1930), Great Wakering, Little Wakering

ROMFORD PLU
Barking, Cranham, Dagenham, Havering-atte-Bower, Hornchurch, Ilford,[13] Noak Hill (1895–1930), Rainham, Romford (1836–94), Romford (1900–30), Romford Rural (1894–1900), Romford Urban (1894–1900), Upminster, Great Warley, Wennington

SAFFRON WALDEN PLU
Arkesden, Ashdon, Great Chesterford, Little Chesterford, Chrishall, Clavering, Debden, Elmdon, Hempstead, Langley, Littlebury, Newport, Quendon, Radwinter, Ricking, Saffron Walden, Great Sampford, Little Sampford, Strethall, Wendens Ambo, Wendon Lofts, Wicken Bonhunt, Widdington, Wimbish

TENDRING PLU
Alresford, Ardleigh, Beaumont cum Moze, Great Bentley, Little Bentley, Bradfield, Brightlingsea (1838–1930), Great Bromley, Little Bromley, Great Clacton, Little Clacton, Dovercourt (1838–1925), Elmstead, Frating, Frinton, Harwich (1925–30), Harwich St Nicholas (1838–1925), Great Holland, Little Holland, Kirby le Soken, Lawford, Manningtree, Mistley, Great Oakley, Little Oakley, Ramsey, St Osyth, Thorpe le Soken, Tendring, Thorrington, Walton le Soken, Weeley, Wix, Wrabness

WITHAM PLU (1835–83)
Great Braxted, Little Braxted, Great Coggeshall, Little Coggeshall, Fairstead, Faulkbourne, Feering, Hatfield Peverel, Inworth, Kelvedon, Markshall, Messing, Rivenhall, Terling, Ulting, Witham, Wickham Bishops

In Other Poor Law Counties:

EDMONTON PLU (Middx)
Waltham Holy Cross

LINTON PLU (Cambs)
Bartlow End,[14] Hadstock

RISBRIDGE PLU (Suffolk)
Ashen, Birdbrook, Helion Bumpstead,[20] Steeple Bumpstead, Haverhill,[17] Kedington,[18] Ovington, Sturmer

ROYSTON PLU (Herts, Cambs)
Great Chishill,[19] Little Chishill,[19] Heydon[19]

BISHOP'S STORTFORD PLU (Herts)
Berden, Birchanger, Elsenham, Farnham, Great Hallingbury, Little Hallingbury, Henham, Manuden, Stansted Mountfitchet, Ugley

SUDBURY PLU (Suffolk)
Alphamstone, Belchamp Otten, Belchamp St Paul, Belchamp Walter, Borley, Bulmer, Bures, Foxearth, Gestingthorpe, Great Henny, Little Henny, Lamarsh, Liston, Middleton, Pentlow, Twinstead, Wickham St Paul, North Wood

17

GLOUCESTERSHIRE and BRISTOL

In Glos Poor Law County:[30]

BARTON REGIS PLU (1836–1904 [called CLIFTON PLU 1840s–80s])
Bristol St George (1836–98), Bristol St James and St Paul Out (1836–96), Bristol St Philip and St Jacob Out (1836–96), Clifton (1836–96), Compton Greenfield (1836–86), Filton, Henbury (1836–1904), Horfield (1836–1904), Shirehampton (1836–1904), Stapleton (1836–98), Stoke Gifford (1836–1904), Westbury-on-Trym (1836–1904), Winterbourne (1836–1904)

BRISTOL INCORPORATION (Glos, Somerset[29])
Bristol (1898–1930), Central Bristol (1896–98), North Bristol (1896–98), Bristol All Saints (until 1896), Bristol Castle Precincts (until 1896), Bristol Christ Church (until 1896), Bristol St Augustine (until 1896), Bristol St Ewen (until 1896), Bristol St James (until 1866), Bristol St James In (1866–96), Bristol St John the Baptist (until 1896), Bristol St Leonard, Bristol St Mary le Port, Bristol St Michael, Bristol St Nicholas, Bristol St Paul (until 1866), Bristol St Paul In (1866–96), Bristol St Peter, Bristol St Philip and St Jacob In, Bristol St Stephen, Bristol St Werburgh (until 1878), Filton (192 –30), Redland (1894–96)

CHELTENHAM PLU
Badgeworth, Charlton Kings, Cheltenham, Coberley, Cowley, Up Hatherley, Leckhampton, Prestbury, Shurdington, Staverton, Swindon, Uckington, Great Witcombe

CIRENCESTER PLU (Glos, Wilts)
Down Ampney, Ampney Crucis, Ampney St Mary, Ampney St Peter, Bagendon, Barnsley, Baunton, Brimpsfield, North Cerney, South Cerney, Cirencester, Coates, Colesbourne, Daglingworth, Driffield, Duntisbourne Abbots, Duntisbourne Rouse, Edgeworth, Elkstone, Fairford, Harnhill, Hatherop, Kempsford, Meysey Hampton, Poulton, Preston, Quenington, Rendcombe, Rodmarton, Sapperton, Siddington, Stratton, Syde, Winstone

DURSLEY PLU
Cam, Coaley, Dursley, Kingswood, North Nibley, Nympsfield, Owlpen, Slimbridge, Stinchcombe, Uley, Wotton under Edge

GLOUCESTER PLU
Ashleworth, Barnwood, Brockworth, Churchdown, Elmore, Gloucester (1896–1930), Gloucester Barton St Mary (until 1896), Gloucester Barton St Michael (until 1885), Gloucester Holy Trinity (until 1896), Gloucester North Hamlet (until 1885), Gloucester South Hamlet (until 1896), Gloucester Pool Meadow (until 1896), Gloucester St Aldate (until 1896), Gloucester St Catherine (until 1896), Gloucester St John the Baptist (until 1896), Gloucester St Mary de Crypt (until 1896), Gloucester St Mary de Grace (until 1896), Gloucester St Mary de Lode (until 1896), Gloucester St Michael (until 1896), Gloucester St Nicholas (until 1896), Gloucester St Owen (until 1896), Down Hatherley, Hempsted, Highnam Over and Linton, Hucclecote, Lassington, Littleworth (until 1896), Longford (1885–1930), Longford St Catherine (1866–85), Longford St Mary (1866–85), Maisemore, Matson, Norton, Prinknash Park, Quedgeley, Sandhurst, Tuffley (until 1900), Twigworth, Upton St Leonards, Whaddon, Ville of Wotton (from 1885), Wotton St Mary (until 1885), Wotton St Mary Within (1885–98), Wotton St Mary Without (1885–1930), Wotton Vill (1894–1930)

NEWENT PLU
Bromsberrow, Corse, Dymock, Hartpury, Highleadon, Kempley, Newent, Oxenhall, Pauntley, Preston, Rudford, Taynton, Tibberton, Upleadon

NORTHLEACH PLU
Aldsworth, Aston Black, Little Barrington, Bibury, Chedworth, Coln Rogers, Coln St Aldwyn, Coln St Dennis, Compton Abdale, Dowdeswell, Eastington, Eastleach Martin, Eastleach Turville, Farmington, Hampnett, Hasleton, Northleach, Salperton, Sevenhampton, Sherborne, Shipton, Southrop, Stowell, Turkdean, Winson, Whittington, Windrush, Withington, Yanworth

CHIPPING SODBURY PLU
Iron Acton, Acton Turville, Alderley, Cold Ashton, Great Badmington, Dodington, Doynton, Dyrham and Hinton, Filton (1894–1930), Frampton Cotterell, Hawkesbury, Horton, West Littleton, Marshfield, Pucklechurch, Chipping Sodbury, Little Sodbury, Old Sodbury, Stoke Gifford (1894–1930), Tormarton, Wapley and Cordrington, Westerleigh, Wick and Abson, Wickwar, Winterbourne (1894–1930), Yate

STOW ON THE WOLD PLU
Adlestrop, Great Barrington, Bledington, Bourton on the Water, Broadwell, Clapton, Condicote, Donnington, Eyford, Icomb, Church Icomb, Longborough, Maugersbury, Naunton, Notgrove, Oddington, Great Rissington, Little Rissington, Wick Rissington, Sezincote, Lower Slaughter, Upper Slaughter, Stow-on-the-Wold, Lower Swell, Upper Swell, Westcote

STROUD PLU
Avening, Bisley (1836–94), Bisley with Lypiatt (1894–1930), Cainscross (1894–1930), Chalford (1894–1930), Cranham, Haywards Field (1858–84), Horsley, Minchinhampton, Miserden, Nailsworth, Painswick, Pitchcombe, Randwick, Rodborough, King's Stanley, Leonard Stanley, Stonehouse, Stroud, Thrupp (1894–1930), Uplands (1894–1930), Whiteshill (1894–1930), Woodchester

TETBURY PLU
Beverstone, Boxwell with Leighterton, Cherington, Didmarton, Kingscote, Newington Bagpath, Oldbury on the Hill (1836– 83), Ozleworth, Shipton Moyne, Tetbury, Tetbury Upton (1894–1930), Weston Birt

18

Gloucestershire *continued*

TEWKESBURY PLU
Ashchurch, Beddington, Deerhurst, Elmstone Hardwicke, Forthampton, Hasfield, Kemerton, Leigh, Oxenton, Stoke Orchard, Tewkesbury, Tirley, Tredington, Twyning, Walton Cardiff, Woolstone

THORNBURY PLU
Alkington, Almondsbury, Alveston, Aust, Berkeley, Breadstone, Charfield, Cromhall, Elberton, Falfield (1894–1930), Ham and Stone, Hamfallow, Hill, Hinton, Littleton upon Severn, Oldbury upon Severn (1894–1930), Olveston, Rangeworthy, Redwick and Northwick, Rockhampton, Thornbury, Tortworth, Tytherington

WESTBURY ON SEVERN PLU
Abenhall, Awre, Blaisdon, Bulley, Churcham, East Dean, Flaxley, Hinders Lane and Dockham (1858–84), Huntley, Littledean, Longhope, Minsterworth, Mitcheldean, Newnham, Westbury on Severn

WHEATENHURST PLU
Arlington, Brookthorpe, Eastington, Frampton on Severn, Fretherne (1836–84), Fretherne with Saul (1884–1930), Frocester, Hardwicke, Harescombe, Haresfield, Longney, Moreton Valence, Saul (1836–84), Standish, Wheatenhurst

WINCHCOMBE PLU
Alderton, Alstone, Beckford, Buckland, Charlton Abbots, Bishop's Cleeve, Didbrook, Dumbleton, Gotherington, Temple Guiting, Guiting Power, Hailes, Hawling, Pinnock and Hyde, Prescott, Roel, Snowshill, Southam and Brockhampton, Stanley Pontlarge, Stanton, Stanway, Sudeley Manor, Toddington, Great Washbourne, Little Washbourne, Winchcombe, Woodmancote, Wormington

In Other Poor Law Counties:
CHEPSTOW PLU (Monmouth)
Alvington, Aylburton, Hewelsfield, Lancaut, Lydney, St Briavels, Tidenham, Woolaston

FARINGDON PLU (Berks)
Lechlade

EVESHAM PLU (Worcs)
Ashton under Hill, Aston Somerville, Aston Subedge, Child's Wickham, Hinton on the Green, Cow Honeybourne, Pebworth, Saintbury, Weston Subedge, Willersley

KEYNSHAM PLU (Somerset)
Bittton, Hanham (1836–94), Hanham Abbots (1894–1930), Kingswood (1894–1930), Mangotsfield (1836–1927), Mangotsfield Rural (1927–30), Mangotsfield Urban (1927–30), Oldland, Siston

MONMOUTH PLU (Monmouth)
English Bicknor, West Dean, Newland, Staunton

ROSS PLU (Hereford)
Lea Bailey (1836–90), Ruardean

SHIPSTON ON STOUR PLU (Warws)
Admington, Batsford, Bourton on the Hill, Chipping Campden, Clopton, Ebrington, Hidcote Bartrim, Ilmington,[31] Lower Lemington, Mickleton, Moreton in Marsh, Quinton, Todenham

STRATFORD ON AVON PLU (Warws)
Clifford Chambers, Dorsington, Marston Sicca, Preston on Stour, Welford, Weston on Avon

HAMPSHIRE

In Hants Poor Law County:[36]

ALRESFORD PLU
New Alresford, Old Alresford, Beauworth, Bighton, Bramdean, Brown Candover, Chilton Candover, Cheriton, Godsfield (1858[37]–1930), Hinton Ampner, Itchen Stoke, Kilmiston, Northington, Ovington, Ropley, Bishops Sutton, Swarraton, Tichborne, West Tisted

ALTON PLU
Alton, Bentley, Bentworth, Binstead, Chawton, Coldrey, Farringdon, Froyle, Grayshott (1902–30), Hartley Mauditt, Headley (1869–1930), Holybourne, Kingsley (1869–1930), Lasham, Medstead, Neatham, Newton Valence, Selborne, Shalden, East Tisted, Whitehill (1929–30), Wield, East Worldham, West Worldham

ALVERSTOKE INCORP (1799–1852), PLU (1852–1930)
Alverstoke

ANDOVER PLU (Hants, Wilts)
Abbots Ann, Amport, Andover, Appleshaw, Barton Stacey, Bullington, Chilbolton, Goodworth Clatford, Upper Clatford, Vernhams Dean, Knights Enham (1894–1930), Faccombe, Foxcott, Fyfield, Grateley, Hurstbourne Tarrant, Kimpton, Linkenholt, Longparish, Monxton, *Park House*,[40] Penton Grafton, Penton Mewsey, Quarley, Shipton Bellinger, Tangley, Thruxton, South Tedworth, Wherwell

BASINGSTOKE PLU (Hants, Berks)
Andwell, Basing, Basingstoke, Bradley, Bramley, Preston Candover, Cliddesden, Deane, Dummer, Eastrop, Ellisfield, Farleigh Wallop, Hartley Wespall, Herriard, Mapledurwell, Mortimer West End (1866[37]–1930), Nateley Scures, Up Nateley, Newnham, Nutley, Oakley, Pamber, Popham, Monk Sherborne, Sherborne St John, Sherfield-on-Loddon, Silchester, Steventon, Stratfield Turgis, Tunworth, Upton Grey, North Waltham, Weston Corbett, Weston Patrick, Winslade, Woodmancott, Wootton St Lawrence, Worting

BOURNEMOUTH PAR (1900–30)
Bournemouth

BOURNEMOUTH AND CHRISTCHURCH PLU (1835–1900)
Bournemouth, Christchurch, Christchurch East (1894–1900), Highcliffe (1894–1900), Holdenhurst, Hurn (1894–1900), Pokesdown (1894–1900), Sopley, Southbourne (1894–1900), Winton (1894–1900)

CATHERINGTON PLU
Blendworth, Catherington, Chalton, Clanfield, Idsworth, Waterloo (1910–30)

CHRISTCHURCH PLU (1900–30)
Christchurch, Christchurch East, Highcliffe, Holdenhurst, Hurn, Pokesdown (1900–02), Sopley, Southbourne (1900–02), Winton (1900–02)

19

DROXFORD PLU
Corhampton, Curdridge (1894–1930), Droxford, Durley, Exton, Hambledon, West Meon, Meonstoke, Soberton, Upham, Shedfield (1894–1930), Swanmore (1894–1930), Bishops Waltham, Warnford

EASTLEIGH PLU (1920–30)
Bishopstoke, Botley, Burlesdon, Chilworth, Eastleigh, Hamble le Rice, Hedge End, Hound, Millbrook, North Stoneham (ent 1920–24, pt 1924–30), West End

FAREHAM PLU
Boarhunt, Cosham (1894–1921), Crofton (1894–1930), Fareham, Hook with Warsash (1894–1930), Portchester, Rowner, Sarisbury (1894–1930), Southwick, Titchfield, Wickham, Widley (1835–94), Widley (1921–30), Wymering (1835–94)

FARNBOROUGH INCORP[38] **(1794–1869)**
Cove, Farnborough, Hawley with Minley, Yateley

FORDINGBRIDGE PLU (Hants, Wilts until 1895, ent Wilts thereafter)
Ashley Walk (1868–1930), Breamore, North Charford, South Charford, Damerham,[39] Fordingbridge, Hale, Martin,[39] Rockbourne, Toyd Farm and Allenford,[39] Whitsbury,[39] Woodgreen

NEW FOREST PLU (Hants, Wilts)
Beaulieu, Bramshaw (Hants, Wilts, 1835–94), Bramshaw (Hants, 1894–1930), Bramshaw (Wilts, 1894–95), East Bramshaw (1895–1930), Calshot,[40] Colbury (1894–1930), Copythorne (1894–1930), Denny Lodge (1868–1930), Dibden, Eling, Exbury, Fawley, Lyndhurst, Marchwood (1894–1930), Minstead, Netley Marsh (1894–1930)

HAVANT PLU
Bedhampton, Farlington, Havant, North Havant (1902–30), North Hayling, South Hayling, Warblington

HARTLEY WINTNEY PLU
Bramshill, Cove (1869–1930), Crondall, Crookham (1894–1930), Dogmersfield, Elvetham, Eversley, Farnborough (1869–1930), Fleet (1894–1930), Greywell, Hartley Wintney, Hawley with Minley (1869–1930), Heckfield, Mattingley, Odiham, Rotherwick, Long Sutton (1869–1930), South Warnborough, Winchfield, Yateley (1869–1930)

HURSLEY PLU
Ampfield (1894–1930), North Baddesley, Chandlers Ford (1894–1930), Farley Chamberlayne, Hursley, Otterbourne

KINGSCLERE PLU
Ashmansworth, Baughurst, Burghclere, Crux Easton, Ecchinswell, Ewhurst, Hannington, Highclere, Kingsclere, Litchfield, Newtown (1894–1930), Sydmonton, Tadley, Wolverton, Woodcott, East Woodhay

LYMINGTON PLU
Boldre, East Boldre (1929–30), Brockenhurst, Hordle, Lymington, Milford (1835–1911), Milford on Sea (1911–30), Milton, Pennington (1911–30), Rhinefield, Sway (1866[37]–1930)

PETERSFIELD PLU
Bramshott[41] (1869–1930), Buriton, Colemore, Priors Dean, Empshott, Froxfield, Greatham, Hawkley, Langrish (1894–1930), Liss, East Meon, Petersfield, Privett, Sheet, Steep

PORTSEA ISLAND PLU (1836–1900)
Portsea, Portsmouth, Great Salterns (1858[37]–1930)

PORTSMOUTH PAR (1900–30)
Portsmouth

RINGWOOD PLU
Broomy (1868–1930), Burley (1868–1930), Ellingham, Harbirdge, Ibsley, Ringwood

ROMSEY PLU (Hants, Wilts until 1895, ent Hants thereafter)
East Dean, Dunwood (1858[37]–1930), Lockereley, Melchet Park,[39] Michelmersh, Mottisfont, Nursling, Plaitford,[39] Romsey Extra, Romsey Infra, Rownhams (1897–1930), Sherfield English, Timsbury, East Wellow, West Wellow[39]

SOUTHAMPTON INCORP (1772–1909), PLU (1909–30)
Bitterne (1924–30), Portswood (1908–12), Shirley (1908–12), pt North Stoneham (1924–30), Southampton (1912–30), Southampton All Saints (1772–1912), Southampton Holy Rood (1772–1912), Southampton St John (1772–1912), Southampton St Lawrence (1772–1912), Southampton St Mary (1772–1912), Southampton St Michael (1772–1912), Southampton St Nicholas (1920–25)

STOCKBRIDGE PLU (Hants, Wilts until 1894, ent Hants thereafter)
Ashley, Bossington, Broughton, Buckholt, Crown Farm (1858[37]–83), West Dean[43] (1835–94), Upper Eldon, Frenchmoor, Houghton, Leckford, Longstock, Kings Somborne, Little Somborne, Stockbridge, East Tytherley, West Tytherley, Nether Wallop, Over Wallop

SOUTH STONEHAM PLU (1835–1920)
Bitterne (1894–1920), Botley, Bursledon, Chilworth, Eastleigh (1894–1920), Hamble le Rice, Hedge End (1894–1920), Hound, Itchen (1903–20), Millbrook, Portswood (1894–1908), St Mary Extra (1835–1903), Shirley (1894–1908), Sholing (1894–1903), North Stoneham, South Stoneham, West End (1894–1920)

Hampshire *continued*

WHITCHURCH PLU
Ashe, Freefolk Manor, Hurstbourne Priors, Laverstoke, Overton, St Mary Bourne, Tufton, Whitchurch

WINCHESTER PLU
Abbots Barton (1894–1930), Avington, Bishopstoke, Chilcombe (1835–94), Chilcombe Within (1894–1902), Chilcombe Without (1894–1930), Compton, Crawley, Easton, Fair Oak (1894–1930), Hunton, Itchen Abbas, Lainston, Littleton, Micheldever, Milland (1835–1902), Morestead, Owslebury, St Faith (1835–94), St Faith Within (1894–1902), St Faith Without (1894–1900), Sparsholt, Stoke Charity, Stoke Park (1899–1930), East Stratton, Twyford, Weeke (1835–94), Weeke Within (1894–1902), Weeke Without (1894–1930), Winchester (1902–30), Winchester St Bartholomew Hyde (1835–1902), Winchester St John (1835–1902), Winchester St Lawrence (1835–1902), Winchester St Mary Kalendar (1835–1902), Winchester St Maurice (1835–1902), Winchester St Michael (1835–1902), Winchester St Peter Cheesehill (1835–1902), Winchester St Peter Colebrook (1835–1902), Winchester St Swithin (1835–1902), Winchester St Thomas (1835–1902), Winnall (1835–1902), Wonston, Headbourne Worthy, Kings Worthy, Martyr Worthy

In Isle of Wight (Hants until 1890, Isle of Wight Adm Co (1890–1930):
ISLE OF WIGHT INCORP (1770–1865), PLU (1865–1930)
Arreton (1865–94), Ashey (1894–1930), Bambridge (1896–1930), Binstead, Bonchurch, Brading, Brixton, Brook, Calbourne, Carisbrooke, Chale, Cowes (1894–1930), East Cowes (1894–1930), Freshwater, Gatcombe, Godshill, Kingston, Mottistone, Newchurch, Newport, Niton, Northwood, Ryde, St Helens, St Lawrence, St Nicholas (1770–1894), Sandown (1894–1930), Shalfleet, Shanklin, East Shanklin (1894–98), Shorwell, Thorley, Totland (1894–1930), Ventnor, Whippingham, Whitwell, Wootton (1770–1894), Yarmouth, Yaverland

In Other Poor Law Counties:
ASH INCORP (Surrey, Hants) (until 1846)
Long Sutton
FARNHAM PLU (Surrey, Hants)
Aldershot, Dockenfield
HUNGERFORD PLU (Berks, Hants, Wilts)
Coombe
NEWBURY PLU (Berks, Hants)
Newtown
WIMBORNE PLU (Dorset, Hants until 1860s, ent Dorset thereafter)
Hampreston

HEREFORDSHIRE

In Heref Poor Law County:[7]
BROMYARD PLU (Heref, Worcs)
Acton Beauchamp,[8] Avenbury, Bredenbury, Brockhampton (1894—1930), Lower Brockhampton (1863—94), Bromyard, Collington, Little Cowarne, Much Cowarne, Cradley, Edvin Loach,[9] Edvin Ralph, Evesbatch, Felton, Bishop's Frome, Grendon Bishop, Grendon Warren (1836—95), Hampton Charles, Linton, Moreton Jeffreys, Norton (1894—1930), Norton with Brockhampton (1836—94), Ocle Pychard, Pencombe (1836—95), Pencombe with Grendon Warren (1895—1930), Saltmarshe (1858—1930), Upper Sapey, Stanford Bishop, Stoke Lacy, Tedstone Delamere, Tedstone Wafer, Thornbury, Ullingswick, Wacton, Whitbourne, Winslow, Wolferlow

DORE PLU
Abbey Dore, Bacton, Craswall, Dulas, Ewyas Harold, Kenderchurch, Kentchurch, Kilpeck, Kingstone, Llancillo, Llanveynoe, Longtown, Madley, Michaelchurch Escley, Newton, Orcop, Peterchurch, Rowlstone, St Devereux, St Margaret's, Thruxton, Treville, Turnastone, Tyberton, Vowchurch, Walterstone, Wormbridge

HEREFORD PLU
Aconbury, Allensmore (soon after 1836[10]—1930), Amberley (1836—97), Bartestree, Little Birch, Bolstone, Breinton, Lower Bullingham, Upper Bullingham (1836—85), Burghill, Callow, Clehonger, Credenhill, Little Dewchurch, Much Dewchurch, Dewsall, Dinedor, Dinmore (1858—1930), Dormington, Eaton Bishop (soon after 1836[10]—1930), Fownhope, Grafton, Hampton Bishop, Haywood (1858—1930), Hereford All Saints, Hereford St the Bishop, Hereford St Martin, Hereford St Nicholas, Hereford St Owen, Hereford St Peter, Hereford The Vineyard (1862—1930), Holme Lacy, Holmer (1884—1930), Holmer and Shelwick (1836—84), Holmer Within (1884—1930), Huntington, Kenchester, Lugwardine, Marden, Mordiford, Moreton on Lugg, Pipe and Lyde, Preston Wynne, Stoke Edith, Stretton Sugwas, Sutton, Tupsley, Wellington, Westhide, Weston Beggard, Withington

KINGTON PLU[10] (Radnor, Heref)
Brilley, Byton (1836—1930), Combe (1836—94), Eardisley, Lower Harpton, Huntington, Kington (1836—94), Kington Rural (1894—1930), Kington Urban (1894—1930), Kinsham (1886—1930), Lower Kinsham (1836—86), Upper Kinsham (1836—86), Knill (1836—1930), Lingen (1836—1930), Lyonshall, Pembridge; Rodd, Nash and Little Brampton (1836—1930); Stapleton (1836—1930), Staunton on Arrow, Titley, Willersley, Willey (1836—1930), Winforton

LEDBURY PLU (Heref, Worcs [1836—97])
Ashperton, Aylton, Bosbury, Coddington, Colwall, Donnington, Eastnor, Egleton, Canon Frome, Castle Frome, Ledbury (1836—84), Ledbury Rural (1894—1930), Ledbury Urban (1894—1930), Little Marcle, Much Marcle, Mathon (1897—1930), Munsley, Parkhold (1836—84), Pixley, Putley, Stretton Grandison, Tarrington, Wellington Heath (1894—1930), Woolhope, Yarkhill

Herefordshire *continued*

LEOMINSTER PLU

Aymestry, Bodenham, Croft, Docklow; Eye, Moreton and Ashton; Eyton, Ford, New Hampton (1858—1930), Hampton Wafer (1858—1930), Hatfield, Hope under Dinmore, Humber, Kimbolton, Kingsland, Laysters, Leominster Borough, Leominster Out, Lucton, Luston, Middleton on the Hill, Monkland, Newton, Orleton, Pudlestone, Shobdon, Stoke Prior, Yarpole

ROSS PLU (Heref, Glos)

Aston Ingham (1836—1930), Ballingham, Brampton Abbotts, Bridstow, Brockhampton, How Caple, King's Caple, Foy, Goodrich, Harewood, Hentland, Hope Mansell, Lea (1883—1930), Lea Lower (1836—83), Lea Upper (1836—83), Linton (1836—1930), Llandinabo, Llangarren, Llanwarne, Marstow, Pencoyd, Peterstow, Ross (1836—94), Ross Rural (1894—1930), Ross Urban (1894—1930), St Weonards, Sellack, Sollers Hope, Tretire with Michaelchurch, Upton Bishop, Walford (1836—1930), Weston under Penyard, Yatton

WEOBLEY PLU

Almeley, Birley, Bishopstone, Blakemere (soon after 1836[11]—1930), Bridge Sollers, Brinsop, Brobury, Canon Pyon, Dilwyn, Eardisland, King's Pyon, Kinnersley, Letton (soon after 1836[11]—1930), Mansell Grange, Mansell Lacy, Moccas (soon after 1836[11]—1930), Monington on Wye, Norton Canon (soon after 1836[11]—1930), Preston on Wye (1836—1930), Sarnesfield, Staunton on Wye (1836—1930), Stretford, Weobley, Wormsley, Yazor

In Other Poor Law Counties:

ABERGAVENNY PLU (Monm, Heref [1836—91]) Fwthog[12]

CLEOBURY MORTIMER PLU (Salop, Worcs, Heref [1836—44]) Farley[13]

HAY PLU (Brecon, Heref, Radnor) Bredwardine, Clifford, Cusop, Dorstone, Whitney

KNIGHTON PLU (Radnor, Salop, Heref) Adforton, Brampton Bryan, Buckton and Coxall, Letton and Newton, Walford

LUDLOW PLU (Salop, Heref) Aston, Burrington, Downton, Elton, Leinthall Starkes, Leintwardine[14] (1895—1930), Leintwardine North Side[14] (1836—95), Ludford,[15] Richards Castle[16] (until 1889), Richards Castle[16] (1889—1930), Wigmore

MONMOUTH PLU (Monm, Glos, Heref) Ganarew, Faraway, Llanrothal, Welsh Bicknor,[17] Welsh Newton, Whitchurch

NEWENT PLU (Glos, Heref [1835—36], Worcs) Aston Ingham (1835—36), Linton (1835—36), Walford (1835—36)

PRESTEIGNE PLU[10] (Brecon, Heref [1836]) Byton (1836), Combe (1836), Lower Kinsham (1836), Upper Kinsham (1836), Knill (1836), Lingen (1836); Ross, Nash and Little Brampton (1836); Stapleton (1836), Willey (1836)

TENBURY PLU (Worcs, Heref, Salop) Brimfield, Little Hereford, Stoke Bliss[18]

HERTFORDSHIRE

In Hertfordshire Poor Law County:[9]

BARNET PLU (Herts, Middx)

Arkley (1894—1930), Chipping Barnet, East Barnet, Barnet Vale (1894—1930), Elstree, Hadley (1894—1930), Monken Hadley,[10] South Mimms,[11] South Mimms Urban (1894—1930), Ridge, Shenley, Totteridge

BERKHAMPSTEAD PLU

Aldbury, Berkhampstead (1835—98), Great Berkhampstead Rural (1898—1930), Great Berkhampstead Urban (1898—1930), Little Gaddesden, Nettleden,[12] Northchurch, Puttenham, Tring (1835—94), Tring Rural (1894—1930), Tring Urban (1894—1930), Wigginton

BUNTINGFORD PLU

Anstey, Ardeley, Aspenden, Broadfield, Buckland, Cottered, Great Hormead, Little Hormead, Layston, Meesden, Rushden, Sandon, Throcking, Wallington, Westmill, Wyddial

HATFIELD PLU

Essendon, Bishop's Hatfield, North Mimms, Northaw

HEMEL HEMPSTEAD PLU

Bovingdon, Flamstead, Flaunden, Great Gaddesden, Hemel Hempstead, King's Langley, Markyate (1897—1930)

HERTFORD PLU

Little Amwell (1866[13]—1930), Aston, Bayford, Bengeo (1835—94), Bengeo Rural (1894—1930), Bengeo Urban (1894—1900), Benington, Little Berkhampstead, Bramfield, Brickendon (1835—94), Brickendon Liberty (1929—30), Brickendon Rural (1894—1929), Brickendon Urban (1894—1900), Datchworth, Hertford (1900—30), Hertford All Saints (1835—1900), Hertford St Andrew (1835—94), Hertford St John (1835—94), Hertingfordbury, Sacombe, St Andrew Rural (1894—1924), St Andrew Urban (1894—1900), St John Rural (1894—1929), St John Urban (1894—1900), Stapleford, Tewin, Unnamed (1894—1900), Walkern, Watton at Stone

HITCHIN PLU

Baldock, Bygrave, Caldecote, Clothall, Codicote, Graveley, Hexton, Hitchin (1835—94), Hitchin Urban (1894—1930), Holwell,[14] Ickleford, Ippollitts, Kimpton, Knebworth, Langley (1894—1930), Letchworth, Lilley, Newnham, Norton (1835—1908), Offley, Pirton, Preston (1894—1930), Radwell, Shephall, Stevenage, King's Walden, St Paul's Walden, Walsworth (1894—1922), Weston, Willian, Great Wymondley, Little Wymondley

ROYSTON PLU (Herts, Cambs, Essex)

Ashwell, Barkway, Barley, South Bassingbourn (1896—97), Hinxworth, Kelsall, South Kneesworth (1896—97), South Melbourn (1896—97), Nuthampstead, Reed, Royston, North Royston (1896—97), Therfield

22

ST ALBANS PLU
Harpenden (1835–98), Harpenden Rural (1898–1930), Harpenden Urban (1898–1930), Redbourn, St Albans, St Albans St Michael (1835–94), St Albans St Peter (1835–94), St Michael Rural (1894–1930), St Michael Urban (1894–98), St Peter Rural (1894–1930), St Peter Urban (1894–98), St Stephen, Sandridge (1835–94), Sandridge Rural (1894–1930), Sandridge Urban (1894–98), Wheathampstead

BISHOP'S STORTFORD PLU
Albury, Braughing, Little Hadham, Much Hadham, Brent Pelham, Furneux Pelham, Stocking Pelham, Sawbridgeworth, Bishop's Stortford, Thorley, High Wych (1901–30)

WARE PLU
Great Amwell, Broxbourne, Eastwick, Gilston, Hoddesdon (1835–94), Hoddesdon Rural (1894–1930), Hoddesdon Urban (1894–1930), Hunsdon, Great Munden, Little Munden, Standon, Stanstead Abbots, Stanstead St Margaret, Thundridge, Ware (1835–94), Ware Rural (1894–1930), Ware Urban (1894–1930), Widford, Wormley

WATFORD PLU
Aldenham, Bushey (1835–94), Bushey (1906–30), Bushey Rural (1894–1906), Bushey Urban (1894–1906), Chorleywood (1898–1930), Abbots Langley, Oxhey (1906–30), Rickmansworth (1835–98), Rickmansworth Rural (1898–1930), Rickmansworth Urban (1898–1930), Sarratt, Watford (1835–94), Watford Rural (1894–1930), Watford Urban (1894–1930)

WELWYN PLU
Ayot St Lawrence, Ayot St Peter, Digswell, Welwyn, Welwyn Garden City (1921–30)

In Other Poor Law Counties:
AMPTHILL PLU (Beds)
Shillington[15]
EDMONTON PLU (Middx)
Cheshunt, Enfield[16]
LUTON PLU (Beds)
Caddington,[17] Kensworth,[18] Studham,[19] Whipsnade[15]

HUNTINGDONSHIRE
In Hunts Poor Law County:[11]

HUNTINGDON PLU
Alconbury, Alconbury Weston, Barham, Brampton, Buckworth, Conington, Coppingford, Easton, Ellington, Steeple Gidding, Godmanchester, Hamerton, Hartford, Huntingdon (1921–30), Huntingdon All Saints (1836–1921), Huntingdon St Benedict (1836–1921), Huntingdon St John (1836–1921), Huntingdon St Mary (1836–1921), Leighton, Ramsey,[20] Great Raveley, Little Raveley, Abbots Ripton, Kings Ripton, Sawtry All Saints (1836–86), Sawtry All Saints and St Andrew (1886–1930), Sawtry St Andrew (1836–86), Sawtry St Judith, Spaldwick, Great Stukeley, Little Stukeley, Upton, Upwood, Wood Walton, Woolley

ST IVES PLU (Hunts, Cambs)
Bluntisham cum Earith, Broughton, Bury, Colne, Fenstanton, Hemingford Abbots, Hemingford Grey, Hilton, Holywell cum Needingworth, Houghton, Old Hurst, Pidley cum Fenton, St Ives, Somersham, Warboys, Wistow, Woodhurst, Wyton

ST NEOTS PLU (Hunts, Beds, Cambs)
Abbotsley, Buckden, Catworth (1885–1930), Great Catworth (1835–85), Little Catworth (1835–85), Diddington, Eynesbury, Eynesbury Hardwicke (1895–1930), Grafham, Kimbolton, Midloe, Offord Cluny, Offord D'Arcy, Great Paxton, Little Paxton, St Neots, St Neots Rural (1895–1930), Southoe, Great Staughton, Stow, Swineshead,[12] Tetworth, Tilbrook,[13] Toseland, Waresley, Hail Weston

In Other Poor Law Counties:
CAXTON PLU (Cambs)
Great Gransden, Papworth St Agnes,[14] Yelling
OUNDLE PLU (Northants)
Elton,[21] Great Gidding, Little Gidding, Luddington in the Brook,[15] Lutton,[15] Thurning,[15] Winwick[16]
PETERBOROUGH PLU (Northants, Cambs/IoE, Lincs)
Alwalton, Caldecote, Chesterton, Denton, Farcet, Fletton (1835–94),[17] Fletton Rural (1894–1930), Folksworth, Glatton, Haddon, Holme, Morborne, Orton Longueville, Orton Waterville, Stanground (1835–1905),[18] Stanground South (1905–30), Stilton, Washingley, Water Newton, Woodston (1835–94),[19] Woodston Rural (1894–1930), Yaxley
STAMFORD PLU (Lincs)
Sibson cum Stibbington
THRAPSTON PLU (Northants)
Brington, Bythorn, Covington, Keyston, Molesworth, Old Weston

23

KENT

In Kent Poor Law County:[32]

EAST ASHFORD PLU

Aldington, Bilsington, Bircholt, Bonnington, Boughton Aluph, Brabourne, Brook, Challock, Chilham, Crundale, Eastwell, Godmersham, Hastingleigh, Hinxhill, Hurst, Kennington, Mersham, Molash, Orlestone (1836–1930), Ruckinge (1836–1930), Sevington, Smeeth, Warehorne (1836–1930), Willesborough, Wye

WEST ASHFORD PLU

Ashford (1836–1930), Bethersden, Charing, Great Chart, Little Chart (1836–1930), Egerton, Hothfield, Kingsnorth, Pluckley, Shadoxhurst, Smarden, Westwell

NORTH AYLESFORD PLU (1835–84), renamed STROOD PLU (1884–1930)

Chalk, Cliffe at Hoo, Cobham, Cuxton, Denton, Frindsbury (1835–94), Frindsbury Extra (1894–1930), Frindsbury Intra (1894–1930), Halling, Higham, Ifield, Luddesdown, Meopham, Northfleet, Nursted, Shorne, Strood (1835–94), Strood Extra (1894–1930), Strood Intra (1894–1930)

BLEAN PLU

Canterbury The Archbishop's Palace Precincts (1835–1912), Canterbury Christchurch (1835–1912), Canterbury St Gregory the Great (1835–1912), Chislet, Hackington, Herne, Herne Bay (1894–1930), Hoath, Reculver, St Cosmus and St Damian in the Blean, St Dunstan (1835–94), St Dunstan Within (1894–1912), St Dunstan Without (1894–1930), Seasalter (1835–94), Staplegate (1835–1912), Sturry, Swalecliffe, Westbere, Whitstable (1835–94), Whitstable cum Seasalter (1894–1930), Whitstable Urban (1894–1930)

BRIDGE PLU

Adisham, Barham, Bekesbourne, Bishopsbourne, Bridge, pt Canterbury Holy Cross Westgate (1835–94), Chartham, Fordwich, Harbledown, Lower Hardres, Upper Hardres, Holy Cross Westgate Without (1894–1912), Ickham and Well, Kingston, Littlebourne, Mint (1858[33]–89), Nackington, Patrixbourne, Petham, St Nicholas Hospital (1858[33]–1930), Stodmarsh, Thanington (1835–94), Thanington Within (1894–1912), Thanington Without (1894–1930), Waltham, Wickhambreux, Womenswold

BROMLEY PLU

Beckenham, Bromley, Chelsfield, Chislehurst, Foots Cray (1836–1925), North Cray, St Mary Cray, St Paul's Cray, Cudham, Downe, Farnborough, Hayes, Keston, Knockholt, Mottingham (1887–1930), Orpington, Sidcup (1925–30), West Wickham

CANTERBURY INCORPORATION

Canterbury (1897–1930), Canterbury All Saints (until 1897), Canterbury Black Prince's Chantry (until 1897)), Canterbury East Bridge Hospital (until 1897), Canterbury Old Castle (until 1897), pt Canterbury Holy Cross Westgate (until 1894), Canterbury St Alphege (until 1897), Canterbury St Andrew (until 1897), Canterbury St Augustine (until 1897), Canterbury St George the Martyr (until 1897), Canterbury St John's Hospital (until 1897), Canterbury St Margaret (until 1897), Canterbury St Martin (until 1897), Canterbury St Mary Bredin (until 1897), Canterbury St Mary Bredman (until 1897), Canterbury St Mary Magdalen (until 1897), Canterbury St Mary North Gate (until 1897), Canterbury St Mildred (until 1897), Canterbury St Paul (until 1897), Canterbury St Peter (until 1897), Canterbury White Friars (until 1897), Holy Cross Westgate Within (1894–97)

CRANBROOK PLU

Benenden, Cranbrook, Frittenden, Goudhurst, Hawkhurst,[35] Sandhurst

DARTFORD PLU

Ash, Bexley, Crayford, Darenth, Dartford, Erith, Eynsford, Farningham, Fawkham, Hartley, Horton Kirby, Kingsdown, Longfield, Lullingstone, Ridley, Southfleet, Stone, Sutton at Hone, Swanscombe, East Wickham (1836–1902), Wilmington

DOVER PLU (renaming in 1840s of RIVER PLU)

Alkham, Buckland (1835–96), Capel-le-Ferne, Charlton (1835–96), East Cliffe (1835–96), West Cliffe, Coldred, Denton, Dover (1896–1930), Dover Castle, Dover St James the Apostle (1835–96), Dover St Mary the Virgin (1835–96), Temple Ewell, Guston, Hougham (1835–96), Hougham Without (1894–1930), East Langdon, West Langdon, Lydden, Oxney, Poulton, Poulton Within (1894–96), Ringwould, River, St Margaret's at Cliffe, Sibertswold, Whitfield, Wootton

EASTRY PLU

Ash, Barfreston, Betteshanger, Chillenden, Deal (1836–1930), Eastry, Elmstone, Eythorne, Goodnestone, Ham, Knowlton, Great Mongeham, Little Mongeham, Nonington, Northbourne, Preston, Ripple, Sandwich St Bartholomew's Hospital (1836–1930), Sandwich St Clement (1836–1930), Sandwich St Mary (1836–1930), Sandwich St Peter (1836–1930), Sholden, Staple, Stourmouth, Sutton, Tilmanstone, Waldershare, Walmer, Wingham, Woodnesborough, Worth

ELHAM PLU

Acrise, Cheriton, Elham, Elmsted, Folkestone (1835–86), Folkestone (before 1891–1930), Folkestone next Sandgate (1894–1930), Folkestone Town (1886–before 1891), Hawkinge, St Leonard Hythe (1836–1930), Lyminge, Lympne, Monks Horton, Newington, Paddlesworth, Postling, Saltwood, Sandgate (1894–1930), Sellindge, Stanford, Stelling, Stelling Minnis (1858[33]–1930), Stowting, Swingfield

FAVERSHAM PLU

Badlesmere, Boughton under Blean, Buckland, Davington, Doddington, Dunkirk, Eastling, Faversham (1835–94), Faversham Within (1894–1930), Faversham Without (1894–1930), Goodnestone, Graveney, Hernhill, Leaveland, Luddenham, Lynsted, Newham, Norton, Oare, Ospringe, Preston next Faversham (1835–94), Preston Within (1894–1930), Preston Without (1894–97), North Preston Without (1897–1930), South Preston Without (1897–1930), Selling, Sheldwich, Stalisfield, Stone, Teynham, Throwley

24

Kent *continued*

GRAVESEND AND MILTON PLU
Gravesend, Milton
GREENWICH PLU (1836–89[29])
Deptford St Nicholas, Deptford St Paul,[30] Greenwich, Woolwich (1836–68)
HOLLINGBOURNE PLU
Bicknor, Boughton Malherbe, Boxley, Bredhurst, Broomfield, Detling, Frinsted, Harrietsham, Headcorn, Hollingbourne, Hucking, Langley, Leeds, Lenham, Otterden, Stockbury, Chart Sutton, East Sutton, Sutton Valence, Thurnham, Ulcombe, Wichling, Wormshill
HOO PLU
Allhallows, Cooling, High Halstow, Hoo, St Mary Hoo, Isle of Grain, Stoke
LEWISHAM PLU (1836–89[29])
Charlton (1836–68), Eltham, Kidbrooke (1836–68), Lee, Lewisham, Mottingham (1836–87), Plumstead (1836–68)
MAIDSTONE PLU
East Barming, West Barming (1866[33]–1930), Bearsted, Boughton Monchelsea, East Farleigh, West Farleigh, Hunton, Linton, Loose, Maidstone, Marden, Nettlestead, Otham, Staplehurst, Teston, Yalding
MALLING PLU
Addington, Allington, Aylesford, Birling, Burham, Ditton, Ightham, Leybourne, East Malling, West Malling, Mereworth, Offham, East Peckham, West Peckham, Ryarsh, Shipbourne, Snodland, Stanstead, Trottiscliffe, Wateringbury, Wouldham, Wrotham
MEDWAY PLU
Chatham, Gillingham, Grange (1835–1906), Lidsing, Rochester Castle Precincts, Rochester St Nicholas, Rochester St Margaret (1835–94), St Margaret Extra (1894–1905), St Margaret Intra (1894–1930)
MILTON PLU
Bapchild, Bobbing, Borden, Bredgar, Lower Halstow, Hartlip, Iwade, Kingsdown, Milsted, Milton, Murston, Newington, Rainham (1835–1929), Rodmersham, Sittingbourne, Tonge, Tunstall, Upchurch
PENSHURST PLU (1835–1840s[34])
Chiddingstone, Cowden, Edenbridge, Hever, Leigh, Penshurst
RIVER PLU–renamed in 1840s DOVER PLU, qv above
ROMNEY MARSH PLU
Blackmanstone, Brenzett, Brookland, Burmarsh, Dymchurch, Eastbridge, Fairfield, Hope All Saints, West Hythe (1835–88), Ivychurch, Lydd, Midley, Newchurch, Orgarswick, New Romney, St Martin's New Romney (1894–1930), Old Romney, St Mary in the Marsh, Snargate, Snave

SEVENOAKS PLU
Brasted, Chevening, Chiddingstone (1840s–1930), Cowden (1840s–1930), Dunton Green (1908–30), Edenbridge (1840s–1930), Halstead, Hever (1840s–1930), Kemsing, Leigh (1840s–1930), Otford, Penshurst (1840s–1930), Riverhead (1894–1930), Seal, Sevenoaks, Sevenoaks Weald (1894–1930), Shoreham, Sundridge, Westerham
SHEPPEY PLU
Eastchurch, Elmley, Harty, Leysdown, Minster in Sheppey, Queenborough, Sheerness (1894–1930), Warden
STROOD PLU–renaming 1884 of NORTH AYLESFORD PLU, qv above where all pars for period 1835–1930 are listed
TENTERDEN PLU
Appledore, Biddenden, Ebony (1835–94), High Halden, Kenardington, Newenden, Rolvenden, Stone (1835–94), Stone cum Ebony (1894–1930), Tenterden, Wittersham, Woodchurch
THANET PLU (sometimes ISLE OF THANET)
Acol, Birchington, Garlinge (1894–1930), Margate St John the Baptist (1836–1930), Minster, Monkton, Northdown (1894–1913), Ramsgate (1836–1930), St Lawrence (1835–94), St Lawrence Extra (1894–1930), St Lawrence Ihtra (1894–1922), St Nicholas at Wade, St Peter (1914–30), St Peter Extra (1894–1914), St Peter Intra (1894–1914), St Peters (1835–94), Sarre, Stonar, Westgate on Sea (1894–1930)
TONBRIDGE PLU
Ashurst, Bidborough, Brenchley, Capel, Hadlow, Hildenborough (1894–1930), Horsmonden, Pembury, Southborough (1894–1930), Speldhurst, Tonbridge (1835–94), Tonbridge Rural (1894–1930), Tonbridge Urban (1894–1930), Tudeley (1835–85), Tunbridge Wells (1894–1930)
WOOLWICH PLU (1868–89[29])
Charlton, Kidbrooke, Plumstead, Woolwich

In Other Poor Law Counties:
RYE PLU (Sussex, Kent)
Broomhill[36]
TICEHURST PLU (Sussex, Kent)
Frant[37]

LANCASHIRE

In Lancs Poor Law County:[117]

ASHTON UNDER LYNE PLU (Lancs, Ches)
Alt (1894—1930), Ashton under Lyne, Audenshaw (1894—1930), Bardsley (1894—1930), Crossbank (1894—1914), Denton, Droylesden, Hartshead (1894—1930), Haughton (1837—94), Hurst (1894—1927), Lees (1894—1930), Little Moss (1894—1930), Mossley (1894—1930), Waterloo (1894—1930), Woodhouses (1894—1930)

BARTON UPON IRWELL PLU (1849—1930)
Barton upon Irwell (1849—94), Barton Moss (1894—1930), Clifton, Davyhulme (1894—1930), Eccles (1894—1930), Flixton, Irlam (1894—1930), Stretford, Swinton (1894—1930), Urmston, Worsley

BLACKBURN PLU
Balderstone, Billington, Blackburn, Church, Clayton le Dale, Clayton le Moors, Darwen (1894—1930), Lower Darwen (1837—94), Over Darwen (1837—94), Dinckley, Eccleshill, Great Harwood, Little Harwood (1837—93), Livesey, Mellor, Osbaldeston, Oswaldtwistle, Pleasington, Ramsgreave, Rishton, Salesbury, Tockholes, Wilpshire, Witton (1837—1900), Yate and Pickup Bank

BOLTON PLU
Astley Bridge (1894—98), Belmont (1894—1925), Bolton (1895—1930), Great Bolton (1837—95), Little Bolton (1837—95), Bradshaw (1837—98), Breightmet (1837—98), Deane (1894—98), Edgeworth (1837—1925), Entwistle (1837—98), Farnworth, Halliwell (1837—95), Harwood (1837—98), Heaton (1837—98), Horwich, Little Hulton, Middle Hulton (1837—98), Over Hulton (1837—98), Kearsley, Darcy Lever (1837—98), Great Lever (1837—98), Little Lever, Longworth (1837—98), Lostock (1837—98), Quarlton (1837—98), Rumworth (1837—95), Sharples (1837—94), Smithills (1894—98), Tonge (1894—98), Tonge with Haulgh (1837—95), Turton, Westhoughton

BURNLEY PLU
Altham, Barley with Wheatley Booth, Barrowford (1894—1930), Barrowford Booth (1837—94), Blacko (1894—1930), Briercliffe (1894—1930), Briercliffe with Extwistle (1837—94), Brierfield (1894—1930), Brunshaw (1894—1911), Burnley, Cliviger,[118] Colne, Dunnockshaw, Foulridge, Goldshaw Booth, Habergham Eaves, Hapton, Heyhouses (1837—1904), Higham with West Close Booth, Huncoat (1837—1929), Ightenhill (1894—1930), Ightenhill Park (1837—94), Great and Little Marsden (1837—94), Nelson (1894—1930), Northtown (1894—1930), Old Laund Booth, Padiham, Read, Reedley Hallows (1894—1930); Reedley Hallows, Filley Close and New Laund Booth (soon after 1837[119]—94); Roughlee Booth, Sabden (1904—30), Simonstone, Trawden, Wheatley Carr Booth, Worsthorne with Hurstwood

BURY PLU
Ainsworth, Ashworth (1837—94), Birtle cum Bamford, Bury, Elton (1837—94), Heap (1837—94), Heywood (1894—1930), Hopwood (1837—94), Outwood (1894—1930), Pilkington (1837—94), Pilsworth (1837—94), Radcliffe, Ramsbottom (1894—1930), Tottington (1894—1930), Tottington Lower End (1837—94), Unsworth (1894—1930), Walmersley cum Shuttleworth, Whitefield (1894—1930)

CATON GILBERT UNION (until 1869)
Bolton le Sands, Borwick, Caton, Claughton, Farleton, Gressingham, Halton, Heysham, Hornby, Nether Kellet, Over Kellet, Netherton, Poulton Barre and Torrisholme, Quernmore, Slyne with Hest, Tatham, Wennington, Wray with Botton

CHORLEY PLU
Adlington, Anderton, Anglezarke, Bretherton (soon after 1837[120]—1930), Brindle, Charnock Richard, Chorley, Clayton le Woods, Coppull, Croston, Cuerdon, Duxbury, Eccleston, Euxton, Heapey, Heath Charnock, Heskin, Hoghton, Leyland, Mawdesley, Rivington, Ulnes Walton, Welsh Whittle, Wheelton, Whittle le Woods, Withnell

CHORLTON PLU
Ardwick (1837—96), Burnage (1837—1910), Chorlton on Medlock (1837—96), Chorlton cum Hardy (1837—1910), Didsbury, Gorton (1837—1910), West Gorton (1894—96), Hulme (1837—96), Levenshulme (1837—1910), South Manchester (1896—1916), Moss Side (1837—1910), Openshaw (1837—1910), Rusholme (1837—96), Stretford (1837—49), Withington (1837—1910)

CLITHEROE PLU (Lancs, Yorks W Riding)
Aighton, Bailey and Chaigley; Little Bowland, Chatburn, Chipping, Clitheroe, Clitheroe Castle (1858—95), Downham, Leagram, Mearley; Little Mitton, Henthorn and Coldcoats; Pendleton, Thornley with Wheatley, Twiston, Whalley, Wiswell, Worston

WEST DERBY PLU
Aintree, Allerton (1837—1922), Bootle cum Linacre, Childwall (1837—1922), Great Crosby, Little Crosby, Croxteth Park (1862—1928), West Derby (1837—1922), West Derby Rural (1895—1928), Everton (1837—1922), Fazakerley (1837—1922), Ford (1905—30), Garston (1837—1922), Ince Blundell, Kirkby, Kirkdale (1837—1922), Litherland, Lunt, Netherton, Orrell (1905—30), Orrell and Ford (1837—1905), Seaforth (1894—1930), Sefton, Thornton, Toxteth Park (1837—57), Walton on the Hill (1837—1922), Waterloo (1894—1930), Wavertree (1837—1922)

FYLDE PLU
Bispham with Norbreck (1837—1918), Blackpool (1894—1930), Bryning with Kellamergh, Carleton, Clifton with Salwick, Little Eccleston with Larbreck, Elswick, Fleetwood (1894—1930), Freckleton, Greenhalgh with Thistleton, Hardhorn with Newton, Kirkham, Layton with Warbreck (1837—94), Lytham (1837—1924), Lytham St Ann's (1924—30), Marton, Medlar with Wesham, Newton with Scales, Poulton le Fylde, Ribby with Wrea, St Anne's on the Sea (1894—1924), Singleton, Thornton; Treales, Roseacre and Wharles; Warton, Weeton and Preese, Westby with Plumptons

26

Lancashire *continued*

GARSTANG PLU
Barnacre with Bonds, Bilsborrow, Bleasdale, Cabus, Catterall, Claughton, Cleveley, Great Eccleston, Forton, Garstang, Hambleton, Holleth, Inskip with Sowerby, Kirkland, Myerscough, Nateby, Pilling, Preesall with Hackinsall, Out Rawcliffe, Upper Rawcliffe with Tarnacre, Stalmine with Staynall, Winmarleigh, Nether Wyresdale

HASLINGDEN PLU
Accrington (1878—1930), New Accrington (1837—78), Old Accrington (1837—78), Bacup (1894—1930), Higher Booths (1837—94), Lower Booths (1837—94); Cowpe Lench, Newhall Hay and Hall Carr (1837—94); Haslingden, Henheads (1837—94), Musbury (1837—94), Newchurch (1837—94), Rawtenstall (1894—1930), Tottington Higher End (1837—94)

LANCASTER PLU
Aldcliffe, Ashton with Stodday, Bolton le Sands (1869—1930), Bulk (1839—1900), Carnforth, Cockerham, Cockersand Abbey (1858—1930), Ellel, Heaton with Oxcliffe, Heysham (1869—1928), Lancaster, Middleton, Morecambe (1924—28), Morecambe and Heysham (1928—30), Overton, Poulton Barre and Torrisholme (1869—1924), Priest Hutton, Scotforth, Silverdale, Skerton (1839—1900), Slyne with Hest (1869—1930), Thurnham, Warton with Lindeth, Over Wyresdale, Yealand Conyers, Yealand Redmayne

LEIGH PLU
Astley, Atherton, Bedford (1837—94), Culceth (1866—1930), Golborne (1850—1930), Kenyon (1866—1930), Leigh (1894—1930), West Leigh (1837—94), Lowton, Newchurch Kenyon (1845—66), Pennington (1837—94), Tyldesley cum Shakerley

LIVERPOOL PAR (1841—1930)
Liverpool

LUNESDALE PLU (1869—1930)
Arkholme with Cawood, Borwick, Burrow with Burrow, Cantsfield, Caton, Claughton, Farleton (1869—87), Gressingham, Halton, Hornby (1866—87), Hornby with Farleton (1887—1930), Ireby, Nether Kellet, Over Kellet, Leck, Melling with Wrayton, Quernmore, Roeburndale, Tatahm, Tunstall, Wennington, Whittington, Wray with Botton

MANCHESTER PLU (1841—50), PAR (1850—1930)
Manchester

OLDHAM PLU
Alkrington (1837—94), Chadderton, Crompton, Middleton, Oldham, Royton, Thornham (1837—94), Tonge (1837—94)

ORMSKIRK PLU
Ainsdale (1894—1925), Altcar, Aughton, Bickerstaffe, Birkdale (1837—1912), Bispham, Burscough, Downholland, Formby, Halsall, Hesketh with Becconsall, Lathom, Lydiate, Maghull, Melling, North Meols, Ormskirk, Rufford, Scarisbrick, Simonswood, Skelmersdale, Southport (1894—1930), Tarleton

PRESCOT PLU
Bold, Cronton, Ditton (1837—1920), Eccleston, Hale, Halewood, Huyton with Roby, Knowsley, Parr (1837—94), Prescot, Rainford, Rainhill, St Helens (1894—1930), Speke, Sutton (1837—94), Tarbock, Whiston, Widnes, Windle, Little Woolton, Much Woolton

PRESTON PLU
Alston, Barton, Bretherton (1837—soon after 1837[119]), Broughton, Cuerdale, Dilworth, Dutton, Elston, Farington, Fishwick (1837—94), Fulwood, Goosnargh, Grimsargh with Brockholes, Haighton, Hothersall, Little Hoole, Much Hoole, Howick, Hutton; Lea, Ashton, Ingol and Cottam; Longton, Penwortham, Preston, Ribbleton, Ribchester, Salmesbury, Walton le Dale, Whittingham (soon after 1837[110]—1930), Woodplumpton

PRESTWICH PLU (1850—1930)
Blackley (1850—96), Beswick (1858—96), Bradford (1850—96), Cheetham (1850—96), Clayton (1894—96), Crumpsall (1850—96), Failsworth, Harpurhey (1850—96), Great Heaton (1850—94), Little Heaton (1850—94), North Manchester (1896—1916), Moston (1850—96), Newton (1850—96), Prestwich

ROCHDALE PLU
Blatchinworth and Calderbrook (1837—94), Butterworth (1837—94), Castleton (1837—94), Castleton by Rochdale (1894—96); Castleton, Lancashire (1894—1900); Littleborough (1894—1930), Milnrow (1894—1930), Norden (1894—1930), Rochdale (1894—1930), Spotland (1837—94), Wardle (1894—1930), Wardleworth (1837—94), Whitworth (1894—1930), Wuerdle and Wardle (1837—94)

SALFORD PLU
Broughton, Pendlebury, Pendleton, Salford

TOXTETH PARK PAR (1857—1922)
Toxteth Park

ULVERSTON PLU
Aldingham, Lower Allithwaite, Upper Allithwaite, Angerton (1858—1930), Barrow in Furness (soon after 1851[119]—1930), Blawith, Broughton East, Broughton West, Cartmel Fell, Claife, Colton, Consiton (1894—1930), Church Coniston (1836—94), Dalton in Furness, Dunnerdale with Seathwaite, Egton with Newland, Grange (1894—1930), Haverthwaite (1927—30), Hawkshead (1894—1930), Hawkshead and Monk Coniston with Skelwith (1836—1930), Lower Holker, Upper Holker, Kirkby Ireleth, Lowick, Mansriggs, Osmotherley, Pennington, Satterwaite, Skelwith (1894—1930), Staveley, Subberthwaite, Torver, Ulverston, Urswick

WARRINGTON PLU
Burtonwood, Cuerdley, Golborne (1837—50), Haydock; Houghton, Middleton and Arbury; Kenyon (1837—45), Newton in Makerfield, Penketh, Poulton with Fearnhead, Rixton with Glazebrook, Great Sankey, Little Sankey (1894—96), Southworth with Croft, Warrington, Winwick with Hulme, Woolston with Martinscroft

WIGAN PLU
Abram, Ashton in Makerfield, Aspull, Billinge and Winstanley (1924—30), Billinge Chapel End (1837—1924), Billinge Higher End (1837—94), Blackrod, Dalton, Haigh, Hindley, Ince in Makerfield, Orrell, Parbold, Pemberton, Shevington, Standish with Langtree, Upholland, Wigan, Winstanley (1837—1924), Worthington, Wrightington

In Other Poor Law Counties:
KENDAL PLU (Westm, Lancs [1836—95])
Dalton
STOCKPORT PLU (Ches, Lancs)
Heaton Norris, Reddish
TODMORDEN PLU (Yorks W Riding, Lancs)
Todmorden and Walsden

LEICESTERSHIRE

In Leics Poor Law County:[17]
ASHBY DE LA ZOUCH PLU (Leics, Derbys)
Appleby[18] (1836—89), Appleby[18] (1889—97), Appleby Magna (1898—1930), Appleby Magna North (1897—98), Appleby Magna South (1897—98), Ashby de la Zouch, Ashby Woulds (1894—1930), Bardon (1862—1930), Blackfordby, Chilcote,[19] Coalville (1894—1930), Coleorton (soon after 1836[20]—1930), Heather, Hugglescote and Donington, Measham,[19] Normanton le Heath, Oakthorpe and Donisthorpe,[21] Osgathorpe (soon after 1836[20]—1930), Packington,[22] Ravenstone[23] (1836—84), Ravenstone with Snibston (1884—1930), Nether Seal[24] (1894—1930), Over Seal[25] (1894—1930), Over and Nether Seal (1836—94), Snarestone, Staunton Harold, Stretton en le Field,[19] Swannington, Swepstone, Thringstone (soon after 1836[20]—1930), Whitwick, Willesley,[19] Worthington (soon after 1836[20]—1930)
BARROW UPON SOAR PLU
Anstey, Anstey Pastures (1858—1930), Barkby, Barkby Thorpe, Barrow upon Soar, Beaumont Leys (1858—1930), Beeby, Belgrave (1837—92), Birstall, Bradgate Park (1858—84), Cossington, Cropston, South Croxton, Gilroes (1858—1930), Leicester Abbey (1858—92), Leicester Frith (1858—1930), Maplewell Longdale (1866—84), Mountsorrel (1884—1930), Mountsorrel North End (1837—84), Mountsorrel South End (1837—84), Newtown Linford, Queniborough, Quorndon, Ratcliffe on the Wreake, Rearsby, Rothley, Rothley Temple (1858—84), Seagrave, Sileby, Swithland, Syston, Thrussington, Thurcaston, Thurmaston (1903—30), North Thurmaston (1837—1903), South Thurmaston (1837—1903), Ulverscroft, Walton on the Wolds, Wanlip, Woodhouse
BILLESDON PLU
Allexton, Billesdon, Burton Overy, Bushby, Carlton Curlieu, Cold Newton, Evington, Frisby, Galby, Glen

Magna, Goadby, Halstead, Houghton on the Hill, Humberstone, Hungerton, Ilston on the Hill, Keyham (soon after 1835[20]—1930), Launde (1858—1930), Loddington, Lowesby, Marefield, Newton Harcourt, East Norton, King's Norton, Noseley (1858—1930), Owston and Newbold, Rolleston, Scraptoft, Skeffington, Skelton Magna, Stoughton, Stretton Magna, Stretton Parva, Thurnby (soon after 1835[20]—1930), Tilton, Tugby, Whatborough, Wistow, Withcote
BLABY PLU
Aylestone (1836—92), Blaby, Braunstone, Braunstone Frith (1861—1930), Cosby, Countesthorpe, Croft, Enderby, Foston, Freakes Ground (1861—92), Glenfield, Glenfield Frith (1861—1930), Glen Parva, Huncote, Kilby, Kirby Frith (1861—1930), Kirby Muxloe, Knighton (1836—92), Knoll and Bassett House (1861—1909), Leicester Forest East, Leicester Forest West (1861—1930), Leicester New Found Pool (1861—92), Lubbesthorpe, Narborough, New Parks (1861—1930), Oadby, Potters Marston, Thurlaston, Whetstone, East Wigston (1894—1930), Wigston Magna
HINCKLEY PLU (Leics, Warws)
Aston Flamville, Barwell, Burbage, Earl Shilton, Elmesthorpe, Higham on the Hill (soon after 1836[20]—1930), Hinckley,[26] Sapcote, Sharnford, Stoke Golding,[27] Stoney Stanton, Wigston Parva (1895—1930)
LEICESTER PLU (1836—96), PAR (1896—1930)
Aylestone (1892—96), Belgrave (1892—96), North Evington (1892—96), West Humberstone (1892—96), Knighton (1892—96), Leicester (1896—1930), Leicester Abbey (1892—96), Leicester All Saints (1836—96), Leicester Augustine Friars (1861—96), Leicester Blackfriars (1861—96), Leicester The Castle View (1836—96), Leicester New Found Pool (1892—96), Leicester The Newarke (1836—96), Leicester St Leonard (1836—96), Leicester St Margaret (1836—96), Leicester St Martin (1836—96), Leicester St Mary (1836—96), Leicester St Nicholas (1836—96)
LOUGHBOROUGH PLU (Leics, Notts)
Belton, Burton on the Wolds, Charley, Cotes, Garendon (1862—1930), Hathern, Holton, Knight Thorpe (1836—1902), Loughborough, Nanpanton (1894—1930), Prestwold, Shepshed, Shepshed Parva (1894—96), Thorpe Acre and Dishley, Long Whatton, Woodthorpe, Wymeswold
LUTTERWORTH PLU (Leics, Warws, Northants [1835—94])
Arnesby, Ashby Magna, Ashby Parva, Bittesby, Bitteswell, Broughton Astley, Bruntingthorpe, Catthorpe, Claybrooke Magna, Claybrooke Parva, Cotesbach, Dunton Bassett, Frolesworth, Gilmorton, North Kilworth, South Kilworth, Kimcote (1835—98), Kimcote and Walton (1898—1930), Knaptoft, Leire, Lutterworth, Misterton, Peatling Magna, Peatling Parva, Shawell, Shearsby, Swinford, Ullesthorpe, Walton in Knaptoft (1835—98), Westrill and Starmore (1895—1930), Wigston Parva (1835—95), Willoughby Waterless

Leicestershire *continued*

MARKET BOSWORTH PLU
Bagworth, Barlestone, Barton in the Beans, Bilstone, Market Bosworth, Cadeby, Carlton, Congerstone, Dadlington, Desford, Gopsall (1861—1930), Groby (1896—1930), Ibstock, Kirkby Mallory, Markfield, Nailstone, Newbold Verdon, Norton juxta Twycross, Odstone, Orton on the Hill, Osbaston, Peckleton, Ratby, Shackerstone, Shenton, Sibson (soon after 1836[20]—1930), Stanton under Bardon, Stapleton (soon after 1836[20]—1930), Sutton Cheney (soon after 1836[20]—1930), Thornton, Twycross, Upton, Witherley

MARKET HARBOROUGH PLU (Leics, Northants)
Husbands Bosworth, Great Bowden (1835—1927), Little Bowden[28] (1835—1927), Cranoe, Fleckney, Foxton, Glooston, Gumley, Kibworth Beauchamp, Kibworth Harcourt, *Church Langton*,[29] East Langton,[29] Thorpe Langton,[29] Tur Langton,[29] West Langton,[29] Laughton, Lubenham, Market Harborough, Mowsley, Saddington, Shangton, Smeeton Westerby, Stonton Wyville, Theddingworth,[30] Welham

MELTON MOWBRAY PLU (Leics, Notts)
Ab Kettleby, Asfordby, Ashby Folville, Barsby, Bescaby (1858—1930), Branston, Brooksby, Nether Broughton, Buckminster, Burrough on the Hill, Burton Lazars, Long Clawson, Coston, Great Dalby, Little Dalby, Old Dalby, Dalby on the Wolds, Eastwell, Eaton, Edmondthorpe, Freeby, Frisby on the Wreak, Gaddesby, Garthorpe, Goadby Marwood, Grimston, Harby, Hoby, Holwell, Hose, Kirby Bellars, Melton Mowbray, Pickwell with Leesthorpe, Ragdale, Rotherby, Saltby, Saxby, Saxelby, Scalford, Sewstern, Shoby (1858—1930), Somerby, Sproxton, Stapleford, Stathern, Stonesby, Sysonby, Sysonby with Eye Kettleby[31] (1894—1930), Thorpe Arnold, Thorpe Satchville, Twyford, Waltham on the Wolds, Wartnaby, Welby, Wycomb and Chadwell, Wyfordby, Wymondham

In Other Poor Law Counties:

ATHERSTONE PLU (Warws, Leics)
Atterton (soon after 1836[20]—1930), Fenny Drayton, Merevale,[32] Ratcliffe Culey (soon after 1836[20]—1930), Sheepy Magna, Sheepy Parva, Witherley

BINGHAM PLU (Notts, Leics)
Barkestone, Plungar

GRANTHAM PLU (Lincs Pts Kestev, Leics)
Belvoir (1861—1930), Bottesford, Croxton Kerrial, Harston, Knipton, Muston, Redmile

OAKHAM PLU (Rutl, Leics)
Cold Overton, Knossington

RUGBY PLU (Warws, Leics [1836—95])
Westrill and Starmore (1836—95)

SHARDLOW PLU (Derbys, Leics, Notts)
Breedon on the Hill, Castle Donington, Diseworth, Hemington, Isley Walton, Kegworth, Langley Priory (1861—1930), Lockington

UPPINGHAM PLU (Rutl, Northants, Leics)
Blaston, Bringhurst, Drayton, Great Easton, Hallaton, Nevill Holt, Horninghold, Medbourne, Slawston, Stockerston, Stoke Dry[33]

LINCOLNSHIRE

In Lincs Poor Law County:[31]

BOSTON PLU [Pts Holl, Pts Lind]
Algar Kirk, Amber Hill[32] (1862—1930), Great Beats (1862—1906), Little Beats (1862—1906), Benington, Bicker, Boston, Great Brand End Plot (1862—91), Little Brand End Plot (1862—91), Brothertoft, Butterwick, Carrington, Copping Syke (1862—1930), Dogdyke (1836—ca 1894), Drainage Marsh (1862—1906), Ferry Corner Plot (1862—1906), Fishtoft, Fosdyke, Frampton, Freiston, The Friths (1866—1906), Frithville, Gibbet Hills (1862—91), Hall Hills (1861—1906), Hart's Grounds (soon after 1836[33]—1930), Kirton, Langriville, Leake (1836—94), Old Leake (1894—1930), Leverton, Mown Rakes (1866—91), North Forty Foot Bank (1862—1906), Pelham's Lands (1862—1930), Pepper Gowt Plot (1862—1906), Royalty Farm (1866—91), Seven Acres (soon after 1836[33]—1906), Shuff Fen (1862—1906), Sibsey, Simon Weir (1862—1906), Skirbeck, Skirbeck Quarter, South of the Witham (1862—1906), Sutterton, Fen, Westville, Wigtoft, Wrangle, Wyberton

BOURNE PLU [Pts Kestev]
Aslackby, Aunby, Baston, Billingborough, Birthorpe, Bourne, Castle Bytham, Little Bytham, Careby, Carlby, Corby, Counthorpe, Creeton (soon after 1836[33]—1930), Market Deeping, Deeping St James, Dowsby, Dunsby, Edenham, Folkingham, Hacconby, Hawthorpe with Bulby[13] (1836—mid cent), Holywell, Horbling, Irnham,[13] Kirkby Underwood, Langtoft, Laughton, Manthorpe, Morton, Pointon, Rippingale, Semperingham, Swayfield, Swinstead, Thurlby, Toft and Lound, Witham on the Hill

CAISTOR PLU [Pts Lind]
Atterby, Bigby, Brocklesby, Buslingthorpe, Cabourne, Caistor, Claxby, Clixby, North Coates, Croxby, Cuxwold, Glentham, Grasby, Holton le Moor, Keelby, North Kelsey, South Kelsey, Kingerby, Kirkby cum Osgodby, Kirmond le Mire, Legsby, Great Limber, Linwood, Lissington, Nettleton, Newton by Toft, Normanby le Wold, Bishop Norton, North Owersby, South Owersby, Market Rasen, Middle Rasen, West Rasen, Riby, Rothwell, Searby cum Ownby, Sixhills, Snitterby, Somerby, Stainton le Vale, Swallow, Swinhope, Tealby, Thoresway, Thorganby, Thornton le Moor, Toft next Newton, East Torrington, Usselby, Waddingham, Walesby, North Willingham

GAINSBOROUGH PLU [Pts Lindsey, Notts]
Blyborough, Blyton cum Wharton, Brampton, Gate Burton, West Butterwick (soon after 1837[33]—1930), Coates, Corringham, Fenton, East Ferry (soon after 1837[33]—1930), Fillingham, Gainsborough, Glentworth, Grayingham, Greenhill and Redhill (1861—1930), Hardwick, Harpswell, Haxey, Heapham, Hemswell, Kettlethorpe, Kexby, Knaith, Laughton, Lea, Marton, Morton, Newton on Trent, Northorpe, Owston (soon after 1837[33]—1912), Owston Ferry (1912—30), Pilham, Scotter, Scotton, Southorpe, Springthorpe, East Stockwith, Stow, Sturton by Stow, Thonock (1895—1930), Torksey, Upton, Walkerith, Wildsworth, Willingham, Willoughton

29

Lincolnshire *continued*

GLANFORD BRIGG PLU [Pts Lind]

Alkborough, Appleby, Ashby (1837—1919), Barnetby le Wold, Barrow upon Humber, Barton upon Humber St Mary (1837—88), Barton upon Humber St Peter (1837—88), Barton upon Humber (1888—1930), Bonby, Bottesford, Broughton, Brumby (1837—1919), Brumby Rural (1919—30), Burringham, Burton upon Stather, East Butterwick, Cadney cum Howsham, Cleatham, Croxton, Crosby (1837—1919), Elsham, South Ferriby, Flixborough, Frodingham (1837—1919), Glanford Brigg, Goxhill, Gunness (soon after 1837[33]—1930), East Halton, West Halton, Hibaldstow, Holme, Horkstow, North Killingholme, South Killingholme, Kirton in Lindsey, Kirmington, Manton, Melton Ross, Messingham, Newstead (1861—1930), Raventhorpe (soon after 1837[33]—1930), Redbourne, Roxby cum Risby, Saxby All Saints, Scawby, Scunthorpe (1837—1919), Scunthorpe and Frodingham (1919—30), Thornton Curtis, Twigmore, Ulceby, Whitton, Winteringham, Winterton, Wootton, Worlaby, Wrawby, Yaddlethorpe (1837—87)

GRANTHAM PLU [Pts Kestev, Leics]

Ancaster, Barrowby, Bassingthorpe, Belton, Bitchfield, Boothby Pagnell, Bracey, Burton Coggles, Carlton Scroop, Colsterworth, Denton, Easton, Great Gonerby, Little Gonerby (1894—1909), Grantham, Grantham Grange (1866—1909), Gunby, Haceby, Harlaxton, Harrowby (1836—94), Harrowby Within (1894—1909), Harrowby Without (1894—1930), Heydour, Honington, Hough on the Hill, Humby (1887—1930), Little Humby (1836—87), Ingoldsby, Keisby, Lenton, Londonthorpe, Manthorpe (1894—1930), Manthorpe cum Little Gonerby (1836—94), Normanton, Osgodby, Pickworth, Great Ponton, Little Ponton, Ropsley, Sapperton, Skillington, Somerby (1836—94), New Somerby (1894—1909), Old Somerby (1894—1930), Spittlegate (1836—94), Spittlegate Within (1894—1909), Spittlegate Without (1894—1930), Stainby, North Stoke, South Stoke, Stroxton, Welby, North Witham, South Witham, Woolsthorpe, Wyville cum Hungerton

GRIMSBY PLU [Pts Lind]

Ashby cum Fenby, Aylesby, Barnoldby le Beck, Beelsby, Bradley, Brigsley, Clee (1894—1928), Clee with Weelsby (1836—94), Cleethorpes, Great Coates, Little Coates (1836—1928), Grimsby (1928—30), Great Grimsby (1836—1928), Habrough, Hatcliffe, Hawerby cum Beesby, Healing, Humberston, Immingham, Irby, Laceby, Wold Newton, East Ravendale, West Ravendale, Scartho (1836—1928), Stallingborough, Waltham, Weelsby (1894—1930)

HOLBEACH PLU [Pts Holl, Norfolk (until 1897), ent Pts Holl thereafter]

Fleet, Gedney, Gedney Hill, Holbeach, Lutton, Little Sutton (1894—1930), Long Sutton or Sutton St Mary (1894—1930), Sutton Bridge (1894—1930), Sutton St Edmund, Sutton St James, Sutton St Mary (1835—94), Tydd St Mary, Whaplode, Central Wingland[12] (1867—1930)

HORNCASTLE PLU [Pts Lind]

Asgarby, West Ashby, Ashby Puerorum, Asterby, East Barkwith, West Barkwith, Baumber, Belchford, Benniworth, Bucknall, Cawkwell, Claxby Pluckacre, Coningsby, Dalderby, Edlington, Bag Enderby, Wood Enderby, Fulletby, Gautby, Goulceby, Greetham, Hagworthingham, Haltham, Hameringham, Hatton, Haven Bank (1861—84), Hemingby, Horncastle, Horsington, Kirkby on Bain, Kirkstead, Langton, Langton by Wragby, Lusby, Mareham le Fen, Mareham on the Hill, Martin, Miningsby, Minting, Moorby, Panton, Ranby, Revesby, Roughton, Salmonby, Scamblesby, Scrafield, Scrivelsby, Somersby, Sotby, Market Stainton, Stixwould, Great Sturton, Tattershall, Tattershall Thorpe, Tetford, Thimbleby, Thornton, West Torrington, High Toynton, Low Toynton, Tumby, Tupholme, Waddingworth, Wildmore (1880—1930), Wilksby, Winceby, Wispington, Woodhall, Woodhall Spa (1894—1930), Wragby

LINCOLN PLU [Pts Kestev, Pts Lind]

Aisthorpe, Apley, Aubourn, Bardney, Barlings, Boothby Graffoe, Boultham, Bracebridge (1836—1920), Bracebridge Heath (1898—1930), Branston, Brattleby, Broxholme, Bullington, Burton, Caenby, Cammeringham, North Carlton, South Carlton, Canwick, Coldstead (1862—1930), Coleby, Doddington, Dunholme, Dunston, Eagle, Eagle Hall (1862—1930), Eagle Woodhouse (1862—86), Faldingworth, East Firsby, West Firsby, Fiskerton, Friesthorpe, Fulnetby (soon after 1836[33]—1930), Goltho, Grange de Lings (1858—1930), Greetwell, Hackthorn, Haddington, Cold Hanworth, Potter Hanworth, Harmston, Heighington, Holton cum Beckering, North Hykeham, South Hykeham, Ingham, Lincoln (1907—30), Lincoln Bishop's Palace (1861—1907), Lincoln Castle Dykings (1858—88), Lincoln Cold Bath House (1861—1907), Lincoln Holmes Common (1863—88), Lincoln Monks Liberty (1861—1930), Lincoln St Benedict (1836—1907), Lincoln St Botolph (1836—1907), Lincoln St John in Newport, Lincoln St Margaret in the Close (1836—1907), Lincoln St Mark (1836—1907), Lincoln St Martin (1836—1907), Lincoln St Mary Magdalen (1836—1907), Lincoln St Mary le Wigford (1836—88), Lincoln St Mary le Wigford with Holmes Common (1888—1907), Lincoln St Michael (1836—1907), Lincoln St Nicholas (1836—1907), Lincoln St Paul in the Bail (1836—1907), Lincoln St Peter at the Arches (1836—1907), Lincoln St Peter in Eastgate (1836—1907), Lincoln St Peter at Gowts (1836—1907), Lincoln St Swithin (1836—1907), Lincoln South Common, Mere, Metheringham, Morton (1862—1930), Navenby, Nettleham, Newball, Nocton, Normanby by Spital, Owmby, Rand, Reepham, Riseholme, Saxby, Saxilby with Ingleby, Scampton, Scothern, Skellingthorpe, Skinnand, Snarford, Snelland, Sprindlington, Stainfield, Stainton by Langworth, Sudbrooke, Swinethorpe, Thorpe in the Fallows, Thorpe on the Hill, Waddington, Washingborough, Welton, Whisby, Wickenby, Cherry Willingham

Lincolnshire *continued*

LOUTH PLU [Pts Lind]
Aby with Greenfield, Alvingham, Authorpe, Beesby in the Marsh, Belleau, Binbrook,[34] Biscathorpe, Brackenborough, Burwell, Burgh on Bain, Calcethorpe, Castle Carlton, Great Carlton, Little Carlton, Little Cawthorpe, Claythorpe, North Coates, North Cockerington, South Cockerington, Conisholme, Covenham St Bartholomew, Covenham St Mary, Donington on Bain, North Elkington, South Elkington, Farforth cum Maidenwell, Fotherby, Fulstow, Gayton le Marsh, Gayton le Wold, Grainsby, Grainthorpe, Grimblethorpe (1858—1930), Grimoldby, Little Grimsby, Hainton, Hallington, Hannah cum Hagnaby, Haugh (1858—1930), Haugham, Holton le Clay, Keddington, Kelstern, Legbourne, Louth, Louth Park, Ludborough, Ludford Magna, Ludford Parva, Mablethorpe, Walmsgate, Welton le Wold, North Willingham, South Willingham, Withcall, Withern with Stain, Worlaby, Wyham cum Cadeby, East Wykeham (1858—1930), Yarburgh
SLEAFORD PLU [Pts Kestev]
Anwick, Asgarby, Ashby de la Launde, Aswarby, Aunsby, Byard's Leap (1861—1930), Billinghay, Blankney, Bloxholm, Brauncewell, Burton Penwardine, Cranwell, Culverthorpe, Dembleby, Digby, Dogdyke (*ca* 1894—1930), Dorrington, Evedon, Ewerby, Great Hale, Little Hale, Haverholme Priory (1861—1930), Heckington, Helpringham, Holdingham, Howell, Kelby, Kirkby Green, Kirkby la Thorpe, North Kyme, South Kyme, Leadenham, Leasingham, Martin, Newton, Osbournby, Quarrington, North Rauceby, South Rauceby, Rowston, Roxholm, Ruskington, Scredington, Scopwick, New Sleaford, Old Sleaford, Spanby, Swarby, Swaton, Temple Bruer with Temple High Grange (1861—1930), Thorpe Tilney, Threckingham, Timberland, Walcot (near Billinghay), Walcot (near Folkingham), Welbourn, Wellingore, Scott Willoughby, Silk Willoughby, Wilsford
SPALDING PLU [Pts Holl, Pts Kestev]
Cowbit, Deeping St Nicholas[10] (1862—1930), Donington (soon after 1835[33]—1930), Gosberton, Moulton, Pinchbeck, Quadring, Spalding, Surfleet, Weston
SPILSBY PLU [Pts Lind] Addlethorpe, Alford, Anderby, Ashby by Partney, Aswardby, Bilsby, Bolingbroke, Bratoft, Brinkhill, Burgh le Marsh, Calceby, Candlesby, Chapel St Leonards (1896—1930), Claxby, Croft, Cumberworth, Dalby, Driby, Eastville, Mavis Enderby, Farlesthorpe, Firsby, Friskney, Gunby, Hagnaby, Halton Holegate, Hareby, Harrington, Hogsthorpe, Hundleby, Huttoft, Ingoldmells, Irby in the Marsh, East Keal, West Keal, East Kirkby, Langton by Spilsby, New Leake (1894—1930), Markby, Midville, Mumby, Northholme (1837—88), Orby, South Ormesby cum Ketsby, Partney, Raithby, Rigsby with Ailby, Sausthorpe, Scremby, Skegness, Skendleby, Spilsby, Great Steeping, Little Steeping, Stickford, Stickney, Sutterby, Sutton in the Marsh, Thorpe St Peter, Toynton All Saints, Toynton St Peter, Ulceby with Fordington, Wainfleet All Saints, Wainfleet St

Mary, Well, Welton le Marsh, West Fen (1880—1930), Willoughby with Sloothby, Winthorpe (1837—1926)
STAMFORD PLU [Pts Kestev, Northants (1835—89), Soke Peterb (1889—1930), Rutl, Hunts]
Barholm, Braceborough, West Deeping, Greatford, Stamford All Saints, Stamford St George, Stamford St John, Stamford St Mary, Stamford St Michael, Stamford Baron St Martin,[30] Stowe, Tallington, Uffington, Wilsthorpe

In Other Poor Law Counties:
DONCASTER PLU [Yorks W Riding, Notts (1837—95), Pts Lind (1837—86)]
Misson[35]
GOOLE PLU [Yorks W Riding, Pts Lind]
Garthorpe, Luddington
NEWARK PLU [Notts, Pts Lind]
Allington,[18] Barkston, Bassingham, Beckingham, Long Bennington, Bennington Grange (1861—1930), Brant Broughton, Carlton le Moorland, Caythorpe, Claypole, Dry Doddington, Fenton, Flawford[36] (1866—84), Foston, Fulbeck, Hougham, Marston, Norton Disney, North Scarle, Sedgebrook, Stapleford, Stragglethorpe, Stubton, Swinderby, Syston, Thurlby, Westborough
PETERBOROUGH PLU [Northants, Hunts (1835—89), Pts Holl, Cambs (1835—89), Soke Peterb (1889—1930), Isle of Ely (1889—1930)]
Crowland
THORNE PLU [Yorks W Riding, Pts Lind]
Althorpe, Amcotts, Belton, Crowle,[37] Eastoft, Epworth, Keadby, Wroot

31

LONDON (City)

CITY OF LONDON PLU (1837–1930)
from 1907: London
1837–1907: All Hallows Barking; All Hallows, Bread Street; All Hallows the Great; All Hallows, Honey Lane; All Hallows the Less; All Hallows, Lombard Street; All Hallows, London Wall; All Hallows Staining; Barnard's Inn (1869–1907); Bridewell Precinct (1869–1907); Christ Church, Newgate Street; Holy Trinity the Less; St Alban, Wood Street; St Alphage London Wall; St Andrew by the Wardrobe; St Andrew Holborn (1869–1907); St Andrew Hubbard; St Andrew Undershaft; St Ann Blackfriars; St Ann and St Agnes; St Antholin; St Augustine Watling Street; St Bartholomew by the Exchange; St Bartholomew the Great (1869–1907); St Bartholomew the Less (1869–1907); St Benet Fink; St Benet Gracechurch; St Benet Paul's Wharf; St Benet Sherehog; St Botolph Aldersgate (1869–1907), St Botolph by Billingsgate; St Botolph Without Aldersgate (1869–1907); St Botolph Without Aldgate (1869–1907); St Botolph Without Bishopsgate; St Bride (1869–1907); St Christopher le Stocks; St Clement, Eastcheap; St Dionis Backchurch; St Dunstan in the East; St Dunstan in the West (1869–1907); St Edmund The King and Martyr; St Ethelburga; St Faith Under St Paul's; St Gabriel Fenchurch; St George Botolph Lane; St Giles Without Cripplegate (1869–1907); St Gregory by St Paul's; St Helen Bishopsgate; St James Duke's Place; St James Garlickhithe; St John the Baptist, Walbrook; St John the Evangelist; St John Zachary; St Katherine Coleman; St Katherine Cree; St Lawrence Jewry; St Lawrence Pountney; St Leonard Eastcheap; St Leonard Foster Lane, St Magnus the Martyr; St Margaret Lothbury; St Margaret Moses; St Margaret New Fish Street; St Margaret Pattens; St Martin Ludgate; St Martin Orgar; St Martin Outwich; St Martin Pomeroy; St Martin Vintry; St Mary Abchurch; St Mary Aldermanbury; St Mary Aldermary; St Mary at Hill; St Mary Bothaw; St Mary le Bow; St Mary Colechurch; St Mary Magdalene, Old Fish Street; St Mary Mounthaw; St Mary Somerset; St Mary Staining; St Mary Woolchurch; St Mary Woolnoth; St Matthew Friday Street; St Michael Bassishaw; St Michael Cornhill; St Michael Crooked Lane; St Michael Queenhithe; St Michael le Querne; St Michael, Paternoster Royal; St Michael, Wood Street; St Mildred, Bread Street; St Mildred Poultry; St Nicholas Acons; St Nicholas Cole Abbey; St Nicholas Olave; St Olave Hart Street; St Olave Old Jewry; St Olave Silver Street; St Pancras, Soper Lane; St Peter Cornhill; St Peter Paul's Wharf; St Peter le Poer; St Peter Westcheap; St Sepulchre (1869–1907); St Stephen Coleman Street; St Stephen Walbrook; St Swithin London Stone; St Thomas Aspostle; St Vedast Foster Lane; Serjeants' Inn (1869–1907); Thavie's Inn (1869–1907); Whitefriars Precinct

EAST LONDON PLU (1837–69) (City of London, Middx)
St Botolph Without Aldersgate; St Botolph Without Aldgate; St Botolph Without Bishopsgate; St Giles Without Cripplegate

WEST LONDON PLU (1837–69)
Barnard's Inn; Bridewell Precinct; St Andrew Holborn; St Bartholomew the Great; St Bartholomew the Less; St Bride; St Dunstan in the West; Serjeants' Inn; Thavie's Inn

LONDON (County)

BATTERSEA PAR (1904–30)
Battersea
BERMONDSEY PAR (1904–30)
Bermondsey
BETHNAL GREEN PAR
Bethnal Green
CAMBERWELL PAR
Camberwell
CHELSEA PAR
Chelsea
FULHAM PAR (1899–1930)
Fulham
FULHAM PLU (1889–99)
Fulham, Hammersmith
GREENWICH PLU
Deptford St Nicholas, Deptford St Paul, Greenwich
HACKNEY PLU
Hackney, Stoke Newington
HAMMERSMITH PAR (1899–1930)
Hammersmith
HAMPSTEAD PAR
Hampstead
HOLBORN PLU
Chartherhouse (1889–1915), Clerkenwell (1899–1915), Finsbury (1915–30), Furnival's Inn, Glasshouse Yard (1901–15); Liberty of Saffron Hill, Hatton Garden, Ely Rents and Ely Place; St Andrew Holborn Above the Bars with St George the Martyr, St Giles in the Fields and St George Bloomsbury (1914–30), St Luke (1889–1915), St Sepulchre (1889–1915), Staple Inn
ISLINGTON PAR
Islington
KENSINGTON PAR
Kensington
LAMBETH PAR
Lambeth
LEWISHAM PLU
Eltham, Lee (1889–1905), Lewisham
MILE END OLD TOWN PAR (1889–1925)
Mile End Old Town
PADDINGTON PAR
Paddington
POPLAR BOROUGH PAR (1907–30)
Poplar Borough
POPLAR PLU (1889–1907)
Bow, Bromley, Poplar
ST GEORGE IN THE EAST PAR (1889–1925)
St George in the East

ST GEORGE'S PLU (1889–1913)
The Close of the Collegiate Church of St Peter, St George Hanover Square, Westminster St Margaret and St John

ST OLAVE PLU (1889–1904)
Bermondsey, Rotherhithe, Southwark St John Horsleydown, Southwark St Olave (1889–96), Southwark St Olave and St Thomas (1896–1904), Southwark St Thomas (1889–96)

ST PANCRAS PAR
St Pancras

ST SAVIOUR'S PLU (1889–1901)
Newington, Southwark Christchurch, Southwark St George the Martyr, Southwark St Saviour

SHOREDITCH PAR
Shoreditch

SOUTHWARK PLU (1901–30)
Newington, Southwark Christchurch, Southwark St George the Martyr, Southwark. St Saviour

STEPNEY PAR (1927–30)
Stepney

STEPNEY PLU (1889–1921)
Limehouse, Ratcliff, Shadwell, Wapping

STEPNEY PLU (1925–27)
Mile End Old Town, St George in the East, Whitechapel

STRAND PLU (1899–1913)
Liberty of the Rolls, St Clement Danes, St Martin in the Fields, St Mary le Strand, St Paul Covent Garden, Precinct of the Savoy

WANDSWORTH PAR (1904–30)
Wandsworth Borough

WANDSWORTH AND CLAPHAM PLU (1889–1904)
Battersea, Clapham, Streatham, Tooting Graveney, Wandsworth

WESTMINSTER PLU (1889–1913)
St Anne Within the Liberty of Westminster, Westminster St James

CITY OF WESTMINSTER PAR (1922–30)
City of Westminster

CITY OF WESTMINSTER PLU (1913–22)
The Close of the Collegiate Church of St Peter, Liberty of the Rolls, St Anne Within the Liberty of Westminster, St Clement Danes, St George Hanover Square, St Martin in the Fields, St Mary le Strand, St Paul Covent Garden, Precinct of the Savoy, Westminster St James, Westminster St Margaret and St John

WHITECHAPEL PAR (1921–25)
Whitechapel

WHITECHAPEL PLU (1889–1921)
Holy Trinity Minories (1889–95), Mile End New Town, Norton Folgate, Old Artillery Ground, St Botolph Without Aldgate, St Katherine by the Tower (1889–95), Spitalfields, Tower of London (1889–1901), Old Tower Without (1889–95), Whitechapel

WOOLWICH PLU
Charlton and Kidbrooke (1901–30), Charlton next Woolwich (1889–1901), Kidbrooke (1889–1901), Plumstead, Woolwich

MIDDLESEX

In Middx Poor Law County:[13]

BRENTFORD PLU
Acton, New Brentford, Old Brentford (1894–1930), Chiswick, Ealing, Greenford, Hanwell (1836–1926), Heston (1836–1927), Heston and Isleworth (1927–30), Isleworth (1836–1927), Perivale (1836–1926), Twickenham, West Twyford (1836–1926)

EDMONTON PLU (Middx, Essex, Herts)
Edmonton, Enfield, Hampstead (1837–48), Hornsey, Southgate (1894–1930), Tottenham, Wood Green (1894–1930)

HENDON PLU
Edgware, Harrow on the Hill, Harrow Weald (1894–1930), Hendon, Kingsbury, Pinner, Great Stanmore, Little Stanmore, Wealdstone (1894–1930), Wembley (1894–1930), Willesden (1835–96)

STAINES PLU
Ashford, East Bedfont, Cranford, Feltham, Hanworth, Harlington, Harmondsworth, Laleham, Littleton, Shepperton, Staines, Stanwell, Sunbury

UXBRIDGE PLU
Cowley, West Drayton, Harefield, Hayes, Hillingdon (1836–94), Hillingdon East (1894–1930), Hillingdon West (1894–1930), Ickenham, Northolt (1836–1928), Norwood, Ruislip, Uxbridge, Yiewsley (1896–1930)

WILLESDEN PAR[14] (1896–1930)
Willesden

In Other Poor Law Counties;

BARNET PLU (Herts, Middx)
Friern Barnet, Finchley, Monken Hadley,[15] South Mimms[16]

KINGSTON PLU (Surrey, Middx)
Hampton, Hampton Wick, Teddington

Middx Poor Law County, in Metropolis (1855–89),. London Poor Law County thereafter:

BETHNAL GREEN PAR
Bethnal Green

CHELSEA PAR
Chelsea

CLERKENWELL PAR[18] (until 1869)
Clerkenwell

FULHAM PLU (1845–89)
Fulham, Hammersmith

HACKNEY PLU
Hackney, Stoke Newington

HAMPSTEAD PAR (1848–89)
Hampstead

HOLBORN PLU
Charterhouse (1877–89), Clerkenwell (1869–89), Furnival's Inn (1858–89), Gray's Inn (1858–89), Holborn St Andrew Above the Bars with St George the Martyr; Liberty of Saffron Hill, Hatton Garden, Ely Rents and Ely Place; St Sepulchre (1845–89), St Luke (1869–89), Staple Inn (1858–89)

ISLINGTON PAR[19]
Islington

KENSINGTON PLU (1837–45), PAR (1845–89)
Fulham (1837–45), Hammersmith (1837–45),
Kensington, Paddington (1837–89)
CITY OF LONDON PLU (London, Middx)
Glasshouse Yard (1869–89)
EAST LONDON PLU (London, Middx)
pt St Botolph Aldersgate (1837–66), Glasshouse
Yard (1866–69)
HMLT/PAR OF MILE END OLD TOWN (1857–89)
Mile End Old Town
PADDINGTON PAR (1845–89)
Paddington
POPLAR PLU
Bow, Bromley, Poplar
ST GEORGE'S PAR,[21] PLU (1870–89)
Close of the Collegiate Church of St Peter (1870–
89), St George Hanover Square, Westminster St
John the Evangelist, Westminster St Margaret
ST GEORGE IN THE EAST PAR
St George in the East
ST GILES IN THE FIELDS AND ST GEORGE
BLOOMSBURY PAR[22]
St Giles in the Field and St George Bloomsbury
ST JAMES PAR[23] (until 1868)
Westminster St James
ST LUKE PAR[24] (until 1869)
St Luke
ST MARGARET AND ST JOHN PARS,[25] PLU
(1867–70)
Westminster St John the Evalgelist, Westminster St
Margaret
ST MARTIN IN THE FIELDS PAR (1835–68)
St Martin in the Fields
ST MARYLEBONE PAR[25]
St Marylebone
ST PANCRAS PAR
St Pancras
SHOREDITCH PAR[23]
Shoreditch
STEPNEY PLU
Limehouse, Mile End Old Town (1836–57), Rat-
cliffe, Shadwell, Wapping
STRAND PLU
Liberty of the Rolls, St Anne Within the Liberty
of Westminster (1837–68), St Clement Danes, St
Martin in the Fields (1868–99), St Mary le Strand,
St Paul Covent Garden, Precinct of the Savoy
WESTMINSTER PLU (1868–89)
St Anne Within the Liberty of Westminster, West-
minster St James
WHITECHAPEL PLU
Holy Trinity Minories, Mile End New Town, Norton
Folgate, Old Artillery Ground, St Botolph Without
Aldgate, St Katherine by the Tower, Spitalfields,
Tower of London, Whitechapel

NORFOLK

In Norfolk Poor Law County:[9]
AYLSHAM PLU
Alby (1836–84), Alby with Thwaite (1885–1930),
Aylsham, Banningham, Little Barningham, Belaugh,
Blickling, Brampton, Burgh, Buxton, Calthorpe,.
Cawston, Colby, Coltishall, Corpusty, Erpingham,
Foulsham, Guestwick, Hackford, Great Hautbois,
Hevingham, Heydon, Hindolveston, Ingworth, Ir-
mingland, Itteringham, Lammas with Little Haut-
bois, Mannington, Marsham, Oulton, Oxnead,
Reepham with Kerdiston, Sall, Saxthorpe, Scottow,
Skeyton, Stratton Strawless, Swanton Abbot,
Themelthorpe, Thurning, Thwaite, Tuttington,
Whitwell, Wickmere, Wolterton, Wood Dalling,
Wood Norton
BLOFIELD PLU
Acle, Beighton, Blofield, Bradeston (1835–84),
Brundall, Buckenham, Burlingham St Andrew, Bur-
lingham St Edmund, Burlingham St Peter, Cantley,
Freethorpe, Halvergate, Hassingham, Hemblington,
Limpenhoe, Lingwood, Moulton St Mary, Great
Plumstead, Little Plumstead, Postwick, Ranworth
with Panxworth, Reedham, Southwood, Strump-
shaw, Thorpe next Norwich, Tunstall, Upton with
Fishley, South Walsham (1897–1930), South Wal-
sham St Mary (1835–97), South Walsham St
Lawrence (1835–97), Wickhampton, Witton,
Woodbastwick
BRINTON INCORPORATION (1738–1860s)
Brinton, Melton Constable
DEPWADE PLU
Alburgh, Ashwellthorpe, Aslacton, Billingford, Bres-
ssingham (1902–30), Brockdish, Bunwell, Burston,
Carleton Rode, Denton, Dickleburgh, Diss, Earsham,
Fersfield (1902–30), Forncett St Mary, Forncett
St Peter, Fritton, Fundenhall, Gissing, Hapton,
Hardwick, Hempnall, Morning Thorpe, Moulton St
Michael, Needham, Pulham St Mary Magdalen, Pul-
ham St Mary the Virgin, Redenham with Harles-
ton, Roydon (1902–30), Rushall, Scole, Shelfan-
ger (1902–30), Shelton, Shimpling, Starston,
Stratton St Mary, Stratton St Michael, Tacolneston,
Tasburgh, Tharston, Thelveton, Thorpe Abbots,
Tibenham, Tivetshall St Margaret, Tivetshall St
Mary, Wacton, Winfarthing (1902–30), Wortwell
DOCKING PLU
Anmer, Bagthorpe, Barmer, Barwick, Great
Bircham, Bircham Newton, Bircham Tofts, Bran-
caster, Broomsthorpe, Burnham Deepdale, Burn-
ham Market (1929–30), Burnham Norton, Burn-
ham Overy, Burnham Sutton cum Burnham Ulph
(1835–1929), Burnham Thorpe, Burnham West-
gate (1835–1929), Choseley (1858[10]–1930),
North Creake, South Creake, Dersingham, Docking,
Fring, Heacham, Holme next the Sea, Houghton,
Hunstanton, New Hunstanton (1894–1930), In-
goldisthorpe, Ringstead, East Rudham, West Rudham, Sedgeford, Shernborne, Snettisham, Stanhoe,
Syderstone, Thornham, Waterden, Titchwell

Norfolk *continued*

DOWNHAM PLU (Norfolk, Cambs/IoE until 1889, ent Norfolk thereafter)
Barton Bendish, Bexwell, Boughton, Crimplesham, Denver, West Dereham, Downham Market, Downham West (1894–1930), Fincham, Fordham, Hilgay, Marham, Roxham, South Runcton, Runcton Holme, Ryston, Shouldham, Shouldham Thorpe, Southery, Stoke Ferry, Stow Bardolph, Stradsett, Tottenhill, Wallington with Thorpland, Watlington, Welney,[11] West Welney[12] (1895–1930), Wereham, Wiggenhall St German, Wiggenhall St Mary Magdalen, Wiggenhall St Mary the Virgin, Wiggenhall St Peter, Wimbotsham, Wormegay, Wretton

ERPINGHAM PLU
Aldborough, Antingham, Aylmerton, Baconsthorpe, Barningham Norwood, Barningham Winter or Barningham Town, East Beckham, West Beckham, Beeston Regis, Bessingham, Bodham, Briston, Cley next the Sea, Cromer, Edgefield, Felbrigg, Gimingham, Glandford with Bayfield, Gresham, Gunton, Hanworth, Hempstead, Holt, Hunworth, Kelling, Knapton, Letheringsett, Matlask, Metton, Mundesley, Northrepps, Overstrand, Plumstead, Roughton, Runton, Salthouse, Sheringham, Upper Sheringham (1901–30), Sidestrand, Southrepps, Stody, Suffield, Sustead, Thorpe Market, Thornage, Thurgarton, Trimingham, Trunch, Weybourne

EAST AND WEST FLEGG INCORP
Ashby with Oby, Billockby, Burgh St Margaret, Caister next Yarmouth, Clippesby, Filby, Hemsby, Martham, Mautby, Ormesby St Margaret with Scratby, Ormesby St Michael, Repps with Bastwick, Rollesby, Runham, Runham Vauxhall (1894–1930), East Somerton, West Somerton, Stokesby with Herringby, Thurne, Winterton

FOREHOE INCORP/PLU
Barford, Barnham Broom, Bawburgh, Bowthorpe, Brandon Parva, Carleton Forehoe, Colton, Costessey, Coston, Crownthorpe, Deopham, Easton, Hackford, Hingham, Kimberley, Marlingford, Morley St Botolph, Morley St Peter, Runhall, Welborne, Wicklewood, Wramplingham

GUILTCROSS PLU (1835–1902)
Banham, Blo' Norton, Bressingham, Bridgham, New Buckenham, Old Buckenham, Eccles, Fersfield, Garboldisham, Gasthorpe, East Harling, West Harling, Kenninghall, North Lopham, South Lopham, Quidenham, Riddlesworth, Roydon, Shelfanger, Wilby, Winfarthing

HENTEAD PLU
Arminghall, Bixley, Bracon Ash, Bramerton, Caister St Edmund, East Carleton, Colney, Cringleford, Flordon, Framingham Earl, Framingham Pigot, Hethel, Hethersett, Holverston, Intwood, Keswick, Ketteringham, Kirby Bedon, Markshall, Great Melton, Little Melton, Mulbarton, Newton Flotman, Poringland, Rockland St Mary, Saxlingham Nethergate, Saxlingham Thorpe, Shotesham All Saints, Shotesham St Mary, Stoke Holy Cross,

Surlingham, Swainsthorpe, Swardeston, Trowse with Newton, Whitlingham, Wreningham

LODDON AND CLAVERING PLU
Aldeby, Alpington, Ashby St Mary, Bedingham, Bergh Apton, Brooke, Broome, Burgh St Peter, Carleton St Peter, Chedgrave, Claxton, Ditchingham, Ellingham, Geldeston, Gillingham, Haddiscoe, Hales, Hardley, Heckingham, Hedenham, Hellington, Howe, Kirby Cane, Kirstead, Langley, Loddon, Mundham, Norton Subcourse, Raveningham, Seething, Sisland, Stockland, Thorpe next Haddiscoe, Thurlton, Thurton, Thwaite, Toft Monks, Topcroft, Wheatacre, Woodton, Yelverton

FREEBRIDGE LYNN PLU
Ashwicken, Babingley, Bawsey, West Bilney, Castle Acre, Castle Rising, Congham, Flitcham with Appleton, Gayton, Gayton Thorpe, Gaywood, Grimston, Harpley, Hillington, Leziate, Great Massingham, Little Massingham, Middleton, Mintlyn, West Newton, Pentney, Roydon, North Runcton, Sandringham, Setchey, West Walton, Westacre, East Winch, West Winch, Wolferton, North Wootton, South Wootton

KING'S LYNN PLU
King's Lynn St Margaret, North Lynn, South Lynn, West Lynn

MITFORD AND LAUNDITCH PLU
Bawdeswell, Beeston with Bittering, Beetley, Billingford, East Bilney, Bintree, Brisley, Bylaugh, Colkirk, Cranworth, East Dereham, Great Dunham, Little Dunham, North Elmham, Elsing, Foxley, Great Fransham, Little Fransham, Garveston, Gateley, Gressenhall, Guist, Hardingham, Hockering, Hoe, Horningtoft, Kempstone, Letton, East Lexham, West Lexham, Litcham, Longham, Lyng, Mattishall, Mattishall Burgh, Mileham, Oxwick with Pattesley, Reymerston, Rougham, Scarning, Shipdham, Southburgh, Sparham, Stanfield, Swanton Morley, Tittleshall, East Tuddenham, North Tuddenham, Twyford, Weasenham All Saints, Weasenham St Peter, Wellingham, Wendling, Westfield, Whinburgh, Whissonsett, Woodrising, Worthing, Yaxham

ST FAITH'S PLU
Alderford, Attlebridge, Beeston St Andrew, Booton, Brandiston, Catton, Crostwick, Drayton, Felthorpe, Frettenham, Hainford, Haveringland, Hellesdon, Honingham, Horsford, Horsham St Faith with Newton St Faith, Horstead with Stanninghall, Morton on the Hill, Norwich St Mary in the Marsh (1836–89), Rackheath, Ringland, Salhouse, Spixworth, Sprowston, Swannington, Taverham, Weston Longville, Great Witchingham, Little Witchingham, Wroxham

SMALLBURGH PLU—Renaming 1870 of TUNSTEAD AND HAPPING INCORP, qv where all pars are listed for both

SWAFFHAM PLU
South Acre, Ashill, Beechamwell, Bodney, East Bradenham, West Bradenham, Buckenham Tofts,

Norfolk: Swaffham *continued*

Caldecote, Cockley Cley, Colveston, Great Cressingham, Little Cressingham, Didlington, Foulden, Gooderstone, Hilborough, Houghton on the Hill, Holme Hale, Ickburgh, Langford, Narborough, Narford, Necton, Newton by Castle Acre, Oxborough, North Pickenham, South Pickenham, Saham Toney, Shingham, Sporle with Palgrave, Stanford. Swaffham, Threxton

THETFORD PLU (Norolk, Suffolk)

Blo' Norton (1902–30), Brettenham, Bridgham (1902–30), Cranwich, Croxton, Feltwell, Feltwell Anchor (1858[10]–1929, Garboldisham (1902–30), Gasthorpe (1902–30), East Harling (1902–30), West Harling (1902–30), Hockwold cum Wilton, Kilverstone, North Lopham (1902–30), South Lopham (1902–30), Lynford, Methwold, Mundford, Northwold, Riddlesworth (1902–30), Rushford, Santon, Great and Little Snarehill (1858[10]–1930), Sturston, Thetford (1924–30), Thetford St Cuthbert[13] (1835–1924), Thetford St Mary[13] (1835–1924), Thetford St Peter (1835–1924), West Tofts, Weeting-with-Bromehill, East Wretham, West Wretham

TUNSTEAD AND HAPPING INCORP (Renamed 1870 SMALLBURGH PLU; pars listed here only for brevity's sake)

Ashmanhaugh, Bacton, Barton Turf, Beeston St Lawrence, Bradfield, Brumstead, Catfield, Crostwight, Dilham, Edingthorpe, Felmingham, Happisburgh, Hempstead with Eccles, Hickling, Honing, Horning, Horsey, Hoveton St John, Hoveton St Peter, Ingham, Irstead, Lessingham, Ludham, Neatishead, Palling, Paston, Potter Heigham, Ridlington, East Ruston, Sco' Ruston, Sloley, Smallburgh, Stalham, Sutton, Swafield, Tunstead, Walcott, North Walsham, Waxham, Westwick, Witton, Worstead

WALSINGHAM PLU

Bale, Barney, East Barsham, North Barsham, West Barsham, Binham, Blakeney, Briningham, Brinton (1860s–1930), Cockthorpe, Dunton cum Doughton, Egmere, Fakenham, Field Dalling, Fulmodeston cum Croxton, Gunthorpe, Helhoughton, Hempton, Hindringham, Holkham, Houghton St Giles, Kettlesbaston, Langham, Melton Constable (1860s–1930), Morston, Pensthorpe, Pudding Norton, Quarles (1858[10]–1930), East Raynham, South Raynham, West Raynham, Great Ryburgh, Little Ryburgh, Saxlingham, Sculthorpe, Sharrington, Shereford, Great Snoring, Little Snoring, Stibbard, Stiffkey, Swanton Novers, Tatterford, Tattersett, Testerton, Thursford, Toftrees, Great Walsingham, Little Walsingham, Warham All Saints, Warham St Mary, Wells next the Sea, Wighton, Wiveton

WAYLAND PLU

Attleborough, Banham (1902–30), Besthorpe, Breckles, New Buckenham (1902–30), Old Buckenham (1902–30), Carbrooke, Caston, Eccles (1902–30), Great Ellingham, Little Ellingham, Griston,

Hargham, Hockham, Illington, Kenninghall (1902–30), Larling, Merton, Ovington, Quidenham (1902–30), Rockland All Saints (1835–85), Rockland All Saints and St Andrew (1885–1930), Rockland St Andrew (1835–85), Rockland St Peter, Roudham, Scoulton, Shropham, Snetterton, Stow Bedon, Thompson, Tottington, Watton, Wilby (1903–30)

YARMOUTH PLU (Norfolk, Suffolk until 1889, Great Yarmouth CB 1889–1930)

Gorleston,[16] Great Yarmouth

In Other Poor Law Counties:

ELY (Cambs/IoE)

Redmere[14] (1858[10]–1930)

HOXNE PLU (Suffolk)

Mendham[15]

WISBECH PLU (Cambs/IoE)

Clenchwarton, Emneth, Outwell,[16] Terrington St Clement, Terrington St John, Tilney All Saints, Tilney St Lawrence, Tilney with Islington, Upwell,[16] Walpole St Andrew, Walpole St Peter, Walsoken, Walsoken Hungate (1894–1930), West Walton

NORTHAMPTONSHIRE

In Northants Poor Law County:[20]

BRACKLEY PLU (Northants, Oxon, Bucks)

Astwell and Falcott, Aynho, Brackley St James (1835–84), Brackley St Peter, Croughton, Culworth, Edgcote (1835–*ca* 1894), Evenley, Eydon, Farthinghoe, Greatworth, Helmdon, Hinton in the Hedges, Marston St Lawrence, Moreton Pinkney, Newbottle (1835–85), Newbottle (1896–1930), Radstone, Steane, Stuchbury, Sulgrave, Kings Sutton (1835–85), Kings Sutton (1896–1930), Kings Sutton with Newbottle (1885–96), Syresham, Thenford, Thorpe Mandeville, Whitfield

BRIXWORTH PLU

Althorp (1861–1930), Cold Ashby (1836–1930), Boughton, Chapel Brampton, Church Brampton, Brington, Brixworth, Coton, Cottesbrooke, Great Creaton, Little Creaton (1835–84), Draughton, Faxton, Guilsborough, East Haddon, Hannington, Harlestone, Haselbech, Holcot, Holdenby, Hollowell, Hanging Houghton, Lamport, Maidwell, Mawsley (1862–1930), Moulton, Moulton Park (1861–1930), Naseby (1836–1930), Old, Overstone (*ca* 1894–1930), Pitsford, Ravensthorpe, Scaldwell, Spratton, Teeton, Thornby (1836–1930), Walgrave

DAVENTRY PLU

Canons Ashby, Ashby St Ledgers, Badby, Braunston, Brockhall, Long Buckby, Byfield, Catesby, Charwell, Daventry, Dodford, Everdon, Farthingstone, Fawsley, Flore, West Haddon, Hellidon, Newnham, Norton, Preston Capes, Staverton, Stowe Nine Churches, Watford, Weedon Beck, Welton, Winwick, Woodford cum Membris, Whilton

36

Northamptonshire *continued*

HARDINGSTONE PLU
Castle Ashby, Brafield on the Green, Cogenhoe, Collingtree, Courtenhall, Denton, Far Cotton (1895—1930), Hackleton, Hardingstone, Horton, Great Houghton, Little Houghton, Milton, Piddington, Preston Deanry, Quinton, Roade, Rotherstone, Whiston, Wootton, Yardley Hastings

KETTERING PLU
Barfield (1862—1930), Barton Seagrave, Beanfield Lawns (1863—1930), Broughton, Burton Latimer, East Carlton, Corby, Cottingham, Cranford St Andrew, Cranford St John, Cransley, Desborough, Geddington, Glendon, Grafton Underwood, Harrington, Kettering, Loddington, Middleton, Newton, Great Oakley, Little Oakley, Orton, Pytchley, Rothwell, Rushton, Stanion, Thorpe Malsor, Warkton, Weekley, Great Weldon (1894—1930), Little Weldon (1894—1930)

NORTHAMPTON PLU
Abington (1835—1913), Great Billing, Little Billing, Bugbrooke, Dallington, Dallington St James (1895—1913), Duston, Duston St James (1895—1913), Harpole, Nether Heyford, Upper Heyford, Kingsthorpe (1835—1913), Kislingbury, Northampton (1909—30), Northampton All Saints (1835—1909), Northampton Priory of St Andrew (1861—1909), Northampton St Giles (1835—1909), Northampton St Peter (1835—1909), Northampton St Sepulchre (1835—1909), Upton, Weston Favell

OUNDLE PLU (Northants, Hunts)
Apethorpe, Armston, Ashton, Barnwell All Saints, Barnwell St Andrew, Benefield, Blatherwycke, Bulwick, King's Cliffe, Cotterstock, Deene, Deenethorpe, Fotheringhay, Glapthorn, Hemington, Lilford cum Wigsthorpe, Luddington,[21] Lutton,[21] Nassington, Oundle, Pilton, Polebrook, Southwick, Stoke Doyle, Tansor, Thorpe Achurch, Thurning,[21] Wadenhoe, Warmington, Great Weldon (1835—94), Little Weldon (1835—94), Winwick,[22] Woodnewton, Yarwell

PETERBOROUGH PLU (Northants [1835—89], Soke Peterb [1889—1930], Cambs [1835—89], Isle of Ely [1889—1930], Lincs Pts Lind, Hunts)
Ailsworth, Borough Fen (1861—1930), Castor, Deeping Gate, Etton, Eye, Fletton Urban (1894—1929), Glinton, Gunthorpe (1835—1929), Helpston, Longthorpe (1908—29), Marholm, Maxey, Newborough, Northborough, Paston (1835—1929), Peakirk, Peterborough (1929—30), Peterborough Minster Close Precincts (1861—1929), Peterborough [St John the Baptist] (1835—94), Peterborough Within (1894—1929), Peterborough Without (1894—1929), Sutton, Upton (1835—1929), Walton (1835—1929), Werrington (1835—1929), Woodstone Urban (1894—1929)

POTTERSPURY PLU (Northants, Bucks [Sept 1835—1930])
Alderton, Ashton, Cosgrove, Furtho, Grafton Regis, Hartwell, Passenham, Paulerspury, Potterspury, Wicken, Yardley Gobion

THRAPSTON PLU (Northants, Hunts)
Great Addington, Little Adington, Aldwincle (1885—1930), Aldwincle All Saints (1835—85), Aldwincle St Peter (1835—85), Brigstock, Chelveston cum Caldecott, Clopton, Denford, Hargrave, Islip, Lowick, Raunds, Ringstead, Slipton, Stanwick, Sudborough, Thrapston, Titchmarsh, Twywell, Woodford

TOWCESTER PLU
Abthorpe, Adstone, Blakesley, Blisworth, Bradden, Easton Neston, Gayton, Cold Higham, Litchborough, Maidford, Green's Norton, Pattishall, Plumpton, Shutlanger, Silverstone, Slapton, Stoke Bruerne, Tiffield, Towcester, Wappenham, Weedon Lois, Whittlebury, Woodend

WELLINGBOROUGH PLU (Northants, Beds)
Mears Ashby, Earls Barton, Bozeat, Great Doddington, Easton Maudit, Ecton, Farndish,[23] Finedon, Grendon, Hardwick, Great Harrowden, Little Harrowden, Higham Ferrers, Higham Park (1862—1930), Irchester, Irthlingborough, Isham, Newton Bromshold, Orlingbury, Overstone (1835—*ca* 1894), Rushden, Strixton, Sywell, Wellingborough, Wilby, Wollaston

In Other Poor Law Counties:

BANBURY PLU (Oxon, Northants, Glos, Warws)
Appletree, Aston le Walls, Banbury,[14] Lower Boddington, Upper Boddington, Chalcombe, Edgcote (*ca* 1894—1930), Middleton Cheney, Chipping Warden, Warkworth

LUTTERWORTH PLU (Leics, Warws, Northants [1835—94])
Welford

MARKET HARBOROUGH PLU (Leics, Northants)
Arthingworth, Ashley, Little Bowden,[24] Brampton Ash, Braybrooke, Clipston, Dingley, East Frandon, Hothorpe, Kelmarsh, Marston Trussel, Great Oxendon, Sibbertoft, Stoke Albany, Sulby, Sutton Bassett, Thorpe Lubenham (1863—1930), Welford (1894—1930), Weston by Welland, Wilbarston

NEWPORT PAGNELL PLU (Bucks, Northants [1836—94])
Hanslope[25]

RUGBY PLU (Warws, Northants)
Barby, Claycoton, Crick, Elkington, Kilsby, Lilbourne, Stanford, Yelvertoft

SOUTHAM PLU (Warws, Northants [1858—95])
Stoneton[26]

STAMFORD PLU (Lincs Pts Kestev, Northants [1835—89], Soke Peterb [1889—1930], Rutl)
Ashton (1835—77), Bainton, Barnack, Collyweston, Duddington, Easton on the Hill, Pilsgate (1835—87), St Martin Without[27] (1894—1930), Southorpe, Stamford Baron,[28] Thornhaugh, Ufford, Wansford, Wittering, Wothorpe

UPPINGHAM PLU (Rutl, Northants)
Fineshade, Gretton, Harringworth, Laxton, Rockingham, Wakerley

NORTHUMBERLAND

In Northumb Poor Law County:[24]

ALNWICK PLU

Abberwick, Acklington, Acklington Park, Acton and Old Felton, Alnmouth, Alnwick, Amble, Bassington, Beanley, Birling, Bolton, Boulmer and Seaton House (1836—88), Broome Park, Brotherwick, Broxfield, Brunton, High Buston, Low Buston, North Charlton, South Charlton, Craster, Crawley, Denwick (1894—1930), Ditchburn, Doxford, Dunstan, Edlingham, Eglingham, Elyhaugh, Embleton, Fallodon, Felton, Glanton, Gloster Hill, Greens and Glantlees, Guyzance, Harehope, Hauxley, Hazon and Hartlaw, Hedgeley, Howick, Learchild, Lemmington, Lesbury, Littlehoughton, Longhoughton, Morwick, Newton by the Sea, Newton on the Moor, Rennington, Rock, Shawdon, Shilbottle, Shipley, Stamford, Sturton Grange, Swarland, Titlington, Togston, Walkmill, Warkworth, Whittle, Woodhouse

BELFORD PLU

Adderstone, Bamburgh, Bamburgh Castle, Beadnell, Belford,[1] Bradford, Budle, Burton, Chathill, Detchant, Easington, Easington Grange, Elford, Ellingham, Elwick,[1] Farne Islands,[2] Fleetham, Glororum, Hoppen (1836—87), Lucker, Middleton, Monks House[2] (1865—1930), Mousen, Newham, Newstead, Outchester, Preston, Ratchwood, Ross,[1] Shoreston, Spindlestone, North Sunderland, Swinhoe, Tughall, Warenford, Warenton

BELLINGHAM PLU

Great Bavington, Little Bavington, Bellingham, Birtley, Carrycoats, Catcherside, East Charlton (1836—86), West Charlton (1836—86), Chirdon, Coldwell, Corsenside, Crookdean, Fawns, Little Harle, West Harle, Hawick, Kirkharle, Kirkwhelpington, Leemailing (1836—86), Nook (1836—86), Otterburn, Plashetts and Tynehead, Ramshope (1836—86), Rochester (1836—86), Rochester Ward (1886—1930), High Shitlington (1836—86), Low Shitlington (1836—86), Smalesmouth, Sweethope, Tarretburn (1836—86), Tarset West, Thockrington, Thorneyburn, Troughend, Wark, Warksburn (1836—86), Wellhaugh, West Whelpington

BERWICK PLU (Northumb, Durham [1836—44])

Ancroft,[3] Berwick upon Tweed, Cornhill on Tweed,[4] Duddo,[4] Felkington,[4] Grindon,[4] Holy Island,[3] Horncliffe,[4] Kyloe,[3] Loanend,[4] Longridge,[4] Norham,[4] Norham Mains,[4] Ord (1891—1930), Shoreswood,[4] Thornton,[4] Tweedmouth,[3] Twizell[4]

CASTLE WARD PLU

Belsay, Berwick Hill, Bitchfield, Bolam, Bolam Vicarage, Bradford, Brenkley, East Brunton, West Brunton, Butterlaw (1836—86), Black Callerton, High Callerton, Little Callerton, Capheaton, Cheeseburn Grange, Coldcoats, Coxlodge (1836—1908), Dalton, Darras Hall, East Denton, West Denton, Dinnington, North Dissington, South Dissington, Eachwick, Fawdon, Fenwick, Gallowhill, Gosforth (1908—30), North Gosforth, South Gosforth (1836—1908), Harlow Hill, Harnham, Hawkwell, Black Heddon, East Heddon,

West Heddon, Heddon on the Wall, Heugh, Higham Dykes, Horton Grange, Houghton and Close House, Ingoe, Kearsley, Kenton, Kirkheaton, Kirkley, Mason, East Matfen, West Matfen, Milbourne, Milbourne Grange, Nesbitt, Newbiggin, Newburn, Newburn Hall, Newham, Ogle, Ouston, Ponteland, Prestwick, Riplington, Rudchester, Ryal, East Shaftoe, West Shaftoe, Shilvington, Shortflatt, Stannington, Sugley, Throckley, Trewick, Twizell, Wallbottle, Wallridge, Whalton, Whitchester, Whorlton, Woolsington

GLENDALE PLU

Akeld, New Bewick, Old Bewick, Brandon, Branton, Branxton, Carham, Chatton, Chillingham, Coldsmouth and Thompson's Walls, Coupland, Crookhouse, Doddington, Earle, Ewart, Fawdon and Clinch (1884—1930); Fawdon, Clinch and Hartside (1836—88); Ford, Grey's Forest, Hepburn, Hethpool, Hotwel, Humbleton, Ilderton; Ingham, Linhope and Greenshawhill (1836—84); Ingham, Linhope, Greenshawhill and Hatside (1884—1930); Kilham, Kirknewton, Lanton, East Lilburn, West Lilburn, Lowick, North Middleton, South Middleton, Middleton Hall, Milfield, Nesbit, Newtown, Paston, Plea Piece, Reaveley, Roddam, Roseden, Selby's Forest, Westnewton, Wooler, Wooperton, Yeavering

HALTWHISTLE PLU

Bellister, Blenkinsopp, Coanwood, Featherstone, Haltwhistle, Hartleyburn, Henshaw, Kirkhaugh, Knarsdale, Lambley, Melkridge, Plenmeller, Ridley, Thirlwall, Thorngrafton, Wall Town, Whitfield

HEXHAM PLU

Acomb, East Acomb (1836—87), West Allen (1897—1930), Allendale, Allendale Common, Anick (1836—87), Anick Grange (1836—87), Apperley (1858—87), Aydon, Aydon Castle, Bearl, Bingfield, Black Carts and Ryehill (1858—1930), Broomhaugh, Broomley, Bywell (1887—1930), Bywell St Andrew (1836—87), Bywell St Peter (1836—87), Chollerton, Clarewood, Cocklaw, Corbridge, Dilston, Duke's Hagg, Eltringham, Espershields, Fallowfield, High Fotherley, Hallington, Halton, Halton Shields (1836—87), Haughton, Haydon, Healey, Hedley, Hedley Woodside (1836—87), Hexham, Hexhamshire High Quarter, Hexhamshire Low Quarter, Hexhamshire Middle Quarter, Hexhamshire West Quarter, Horsley, Humshaugh, Masters Close (1858—87), Mickley, Nafferton, Newbiggin (1836—87), Newbrough, Newlands, Newton, Newton Hall, Ovingham, Ovington, Portgate, Prudhoe, Prudhoe Castle, Riding, Sandhoe, Shotley High Quarter, Shotley Low Quarter, Simonburn, Slaley, Spital, Stelling, Stocksfield Hall (1836—87), Styford, Thornborough, Wall, Warden, Welton, Great Whittington, Little Whittington, Whittle, Whittonstall, Wylam

MORPETH PLU (Northumb, Durham [1836—44])

High Angerton, Low Angerton, Ashington (1896—1930), Ashington and Sheepwash (1836—96), Bedlington,[25] Benridge, Bigge's Quarter, Bockenfield, Bothal Demesne, Bullers Green (1836—86), Bullock's Hall, Cambo, Causey Park, East Chevington, West Chevington, Cockle Park, Corridge, Cresswell, Dean-

38

Northumberland: Morpeth *continued*

ham, Earsdon, Earsdon Forest, Edington, Ellington, Eshott, Fenrother, Freeholders' Quarter, Hadston, Hartburn, Hartburn Grange, Hebron, Hepscott, Highlaws, High and Low Highlaws, Hirst, Horlsley Moor, Long Horsley Common, Longhirst, Longshaws, Longwitton, Lynmouth, Meldon, North Middleton, South Middleton, Mitford, Molesdon, Morpeth, Morpeth Castle, Newbiggin by the Sea, Netherwitton, Newminster (1894—1930), Newminster Abbey (1836—94), Newton Park, Newton Underwood, Nunriding, Old Moor, Pegswood, Pigdon, Riddell's Quarter, Rivergreen, North Seaton, Spital Hill, Stanton, Sheepwash (1896—1930), East and West Thirston with Shothaugh, East Thornton, West Thornton, Throphill, Todridge, Tranwell (1894—1930), Tranwell and High Church (1836—94), Tritlington, Ulgham, Wallington Demesne, Whitridge, Widdrington, Witton Shields, Woodhorn, Woodhorn Demesne

NEWCASTLE UPON TYNE PLU (1836—1914), PAR (1914—30)

Benwell (1836—1914), Byker (1836—1914), Elswick (1836—94), Fenham (1836—1914), Heaton (1836—1914), Jesmond (1836—1914), Newcastle upon Tyne (1914—30), Newcastle upon Tyne All Saints (1836—1914), Newcastle upon Tyne St Andrew (1836—1914), Newcastle upon Tyne St John (1836—1914), Newcastle upon Tyne St Nicholas (1836—1914), Westgate (1836—1914)

ROTHBURY PLU

Alnham, Alwinton, Barrow, Bickerton, Biddlestone, Brinkburn High Ward, Brinkburn Low Ward, Brinkburn South Side (1836—89), Burradon, Caistron, Callaly and Yetlington, Cartington, Clennell, Coatyards, Debdon (1836—89), Debdon (1896—1930), Dueshill (1836—89), Elsdon, Ewesley, Fairhaugh, Fairnley, Fallowlees, Farnham, Flotterton, Greenleighton, Harbottle, Hartington, Hartington Hall, Harwood, Healey and Combhill, Hepple, Hepple Demesne (1836—89), Hesleyhurst, Hollinghill, Holystone, Kidland, Lee Ward (1836—89), Linbridge, Linsheeles, Longframlington, Lorbottle, Monkridge, Mount Healey, Netherton North Side, Netherton South Side, Newtown, Nunnykirk, Pauperhaugh (1836—89). Peels, Prendwick, Raw, Ritton Colt Park, Ritton White House, Rothbury, Rothley, Great Ryle, Little Ryle, Scrainwood, Sharperton, Snitter, Thropton, Todburn, Tosson (1889—1930), Great Tosson and Rye Hill (1836—89), Tosson Little (1836—89), High and Low Trewhitt, Unthank, Warton, Whittingham, Whitton, Wingates, Woodside, Wreighill

TYNEMOUTH PLU

Backworth, Bebside (1836—1920), Blyth (1920—30), Burradon, Camperdown (1899—1912), Chirton (1836—1908), Cowpen (1836—1920), Cramlington, Cullercoats (1836—1908), Earsdon, East Hartford, West Hartford, Hartley (1836—1912), Holywell, Horton, Longbenton, Monkseaton (1836—1913), Murton, Newsham and South Blyth (1836—1920), Preston (1836—1908), Seaton Delaval, Seghill, North

Shields (1836—1908), Tynemouth, Unnamed (1894—1908), Walker (1894—1910), Wallsend, Weetslade (1894—1930), Whitley (1836—1913), Whitley and Monkseaton (1913—30), Willington (1894—1910), Willington Quay (1894—1910)

NOTTINGHAMSHIRE

In Notts Poor Law County:[15]

BASFORD PLU (Notts, Derbys)

Annesley, Arnold, Awsworth (1894—1930), Barton in Fabis, Basford (1836—99), Beeston, Bestwood Park (1877—1930), Bilborough, Bradmore, West Bridgford, Brinsley (1896—1930), Bulwell (1836—99), Bunny, Burton Joyce, Calverton, Carlton, Clifton with Glapton, Colwick, Cossall, Eastwood, Felley, Gamston, Gedling, Gotham, Greasley, Hucknall Torkard, Kimberley (1896—1930), Kirkby in Ashfield, Lambley, Linby, Newstead, Nuthall, Papplewick, Ruddington, Selston, Standard Hill (1862—97), Stoke Bardolph, Strelley, Thrumpton, Trowell, Wilford (1836—94), North Wilford (1894—97), South Wilford (1894—1930), Wollaton, Woodborough

BINGHAM PLU (Notts, Leics)

Aslockton, Barnston cum Langar, Bingham, East Bridgford, Clipston, Car Colston, Colston Bassett, Cotgrave, Cropwell Bishop, Cropwell Butler, Edwalton, Elton, Flawborough, Flintham, Granby, Hawksworth, Hickling, Holme Pierrepont, Keyworth, Kinoulton, Kneeton, Langar cum Barnstone, Lodge on the Wolds (1858—96), Normanton on the Wolds, Orston, Owthorpe, Plumtree, Radcliffe on Trent, Saxondale, Scarrington, Screveton, Shelford, Shelton, Sibthorpe, Stanton on the Wolds, Tithby, Thoroton, Tollerton, Whatton, Widmerpool, Wiverton Hall (1858—1930)

MANSFIELD PLU (Notts, Derbys)

Blidworth, Fulwood (1861—1930), Haywood Oaks (1861—1930), Hucknall under Huthwaite, Lindhurst (1861—1930), Mansfield, Mansfield Woodhouse, Pinxton,[16] Skegby, Sookholme, Sutton in Ashfield, Teversal, Warsop

NEWARK PLU (Notts, Leics)

Alverton, Balderton, Barnby in the Willows, Besthorpe, Broadholme (soon after 1836[17]—1930), North Clifton (soon after 1836[17]—1930), South Clifton, Coddington, North Collingham, South Collingham, Cotham, Farndon, Flawford[18] (1866—84), Girton, Harby (soon after 1836[17]—1930), Hawton, Kilvington, Langford, Meering (1858—1930), West Newark (1894—1930), Newark upon Trent, South Scarle, Spalford, Staunton, Thorney (soon after 1836[17]—1930), Wigsley (soon after 1836[17]—1930), Winthorpe

NOTTINGHAM PLU (1836—97), PAR (1897—1930)

Nottingham (1897—1930), Nottingham St Mary (1836—97), Nottingham St Nicholas (1836—97), Nottingham St Peter (1836—97)

39

RADFORD PLU (1836—97)
Brewhouse Yard, Lenton, Radford, Sneinton
EAST RETFORD PLU
Askham, Babworth, Barnby Moor, Bevercotes, Bothamsall, Clarborough, Clayworth, Cottam, Darlton, East Drayton, West Drayton, Dunham, Eaton, Elkesley, Everton, Fledborough, Gamston, Gringley on the Hill, Grove, Habblesthorpe (1836—84), Haughton, Hayton, Headon cum Upton, Laneham, North Leverton (1836—84), North Leverton with Habblesthorpe (1884—1930), South Leverton, Littleborough, Lound, East Markham, Markham Clinton or West Markham, Marnham, Mattersey, Normanton on Trent, Ordall (1836—1921), Ragnall, Rampton, Ranskill, East Retford, North Retford (1894—1921), West Retford (1836—1921), Scaftworth, Scrooby, Stokeham, Sturton le Steeple, Sutton, Torworth, Treswell, Tuxford, North Wheatley, South Wheatley, Wiseton
SOUTHWELL PLU
Averham, Bathley, Bilsthorpe, Bleasby, Boughton, Budby (1836—99), Bulcote, Carlton on Trent, Caunton, Caythorpe, Clipstone, Cromwell, Eakring, Edingley, Edwinstowe, Egmanton, Elston, Epperstone, Farnsfield, Fiskerton (1836—84), Fiskerton cum Morton (1884—1930), Gonalston, Grassthorpe, Gunthorpe, Halam, Halloughton, Hockerton, Holme, Hoveringham, Kelham, Kersall, Kirklington, Kirton, Kneesall, Laxton, Lowdham, Maplebeck, Morton (1836—84), North Muskham, South Muskham, Norwell, Norwell Woodhouse, Ollerton, Ompton, Ossington, Oxton, Park Leys (1858—99), Perlethorpe (1836—99), Perlethorpe cum Budby (1899—1930), Rolleston, Rufford, Southwell, Staythorpe, East Stoke, Sutton on Trent, Syerston, Thorpe, Thurgarton, Upton, Walesby, Wellow, Weston, Winkburn
WORKSOP PLU (Notts, Derbys, Yorks W Riding)
Blyth,[19] Carburton, Carlton in Lindrick, Cuckney, Harworth, Hodsock, Holbeck, Nether Langwith, Norton, Styrrup, Wallingwells[20] (1862—1930), Welbeck (1862—1930), Woodhouse Hall (1862—1930), Worksop

In Other Poor Law Counties:
DONCASTER PLU (Yorks W Riding, Notts [1837—95], Lincs Pts Lind [1837—86])
Auckley,[21] Finningley,[22] Misson[23]
GAINSBOROUGH PLU (Lincs Pts Lind, Notts)
Beckingham, Bole, West Burton, Misterton, Saundby, West Stockwith, Walkeringham
LOUGHBOROUGH PLU (Leics, Notts)
Costock, East Leake, West Leake, Normanton on Soar, Rempstone, Stanford on Soar, Sutton Bonington, Thorpe in the Glebe, Willoughby on the Wolds, Wysall
MELTON MOWBRAY PLU (Leics, Notts)
Upper Broughton
SHARDLOW PLU (Derbys, Leics, Notts)
Bramcote, Chilwell, Kingston on Soar, Ratcliffe on Soar, Stapleford, Toton

OXFORDSHIRE

In Oxon Poor Law Co:[27]
BANBURY PLU (Oxon, Northants, Glos, Warws)
East Adderbury, West Adderbury, Alkerton, Banbury,[28] Barford St John, Barford St Michael, Bloxham, Bodicote, Bourton, Broughton, Clattercott, Claydon, Cropredy, Drayton, Epwell, Grimsbury (1894—1930), Hanwell, Horley, Hornton, Milcombe, Milton, Mollington,[29] Neithrop,[30] North Newington, South Newington, Hook Norton, Prescote, Shenington, East Shutford, West Shutford, Sibford Ferris, Sibford Gower, Swalcliffe, Tadmarton, Wardington, Wigginton, Wroxton
BICESTER PLU (Oxon, Bucks)
Ambrosden, Ardley, Arncott, Bicester King's End, Bicester Market End, Blackthorn, Bletchingdon, Bucknell, Caversfield,[31] Charlbury, Chalton-on-Otmoor, Chesterton, Cottisford, Fawler, Fencott and Murcott, Finmere, Finstock, Fringford, Fritwell, Godington, Hardwick, Hethe, Lower Heyford, Upper Heyford, Islip, Kirtlington, Launton, Merton, Middleton Stoney, Mixbury, Newton Purcell, Noke, Oddington, Piddington, Shelswell, Somerton, Souldern, Stoke Lyne, Stratton Audley,[32] Tusmore, Wendlebury, Weston-on-the-Green
HEADINGTON PLU (Oxon, Bucks until 1844, ent Oxon thereafter)
Beckley,[33] Chippinghurst, Cowley (1836—1929), Cowley St John (1894—1926), Cuddesdon, Denton, Elsfield, Forest Hill (1836—81), Forest Hill with Shotover (1881—1930), Garsington, Headington, Holton, Horspath, Horton cum Studley, Iffley, Littlemore, Marston, Oxford St Clement (1836—1926), Oxford St Giles (1836—1926), Oxford St John the Baptist (1836—1926), St Giles and St John (1926—30), Shotover (1858[34]—81), Stanton St John, Stowood, Studley,[33] Wheatley, Woodeaton
HENLEY PLU (Oxon, Berks, Bucks)
Badgemore (1894—1930), Bix, Brightwell Baldwin, Britwell (1912—30), Britwell Prior (1835—1912), Britwell Salome (1835—1912), Caversham, Checkendon, Cuxham, Eye and Dunsdem, Greys (1894—1905), Harpsden, Henley-on-Thames, Ipsden, Kidmore (1894—1902), Kidmore End (1902—30), Nettlebed, Nuffield, *Pepton*,[35] Pishill (1835—1922), Pishill with Stonor (1922—30), Pyrton, Rotherfield Greys, Rotherfield Peppard, Shiplake, Stonor (1896—1922), Swyncombe, Watlington
CHIPPING NORTON PLU (Oxon, Glos, Warws)
Ascott-under-Wychwood, Bruern, Chadlington, Charlbury, Chastleton, Chilson, Churchill, Cornbury Park, Cornwell, Enstone, Fawler, Fifield, Finstock, Heythrop, Idbury, Kingham, Langley, Leafield, Lyneham, Milton-under-Wychwood, Chipping Norton, Over Norton, Great Rollright, Little Rollright, Salford, Sarsden, Shipton-under-Wychwood, Spelsbury, Swerford, Great Tew, Little Tew, Wychwood

Oxfordshire *continued*

OXFORD INCORPORATION (Oxon/Oxf. CB,
Berks until 1889, ent Oxf. CB thereafter)
Holywell (until 1926), Oxford (1926–30), Oxford All Saints (until 1895), Oxford St Aldate[36] (until 1926), Oxford St Ebbe (until 1926), Oxford St Martin (until 1895), Oxford St Martin and All Saints (1895–1926), Oxford St Mary Magdalene (until 1926), Oxford St Mary the Virgin (until 1926), Oxford St Michael (until 1926), Oxford St Peter in the East (until 1926), Oxford St Peter le Bailey (until 1926), Oxford St Thomas (until 1926)
THAME PLU (Oxon, Bucks)
Adwell, Albury, Ascott, Aston Rowant, Attington, Chalgrove, Chilworth, Chinnor, Crowell, Easington, Emmington, Great Haseley, Ickford,[37] Kingsey, Lewknor,[38] Great Milton, Little Milton, Shirburn, Stoke Talmage, Sydenham, Tetsworth, Thame, Thomley, Tiddington, Warpsgrove, Waterstock, Waterperry, South Weston, Wheatfield
WITNEY PLU (Oxon, Glos, Berks until 1844, ent Oxon thereafter)
Alvescot, Asthall, Aston and Cote, Bampton, Black Bourton, Brighthampton, Broadwell, Broughton Poggs,[39] Burford, Chimney, Clanfield, Cogges, Crawley, Curbridge, Ducklington, Eynsham, Filkins (1835–86), Filkins (1896–1930), Fulbrook, Hailey, Handborough, Hardwick, Holwell, Kelmscot, Kencot, North Leigh, South Leigh, Lew, Minster Lovell, Northmoor, Brize Norton, Osney Hill (1858[34]–1930), Ramsden, Shifford, Shilton,[40] Standlake, Stanton Harcourt, Swinbrook, Taynton, Upton and Signet, Westwell, Widford,[41] Wilcote, Witney, Yelford
WOODSTOCK PLU
Asterleigh (1835–94), Middle Aston, North Aston, Steeple Aston, Steeple Barton, Westcott Barton, Begbroke, Bladon, Blenheim Park, Cassington, Clifton Hampden, Combe, Cutteslowe (1858[34]–1930), Deddington, Glympton, Gosford, Hampton Gay, Hampton Poyle, *Hempton*,[42] Hensington (1835–94), Hensington Within (1894–1930), Hensington Without (1894–1930), Kiddington (1835–94), Kiddington with Asterleigh (1894–1930), Kidlington, Rousham, Sandford St Martin, Shipton-on-Cherwell, Stonesfield, Tackley, Duns Tew, Thrup, Water Eaton, Wolvercott, Woodstock, Old Woodstock (1894–1930), Nether Worton, Over Worton, Wootton, Yarnton

In Other Poor Law Cos:
ABINGDON PLU (Berks, Oxon)
Marsh Baldon, Toot Baldon, Binsey, Burcott, Chislehampton, Clifton Hampden, Culham, Drayton St Leonard, Nuneham Courtenay, Sandford-on-Thames, Seacourt[24] (1836–94), Stadhampton, Unnamed[24] (1894–1929)
BRACKLEY PLU (Northants, Oxon)
Finmere, Mixbury

BRADFIELD PLU (Berks, Oxon)
Goring, Mapledurham, Whitchurch[43]
BUCKINGHAM PLU (Bucks, Oxon until 1844, ent Bucks thereafter)
Lillingstone Lovell,[44] pt Stowe (Boycott)[44]
FARINGDON PLU (Berks, Oxon)
Little Faringdon,[45] Grafton, Langford,[45] Radcot
WALLINGFORD PLU (Berks, Oxon)
Benson, Berrick Salome, Crowmarsh Gifford, Dorchester, Ewelme, Mongewell, Newington, Newnham Murren, North Stoke, South Stoke, Warborough
WYCOMBE PLU (Bucks, Oxon)
Chinnor, Ibstone,[46] Lewknor Uphill[47] (1835–85), Stokenchurch

RUTLAND

In Rutl Poor Law County:[5]
OAKHAM PLU (Rutl, Leics)
Ashwell, Barleythorpe (1894–1930), Barrow, Braunston, Brooke, Burley, Cottesmore, Edith Weston, Egleton, Empingham, Exton, Greetham, Gunthorpe, Hambleton, Horn, Langham, Leighfield (1861–1930), Lyndon, Manton, Martinsthorpe, Normanton, Oakham (1894–1930), Oakham (1894–1930), Oakham Deanshold with Barleythorpe (1836–94), Oakham Lordship (1836–94), Market Overton, Stretton, Teigh, Thistleton, Tickencote, Whissendine, Whitwell
UPPINGHAM PLU (Rutl, Leics, Northants)
Ayston, Barrowden, Beaumont Chase (1861–1930), Belton, Bisbrooke, Caldecott, Glaston, Liddington, North Luffenham, South Luffenham, Morcott, Pilton, Preston, Ridlington, Seaton, Stoke Dry,[3] Thorpe by Water,[3] Uppingham, Wardley, Wing

In Other Poor Law Counties:
STAMFORD PLU (Lincs Pts Kestev, Northants, Soke Peterb [1899—1830], Rutl, Hunts)
Great Casterton, Little Casterton, Clipsham, Essendine, Ketton, Pickworth, Ryhall, Tinwell, Tixover

41

SHROPSHIRE

In Salop.Poor Law County:[16]

ATCHAM PLU (Salop, Montg)
Acton Burnell, Alberbury Lower Quarter (1836—86), Alberbury with Cardeston (1886—1930), Albrighton, Astley, Atcham, Battlefield, Berrington, Bicton (1885—1930), Buildwas (1895—1930), Cardeston (1836—86), Condover, Cound, Cressage, Eaton Constantine, Fitz, Ford, Frodesley, Habberley, Great Hanwood, Harley, Haughton Demesne (1858—85), Hughley, Kenley, Leighton, Melverley, Meole Brace (1871—1930), Minsterley, Montford, Pitchford, Pontesbury, Church Preen, Preston Gubbals, Church Pulverbatch, Ruckley and Langley, Sheinton, Shrawardine, Shrewsbury (1924—30), Shrewsbury Holy Cross with St Giles (1871—1924), Shrewsbury St Alkmund (1871—1930), Shrewsbury St Chad (1871—1924), Shrewsbury St Julian (1871—1924), Shrewsbury St Mary (1871—1924), Stapleton, Sutton, Uffington, Unnamed (1894—1901), Unnamed (1894—1901), Uppington, Upton Magna, Westbury, Withington, Woolaston, Wroxeter

BRIDGNORTH PLU
Acton Round, Alveley, Astley Abbots, Aston Eyre, Billingsley, Bridgnorth St Leonard, Bridgnorth St Mary Magdalen, Burwarton, Chelmarsh, Chetton, Claverley, Cleobury North, Deuxhill, Ditton Priors, Eardington, Glazeley, Middleton Scriven, Monkhopton, Morville, Neenton, Oldbury, Quatford, Quatt (1836—soon after 1836[17]), Quatt Jarvis (soon after 1836[17]—1930), Quatt Malvern (soon after 1836[17]—1930), Romsley, Rudge (1895—1930), Sidbury, Stanton Long, Tasley, Upton Cressett, Worfield

CHURCH STRETTON PLU
Acton Scott, Cardington, Easthope, Eaton under Haywood, Hope Bowdler, Leebotwold, Longnor, Rushbury, Shipton, Sibdon Carwood, Smethcott, All Stretton (1899—1930), Church Stretton, Little Stretton (1899—1930), Wistanstow, Woolstaston

CLEOBURY MORTIMER PLU (Salop, Worcs, Heref [1836—44])
Aston Botterell, Cleobury Mortimer, Coreley, Farlow,[7] Highley, Hopton Wafers, Kinlet, Loughton, Milson, Neen Savage, Neen Sollars, Silvington, Stottesdon, Wheathill, Woodhouse (1862—1930)

CLUN PLU (Salop, Montg [1836—84])
Bishop's Castle (1884—94), Bishop's Castle Borough (1836—84), Bishop's Castle Out (1836—84), Bishop's Castle Rural (1894—1930), Clun, Clunbury, Clungunford, Dinmore (1862—84), Edgton, Hill End (1862—84), Hopesay, Hopton Castle, Horderley Hall (1862—84), Lydbury North, Lydham,[18] Mainstone,[18] More, Mucklewick (soon after 1836[19]—84), Myndtown, Norbury, Old Church Moor (1862—84), Ratlinghope, Shelve, Snead,[20] Wentnor

DRAYTON PLU—see MARKET DRAYTON PLU

ELLESMERE PLU (Salop, Flints)
Baschurch, Cockshutt (1896—1930), Ellesmere (1836—94), Ellesmere Rural (1894—1930), Ellesmere Urban (1894—1930), Hadnall, Hordley, Myddle, Great Ness, Little Ness, Petton, Welshampton

LUDLOW PLU[21] (Salop, Heref)
Abdon, Ashford Bowdler, Ashford Carbonnell, Bitterley, Bromfield, Caynham, Clee St Margaret, Culmington, Diddlebury, East Hamlet (1884—1930), Halford, Heath, Holdgate, Hope Bagot, Hopton Cangeford, Leintwardine (North Side),[22] Ludford,[23] Ludlow [St Lawrence],[6] Ludlow Castle (1862—1901), Munslow, Onibury, Richard's Castle[13] (1836—89), Richard's Castle (1889[13]—1930), Stanton Lacy, Stoke St Milborough, Stokesay, Tugford, Cold Weston

MADELEY PLU
Barrow, Benthall, Broseley, Buildwas (1836—95), Dawley Magna, Linley, Madeley, Posenhall, Stirchley, Little Wenlock, Much Wenlock, Willey

MARKET DRAYTON PLU (orig, 'DRAYTON') (Salop, Staffs)
Adderley, Cheswardine, Market Drayton (1914—30), Drayton in Hales (1836—1914), Child's Ercall, Hinstock, Hodnet, Moreton Say, Norton in Hales, Stoke upon Tern, Sutton upon Tern (1914—30), Tittenley,[24] Woore

NEWPORT PLU (Salop, Staffs)
Cherrington, Chetwynd (1836—94), Chetwynd Aston (1836—94), Chetwynd Aston Rural (1894—1930), Chetwynd Aston Urban (1894—96), Chetwynd Rural (1894—1930), Chetwynd Urban (1894—96), Church Aston (1836—94), Church Aston Rural (1894—1930), Church Aston Urban (1894—96), Edgmond, Lilleshall, Longford, Newport, St George's (1898—1930), Tibberton, Woodcote

OSWESTRY PLU (local act 1791)
West Felton, Kinnerley, Knockin, Llanyblodwel, Llanymench,[25] Oswestry Rural, Oswestry Town (1791—1880s), Oswestry Urban (1880s—1930), Ruyton of the Eleven Towns, St Martin's, Selattyn, Sychtyn, Weston Rhyn (1897—1930), Whittington

SHIFNAL PLU (Salop, Staffs)
Albrighton, Badger, Beckbury, Bobbington,[26] Boningale, Boscobel (1858—1930), Donington, Kemberton, Priorslee (1898—1930), Ryton, Sheriff Hales, Shifnal, Stockton, Sutton Maddock, Tong

SHREWSBURY INCORP (local act, 1784—1870)/PLU (1870—71)
Meole Brace, Shrewsbury Holy Cross with St Giles, Shrewsbury St Alkmund, Shrewsbury St Chad, Shrewsbury St Julian, Shrewsbury St Mary

WELLINGTON PLU
Bolas Magna, Ercall Magna, Eyton on the Weald Moors, Hadley (1898—1930), Kinnersley, Longdon upon Tern, Preston upon the Weald Moors, Rodington, Waters Upton, Wellington (1836—94), Wellington Rural (1894—1930), Wellington Urban (1894—1930), Wombridge, Wrockwardine, Wrockwardine Wood (1884—1930)

42

WEM PLU
Broughton, Clive, Grinshill, Ightfield (1836—54), Lee Brockhurst, Loppington, Moreton Corbet, Prees, Shawbury, Stanton upon Hine Heath, Wem (1836—1900), Wem Rural (1900—30), Wem Urban (1900—30), Weston under Redcastle, Whixall (1894—1930)

WHITCHURCH INCORP (1792—1854) (Salop), PLU (1854—1930) (Salop, Ches, Flints)
Ightfield (1854—1930), Whitchurch (1792—1894), Whitchurch Rural (1894—1930), Whitchurch Urban (1894—1930)

In Other Poor Law Counties:
BROMSGROVE PLU[27] (Worcs, Salop [1836—44], Warws, Staffs)
Hunnington, Romsley
WEST BROMWICH PLU[27] (Staffs, Salop [1836—44], Worcs)
Oldbury, Warley Salop
KIDDERMINSTER PLU (Worcs, Staffs [1836—95], Salop [1836—95])
Dowles[28]
KNIGHTON PLU (Radnor, Heref, Salop)
Bedstone, Bettws y Crwyn, Bucknell,[29] Llanfair Waterdine, Stowe
MONTGOMERY PLU (Montg, Cardigan, Merioneth, Salop)
Brompton and Rhiston, Chirbury, Worthen
SEISDON PLU (Staffs, Salop [1836—95])
Bobbington,[26] Rudge (1836—95)
STOURBRIDGE PLU[27] (Worcs, Salop [1836—44], Staffs)
Cakemore (1836—1919), Halesowen, Hasbury, Hawne, Hill (1836—1919), Illey, Lapal, Ridgacre
TENBURY PLU (Worcs, Salop, Heref)
Boraston, Burford, Greete, Nash, Whitton

SOMERSET

In Somerset Poor Law County:[16]
LONG ASHTON PLU (1899[17]—1930, renaming of BEDMINSTER PLU, qv)
AXBRIDGE PLU
Chapel Allerton, Axbridge, Badgworth, Banwell, Berrow, Biddisham, Blagdon, Bleadon, Brean, East Brent, Brent Knoll, Burnham, Burhham Without (1896—1930), Burrington, Butcombe, Charterhouse, Cheddar, Christon, Churchill, Compton Bishop, Congresbury, Highbridge (1894—96), North Highbridge (1896—1930), South Highbridge (1896—1930), Hutton, Kewstoke, Locking, Loxton, Lympsham, Mark, Nyland cum Batcombe, Puxton, Rowberrow, Shipham, Uphill, Weare, Wedmore, Weston-super-Mare, Wick St Lawrence, Winscombe, Worle, Wrington

BATH PLU
Bath (1900—30), Bath St James (1836—1900), Bath St Michael (1836—1900), Bath St Peter and St Paul (1836—1900), Bathampton, Batheaston, Bathford, Bathwick (1836—1900), Charlcombe, Claverton, English Combe, Monkton Combe, Combe Hay, Dunkerton, Freshford (1882—1930), Hinton Charterhouse, Langridge, Lyncombe and Widcombe (1836—1900), St Catherine, South Stoke, Swainswick, Twerton or Twiverton (1836—1911), Walcot (1836—1900), Wellow, Weston, Wooley
BEDMINSTER PLU (1836—99[17], renamed LONG ASHTON PLU [as such 1899—1930])
Long Ashton, Backwell, Barrow Gurney, Bedminster (1836—96), Bedminster Without (1894—late 1890s[18]), Bishopsworth (late 1890s[18]—1930), Brockley, Chelvey (1836—96), Clapton, Clevedon, Dundry, Easton-in-Gordano, Flax Bourton, Kenn, Kingston Seymour, Abbots Leigh, Nailsea, Portbury, Portishead, Tickenham, Walton-in-Gordano, North Weston (1894—1930), Weston-in-Gordano, Winford, Wraxall, Yatton

BRIDGWATER PLU
Aisholt, Ashcott, Bawdrip, Bridgwater, Bridgwater Without (1894—1930), Broomfield, Cannington, Catcott, Charlynch, Chedzoy, Chilton Common (1858[19]—1907), Chilton Polden, Chilton Trinity, Cossington, Durleigh, Edington, Edstock and Beer (1836—86), Enmore, Fiddington, Goathurst, Greinton, Huntspill, Lyng, Middlezoy, Moorlinch, Othery, Otterhampton, Pawlett, North Petherton, Puriton, St Michaelchurch, Shapwick, Spaxton, Stawell, Stockland Bristol, Nether Stowey, Over Stowey, Sutton Mallet, Thurloxton, Wembdon, Westonzoyland, Woolavington

CHARD PLU (Somerset, Devon, Dorset)
Ashill, Broadway, Buckland St Mary, Chaffcombe, Chard, Chard Borough, Chillington, Combe St Nicholas, Crewkerne, West Crewkerne (1894—1930), Cricket Malherbie, Cricket St Thomas, Cudworth, Dinnington, Donyatt, West Dowlish, Dowlish Wake, Hinton St George, Ilminster, Ilminster Without (1899—1930), Ilton, Kingstone, Knowle St

Somerset: Chard *continued*

Giles, Lopen, Merriot, Misterton (1896–1930), Seavington St Mary, Seavington St Michael, Shepton Beauchamp, Stocklinch (1884–1930), Stocklinch Magdalen (1836–84), Stocklinch Ottersey (1836–84), Wambrook,[20] Wayford, Whitelackington, Whitestaunton, Winsham

CLUTTON PLU

Cameley, Camerton, Chelwood, Chew Magna, Chew Stoke, Chilcompton, Clutton, Compton Martin, Farmborough, Farrington Gurney, East Harptree, West Harptree, Hinton Blewitt, High Littleton, Litton, Nempnett Thrubwell, Midsomer Norton, Norton Hawkfield (1836–96), Norton Malreward, Paulton, Publow, St Thomas in Pensford (1836–84), Stanton Drew, Ston Easton, Stowey, Timsbury, Ubley, North Widcombe

DULVERTON PLU

Brompton Regis, Brushford, Dulverton, Exford, pt Exmoor,[21] Exton, Hawkridge, Huish Champflower, Skilgate, Upton, Winsford, Withiel Florey (1896–1930), Withypool

FROME PLU

Babington (1845–1930), Beckington, Berkley, Buckland Dinham, Cloford, Elm, Farleigh Hungerford, Foxcote, Frome, Hardington, Hemington, Kilmersdon, Laverton, Leigh-upon-Mendip, Lullington, Marston Bigot, Mells, Norton St Philip, Nunney, Orchardleigh, Rodden, Rode, Selwood (1894–1930), Standerwick (1836–85), Tellisford, Wanstrow, Whatley, Witham Friary, Woolverton, Writhlington

KEYNSHAM PLU (Somerset, Glos)

Brislington, Burnett, Queen Charlton, Compton Dando, Corston, Kelston, Keynsham, Marksbury, Newton St Loe, Priston, Saltford, Stanton Prior, North Stoke, Whitchurch

LANGPORT PLU

Aller, Babcary, Barrington, Barton St David, Beer Crocombe, South Bradon (1836–85), Charlton Adam (1836–87), Charlton Mackerell, Compton Dundon, Curry Mallet, Curry Rivel, Drayton, Earnshill, Fivehead, High Ham, Huish Episcopi, Isle Abbots, Isle Brewers, Keinton Mandeville, Kingsbury Episcopi, Kingsdon, Kingweston, Langport, Muchelney, Pitney, Puckington, Somerton, Long Sutton, Swell

SHEPTON MALLET PLU

Ashwick, Babington (1835–45), Batcombe, Binegar, West Bradley (1882–1930), East Cranmore, West Cranmore, Croscombe, Ditcheat, Doulting, Downhead, Emborough, Evercreech, Holcombe, Hornblotton, Lamyat, East Lydford, West Lydford, Milton Clevedon, East Pennard, Pilton, Pylle, Shepton Mallet, Stoke Lane, Stratton-on-the-Fosse, Upton Noble

TAUNTON PLU (Somerset, Devon until 1896, ent Somerset thereafter)

Angersleigh, Ash Priors, West Bagborough, Bickenhall, Cheddon Fitzpaine, Churchstanton,[22] Combe

Florey, Corfe, Cothelstone, Creech St Michael, Curland, North Curry, Durston, Halse, West Hatch, Hatch Beauchamp, Heathfield, Bishop's Hull (1836–85), Bishop's Hull Within (1885–1921), Bishop's Hull Without (1885–1930), Kingston, Bishop's Lydeard, Lydeard St Lawrence, West Monkton, Norton Fitzwarren, Orchard Portman, Otterford, Pitminster, Ruishton, Stoke Fitzpaine, Staplegrove, Stoke St Gregory, Stoke St Mary, Taunton St James (1836–85), Taunton St James Within (1885–1921), Taunton St James Without (1885–1930), Taunton St Mary Magdalene (1836–85), Taunton St Mary Magdalene Within (1885–1921), Taunton St Mary Magdalene Without (1885–1930), Thorn Falcon, Thurlbear, Tolland, Trull, Wilton (1836–1921)

WELLINGTON PLU (Somerset, Devon)

Ashbrittle, Bathealton, Bradford, West Buckland, Chipstable, Fitzhead, Hillfarrance (1836–84), Kittisford, Langford Budville, Milverton, Nynehead, Oake, Raddington, Runnington, Sampford Arundel, Stawley, Thorne St Margaret, Wellington, Wiveliscombe, Wiveliscombe Without (1894–1930)

WELLS PLU

Baltonsborough, West Bradley (1836–82), Butleigh, Chewton Mendip, Dinder, Glastonbury, Godney (1904–30), Green Oare (1858[19]–85), Meare, West Pennard, Priddy, Sharpham (1894–1930), Rodney Stoke, Street, Walton, Wells St Andrew, Wells St Cuthbert In, Wells St Cuthbert Out, Westbury, Wookey, North Wootton

WILLITON PLU

Bicknoller, Brompton Ralph, Carhampton, Clatworthy, Old Cleeve, Crowcombe, Culbone, Cutcombe, Dodington, Dunster, Elworthy, Holford, Kilton (1836–86), Kilton with Lilstock (1886–1930), Kilve, Lilstock (1836–86), Luccombe, Luxborough, Minehead, Minehead Without (1894–1930), Monksilver, Nettlecombe, Oare, Porlock, East Quantoxhead, West Quantoxhead, St Decuman's (1836–1902), Sampford Brett, Selworthy, Stogumber, Stogursey, Stoke Pero, Stringston, Timberscombe, Treborough, Watchet (1902–30), Williton (1902–30), Withiel Florey (1836–96), Withycombe, Wootton Courtney

WINCANTON PLU (Somerset, Dorset until 1896, ent Somerset thereafter)

Alford, Ashford, North Barrow, South Barrow, Blackford, Bratton Seymour, North Brewham, South Brewham, Bruton, North Cadbury, South Cadbury, Queen Camel, Castle Cary, Charlton Horethorne, Charlton Musgrove, North Cheriton, Abbas Combe, Compton Pauncefoot, Corton Denham, Cucklington, Eastrip (1858[19]–85), Four Towers (1858[19]–85), Henstridge, Holton, Horsington, Lovington, Maperton, Milborne Port, Penselwood, Pitcombe, Shepton Montague, Sparkford, Stoke Trister, Stowell, Sutton Montis, Weston Bampfylde, Wheathill, Wincanton, Yarlington

44

Somerset *continued*

YEOVIL PLU

Ash (1895–1930), Ashington, Barwick, Brympton, West Camel, Chilthorne Domer, Chilton Cantelo, East Chinnock, Middle Chinnock[10] (1836–84), West Chinnock,[10] Chiselborough, Closworth, East Coker, West Coker, Hardington Mandeville, Haselbury Plucknett, Ilchester, Limington, Long Load (1895–1930), Lufton, Marston Magna (1894–1930), Martock, Montacute, Mudford, Northover, Norton sub Hamdon, Odcombe, Pendomer, North Perrott, South Petherton, Podimore, Preston Plucknett, Rimpton (1896–1930), Sock Dennis (1858[19]–1930), Stoke sub Hamdon, Sutton Bingham, Thorne, Tintinhull, Yeovil, Yeovil Without (1894–1930), Yeovilton

In Other Poor Law Counties:

BEAMINSTER PLU (Dorset, Somerset until 1896, ent Dorset thereafter)
Misterton (1836–96), Seaborough[23]
BRADFORD PLU (Wilts, Somerset until 1882, ent Wilts thereafter)
Freshford (1836–82)
MERE PLU (Wilts, Somerset until 1896, ent Wilts thereafter)
Maiden Bradley,[24] Kilmington,[25] Stourton[24]
SOUTH MOLTON PLU (Devon, Somerset until 1884, ent Devon thereafter)
pt Exmoor[21]
SHERBORNE PLU (Dorset, Somerset until 1896, ent Dorset thereafter)
Goathill,[23] Marston Magna (1836–94), Poyntington,[23] Rimpton (1836–96), Sandford Orcas,[23] Trent[23]

STAFFORDSHIRE

In Staffs Poor Law County:[50]
ALSTONFIELD GILBERT UNION (until 1869)
Alstonfield, Butterton, Grindon, Wetton
WEST BROMWICH PLU (Staffs, Salop [1836—44], Worcs, Birm CB [1928—30])
West Bromwich, Handsworth (1836—1911), Perry Barr,[51] Warley Woods (1928—30)
BURTON UPON TRENT PLU (Staffs, Derbys)
Anslow, Barton under Needwood, Branston, Burton Extra (1837—1904), Burton upon Trent,[52] Dunstall, Foston and Scropton,[23] Hanbury, Horninglow (1837—1904), Outwoods (1894—1930), Rolleston,[53] Stapenhill,[33] Stretton, Tatenthill, Tutbury, Winshill,[33] Wychnor
CANNOCK PLU (1870s[54]—1930)
Acton Trussell and Bednall, Brewood, Bushbury, Cannock, Cheslyn Hay, Church Eaton, Coppenhall, Dunston, Essington, Featherstone, Hatherton, Hilton, Huntington, Kinvaston, Lapley, Norton Canes, Penkridge, Saredon, Shareshill, Stretton, Teddesley Hay, Great Wyrley
CHEADLE PLU
Alton, Bradley in the Moors, Cauldon, Caverswall, Cheadle, Checkley, Cheddleton, Consall, Cotton, Denstone, Dilhorne, Draycott in the Moors, Farley, Forsbrook (1896—1930), Ipstones, Kingsley, Oakamoor (1896—1930)
DUDLEY PLU (Staffs, Worcs)
Coseley (1903—30), Dudley Castle Hill[55] (1867—1929), Rowley Regis, Sedgley, Tipton
LEEK PLU
Bradnop and Cawdry, Butterton, Endon and Stanley (1894—1930); Endon, Longsdon and Stanley (1837—94); Fawfieldhead, Grindon (1869—1930), Heathylee, Heaton, Hollinsclough, Horton, Leek (1894—1930), Leek and Lowe (1837—95), Leekfrith, Longnor, Longsdon (1894—1930), Lowe (1895—1930), Norton in the Moors, Onecote, Quarnford, Rudyard, Rushton James, Rushton Spencer, Sheen, Smallthorne (1894—1922), Tittesworth, Warslow and Elkstones
LICHFIELD PLU
Alrewas, Alrewas Hays (1858—85), Armitage, Brereton (1894—1930), King's Bromley, King's Bromley Hays (1858—1922), Burntwood (1929—30); Burntwood, Edial and Woodhouses (1836—1929); Colton, Curborough and Elmhurst, Elford, Farewell and Chorley, Fisherwick, Fradley (1836—85), Freeford (1858—1930), Fulfen (1858—1930), Hammerwich, Haselour (1858—1930), Longdon, Ogley Hay (soon after 1836[56]—1930), Ogley Hay Rural (1896—1930), Orgreave (1836—85), Pipehill (1836—94), Hamstall Ridware, Mavesyn Ridware, Pipe Ridware, Rugeley, Shenstone, Shire Oak (1894—1930), Streethay, Swinfen and Packington, Tamhorn (1858—1930), Wall, Weeford, Whittington, Yoxall

Staffordshire *continued*

NEWCASTLE UNDER LYME PLU
Audley, Balterley, Betley, Chapel and Hill Chorlton, Clayton (1896—1930), Hardings Wood (1894—1930), Keele, Madeley, Maer, Newcastle under Lyme, Whitmore

PENKRIDGE PLU (1836—70s[54])
Acton Trussell and Bednall, Brewood, Bushbury, Cannock, Cheslyn Hay, Church Eaton, Coppenhall, Dunston, Essington, Featherstone, Hatherton, Hilton, Huntington, Kinvaston, Lapley, Norton Canes, Penkridge, Saredon, Shareshill, Stretton, Teddesley Hay, Great Wyrley

SEISDON PLU (Staffs, Salop [1836—95])
Bobbington,[57] Codsall, Enville, Himley, Kinver, Pattingham,[57] Lower Penn, Upper Penn, Swindon (1896—1930), Tettenhall, Trysull and Seisdon, Wombourn, Woodford Grange (1861—1930), Wrottesley (1894—1930)

STAFFORD PLU
Baswich, Bradley, Brocton, Castle Church, Chartley Holme (1858—1930), Colwich, Cresswell (1958—1930), Ellenhall (soon after 1836[56]—1930), Fradswell, Gayton, Haughton, Hopton and Coton, Ingestre, Marston, Ranton, Ranton Abbey (1858—85), Salt and Enson, Seighford, Stafford (1894—1930), Stafford St Mary and St Chad (1836—94), Stowe, Tillington (1858—1917), Tixall, Weston upon Trent, Whitgreave, Worston (1858—1930), Yarlet (1858—1930)

STOKE AND WOLSTANTON PLU (1922—30)
Bagnall, Burslem, Chesterton, Kidsgrove, Newchapel, Silverdale, Stoke upon Trent, Wolstanton

STOKE ON TRENT PLU (1836—1922)
Bagnall (1896—1922), Fenton (1894—1922), Florence (1894—96), Hanley (1894—1922), Longton (1894—1922), Normancot (1894—96), Stoke upon Trent, Stoke Rural (1894—1922), East Vale (1894—96)

STONE PLU
Barlaston, Chebsey, Cold Norton, Eccleshall, Fulford (1897—1930), Hilderstone (1897—1930), Milwich, Sandon, Standon, Stone, Stone Rural (1894—1930), Swynnerton, Trentham

TAMWORTH PLU (Staffs, Warws, Derbys)
Canwell, Clifton Campville and Haunton, Croxall,[58] Drayton Bassett,[59] Edingale, Fazeley, Harlaston, Hints, Hopwas Hays (1865—1930), Statfold, Syerscote, Tamworth,[46] Thorpe Constantine, Wiggington

UTTOXETER PLU (Staffs, Derbys)
Blithfield, Bramshall, Abbot's Bromley, Croxden, Denstone (soon after 1837[56]—1930), Gratwich, Kingston, Leigh, Marchington, Marchington Woodlands, Newborough, Rocester, Uttoxeter, Uttoxeter Rural (1896—1930)

WALSALL PLU
Aldridge, Great Barr, Bentley, Darlaston, Pelsall, Rushall, Walsall (1894—1930), Walsall Borough (1836—94), Walsall Foreign (1836—94), Walsall Wood (1894—1930)

WOLSTANTON AND BURSLEM PLU (1838—1922)
Burslem, Chell (1894—1922), Chesterton (1894—1930), Goldenhill (1894—1922), Kidsgrove (1894—1922), Milton (1894—1922), Newchapel (1894—1922), Silverdale (1894—1922), Tunstall (1894—1922), Wolstanton

WOLVERHAMPTON PLU
Bilston, Heathtown (1894—1922), Short Heath (1894—1930), Wednesfield, Willenhall, Wolverhampton

In Other Poor Law Counties:

ASHBOURNE PLU (Derbys, Staffs)
Alstonfield (1869—1930), Blore with Swinscoe, Calton, Calwich, Ellastone, Ilam, Mayfield, Musden Grange (1858—86), Okeover, Prestwood, Ramshorn, Stanton, Waterfall, Wetton (1869—1930), Woodhouses (1845—1916), Wootton

BROMSGROVE PLU (Worcs, Warws [1836—44], Salop [1836—44])
Clent[60]

CONGLETON PLU (Ches, Staffs)
Biddulph

DRAYTON PLU—see MARKET DRAYTON PLU

KIDDERMINSTER PLU (Worcs, Staffs [1836—95], Salop [1836—95])
Upper Arley,[61] Broom[60]

KING'S NORTON PLU (Worcs, Staffs, Warws [1836—89], Birm CB [1889—1911])
Harborne (1836—1912), Smethwick (1894—1930)

MARKET DRAYTON PLU (cr as 'DRAYTON', soon after 'MARKET DRAYTON') (Salop, Staffs, Ches [1836—95])
Ashley (soon after 1836[56]—1930), Mucklestone,[62] Tyrley

NEWPORT PLU (Salop, Staffs)
Adbaston, Forton, Gnosall, Norbury, High Offley, Weston Jones

SHIFNAL PLU (Salop, Staffs)
Blymhill, Patshull, Sheriff Hales,[63] Weston under Lizard

STOURBRIDGE PLU (Worcs, Salop [1836—44], Staffs)
Amblecote, Brierley Hill (1894—1930), Kingswinford, Quarry Bank (1894—1930)

SUFFOLK

In Suffolk Poor Law County:[10]

BLYTHING PLU
Aldringham with Thorpe, Benacre, Blyford, Blythburgh, Bramfield, Brampton, Carlton (1835–85), Chediston, Cockley, South Cove, Covehithe, Cratfield, Darsham, Dunwich, Easton Bavants, Frostenden, Halesworth, Henham, Henstead, Heveningham, Holton, Huntingfield, Kelsale (1835–85), Kelsale cum Carlton (1885–1930), Knodishall, Leiston, Linstead Magna, Linstead Parva, Middleton, Peasenhall, Reydon, Rumburgh, Sibton, Sotherton, Southwold, Spexhall, Stoven, Theberton, Thorington, Ubbeston, Uggeshall, Walberswick, Walpole, Wangford, Wenhaston, Westhall, Westleton, Wissett, Wrentham, Yoxford

BOSMERE AND CLAYDON PLU
Akenham, Ashbocking, Ashfield with Thorpe, Badley, Barham, Barking, Battisford, Baylham, Great Blakenham, Little Blakenham, Bramford, Great Bricett, Claydon, Coddenham, Creeting All Saints (1835–84), Creeting St Mary, Creeting St Olave (1835–84), Crowfield, Darmsden (orig sep rated, status not sustained), Debenham, Flowton, Framsden, Gosbeck, Helmingham, Hemingstone, Henley, Mickfield, Needham Market (1907–30), Nettlestead, Offton, Pettaugh, Ringshall, Somersham, Earl Stonham, Little Stonham, Stonham Aspall, Swilland, Whitton (1894–1930), Willisham, Winston

BURY ST EDMUNDS PLU
In 1907 this PLU gained all the pars of Thingoe PLU (qv); prev this PLU contained Bury St Edmunds (1895–1930), Bury St Edmunds St James (1835–95), Bury St Edmunds St Mary (1835–95)

COSFORD PLU
Aldham, Bildeston, Boxford, Brettenham, Chelsworth, Cockfield, Edwardstone, Brent Eleigh, Monks Eleigh, Elmsett, Groton, Hadleigh, Hadleigh Hamlet, Hitcham, Kersey, Kettlebaston, Lavenham, Layham, Lindsey, Milden, Naughton, Nedging, Polstead, Preston St Mary, Semer, Thorpe Morieux, Wattisham, Whatfield

HARTISMERE PLU
Aspall, Athelington (1907–30), Bacton, Badingham (1907–30), Bedfield (1907–30), Bedingfield (1907–30), Botesdale, Braiseworth, Brome, Brundish (1907–30), Burgate, Cotton, Denham (1907–30), Dennington (1907–30), Eye, Finningham, Fressingfield (1907–30), Gislingham, Horham (1907–30), Hoxne (1907–30), Laxfield (1907–30), Mellis, Mendham (1907–30), Mendlesham, Metfield (1907–30), Oakley, Occold, Palgrave, Redlingfield, Rickinghall Superior, Rishangles, Saxstead (1907–30), Monk Soham (1907–30), Southolt (1907–30), Stoke Ash, Stradbroke (1907–30), Stuston, Syleham (1907–30), Tannington (1907–30), Thorndon, Thornham Magna, Thornham Parva, Thrandeston, Thwaite, Westhorpe, Wetheringsett cum Brockford, Weybread (1907–30), Wickham Skeith, Wilby (1907–30), Wingfield (1907–30), Worlingworth (1907–30), Wortham, Wyverstone, Yaxley

HOXNE PLU (1835–1907)
Athelington, Badingham, Bedfield, Bedingfield, Brundish, Denham, Dennington, Fressingfield, Horham, Hoxne, Laxfield, Mendham,[11] Metfield, Saxstead, Monk Soham, Southolt, Stradbroke, Syleham, Tannington, Weybread, Wilby, Wingfield, Withersdale (1835–85), Worlingworth

IPSWICH PLU
Ipswich (1903–30), Westerfield (1835–94), Westerfield in Ipswich (1894–1903), Whitton cum Thurleston (1835–1903), and the following pars in Ipswich, all in the PLU 1835–1903: St Clement, St Helen, St Lawrence, St Margaret, St Mary at the Elms, St Mary at the Quay, St Mary at the Tower, St Mary Stoke, St Matthew, St Nicholas, St Peter, St Stephen

MILDENHALL PLU
Barton Mills, Cavenham, Elveden, Eriswell, Freckenham, Herringswell, Icklingham, Kentford, Lakenheath, Mildenhall, Tuddenham, Wangford, Worlington

MUTFORD AND LOTHINGLAND PLU
Ashby, Barnby, Belton, Blundeston, Bradwell, Burgh`Castle, Carlton Colville, Corton, Flixton, Fritton, Gisleham, Gunton, Herringfleet, Hopton, Kessingland, Kirkley (1835–1907), Lound, Lowestoft, Mutford, Oulton, Oulton Broad (1907–19), Pakefield, Rushmere, Somerleyton

NEWMARKET PLU (Suffolk, Cambs)
Dalham, Wood Ditton,[12] Exning, Gazeley, Higham Green, Lidgate, Moulton, Newmarket All Saints,[13] Newmarket St Mary,[14] Ousden

PLOMESGATE PLU
Aldeburgh, Benhall, Blaxhall, Brandeston, Bruisyard, Butley, Campsey Ash, Chillesford, Cransford, Cretingham, Easton, Eyke, Farnham, Framlingham, Friston, Gedgrave, Great Glemham, Little Glemham, Hacheston, Havergate Island, Hazlewood, Hoo, Iken, Kenton, Kettleburgh, Letheringham, Marlesford, Monewden, Orford, Parham, Rendham, Rendlesham, Saxmundham, Snape, Earl Soham, Sternfield, Stratford St Andrew, Sudbourne, Swefling, Tunstall, Wantisden, Wickham Market

RISBRIDGE PLU (Suffolk, Essex)
Barnardiston, Great Bradley, Little Bradley, Clare, Cowlinge, Denston, Hundon, Haverhill,[15] Kedington,[16] Poslingford, Monks Risbridge, Stansfield, Stoke by Clare, Stradishall, Great Thurlow, Little Thurlow, Wickhambrook, Withersfield, Wixoe, Great Wratting, Little Wratting

SAMFORD PLU
Belstead, Bentley, East Bergholt, Brantham, Burstall, Capel St Mary, Chattisham, Chelmondiston, Copdock, Erwarton, Freston, Harkstead, Higham, Hintlesham, Holbrook, Holton St Mary, Raydon, Shelly, Shotley, Sproughton, Stratford St Mary, Stutton, Tattingstone, Washbrook, Great Wenham, Little Wenham, Wherstead, Woolverstone

47

Suffolk *continued*

STOW PLU

Great Ashfield, Badwell Ash, Boyton, Buxhall, Combs, Creeting St Peter, Drinkstone, Elmswell, Felsham, Great Finborough, Little Finborough, Gedding, Gipping, Harleston, Haughley, Hessett, Hinderclay, Hunston, Langham, Old Newton, Norton, Onehouse, Rattlesden, Rickinghall Inferior, Shelland, Stowlangtoft, Stowmarket, Stowupland, Thurston, Tostock, Walsham-le-Willows, Wattisfield, Wetherden, Woolpit

SUDBURY PLU (Suffolk, Essex)

Acton, Alpheton, Assington, Ballingdon,[17] Boxted, Bures St Mary,[18] Cavendish, Chilton, Great Cornard, Little Cornard, Glemsford, Hartest, Hawkedon, Lawshall, Long Melford, Nayland (1835–84), Nayland with Wissington (1884–1930), Newton, Shimpling, Somerton, Stanstead, Stoke by Nayland, Sudbury (1880s–1930), Sudbury All Saints (1835–80s), Sudbury St Bartholomew, Sudbury St Gregory (1835–80s), Sudbury St Peter (1835–80s), Great Waldingfield, Little Waldingfield, Wissington (1835–84)

THINGOE PLU (1836–1907)

Ampton, Bardwell, Barrow, Great Barton, Bradfield Combust, Bradfield St Clare, Bradfield St George, Brockley, Chedburgh, Chimney Mills (1858–97), Chevington, Culford, Denham, Depden, Flempton, Fornham All Saints, Fornham St Genevieve, Fornham St Martin, Hardwick, Hargrave, Hawstead, Hengrave, Horningsheath, Ickworth, Ingham, Ixworth, Ixworth Thorpe, Lackford, Great Livermere, Little Livermere, Nowton, Pakenham, Rede, Risby, Rougham, Rushbrooke, Great Saxham, Little Saxham, Stanningfield, Stanton, West Stow, Timworth, Troston, Great Welnetham, Little Welnetham, Westley, Whepstead, Wordwell

WANGFORD PLU

Barsham, Beccles, Bungay (1910–30), Bungay Holy Trinity (1835–1910), Bungay St Mary (1835–1910), North Cove, South Elmham All Saints and St Nicholas, South Elmham St Cross, South Elmham St James, South Elmham St Margaret, South Elmham St Michael, South Elmham St Peter, Ellough, Flixton, Homersfield, Ilketshall St Andrew, Ilketshall St John, Ilketshall St Lawrence, Ilketshall St Margaret, Mettingham, Redisham, Ringsfield, Shadingfield, Shipmeadow, Sotterley, Weston, Willingham, Worlingham

WOODBRIDGE PLU

Alderton, Alnesbourn Priory, Bawdsey, Great Bealings, Little Bealings, Boulge, Boyton, Bredfield, Brightwell, Bromeswell, Bucklesham, Burgh, Capel St Andrew, Charsfield, Clopton, Culpho, Dallinghoo, Dallinghoo Wield, Debach, Falkenham, Felixstowe, Foxhall, Grundisburgh, Hasketon, Hemley, Hollesley, Kesgrave, Kirtton, Levington, Martlesham, Melton, Nacton, Newbourne, Otley, Pettistree, Playford, Purdis Farm, Ramsholt, Rushmere (1836–1903), Rushmere St Andrew (1894–1930),

Shottisham, Stratton Hall, Sutton, Trimley St Martin, Trimley St Mary, Tuddenham, Ufford, Waldringfield, Walton (1835–1914), Witnesham, Woodbridge

In Other Poor Law Counties:

DEPWADE PLU (Norfolk)

Earsham[19]

THETFORD PLU (Norfolk)

Barham, Barningham, Brandon, Euston, Fakenham Magna, Hepworth, Honington, Hopton, Kenttishall, Rushford,[20] Rymer (1835–81), Santon Downham, Sapiston, Thelnetham, Thetford St Cuthbert,[20] Thetford St Mary,[20] Coney Weston, Market Weston

YARMOUTH PLU (Norfolk)

Gorleston[21]

SURREY

In Surrey Poor Law County:[16]

ASH PAR (local act, until 1846)

Ash and Normandy, Dockenfield, Frensham, Frimley, Seale

CHERTSEY PLU

Bisley, Byfleet, Chertsey, Chobham, Horsell, Pyrford, Thorpe (1894–1930), Walton upon Thames, Weybridge, Windlesham

CROYDON PLU

Addington, Beddington, Coulsdon, Croydon, Merton, Mitcham, Morden, Penge, Sanderstead, Wallington (1866–1930), Woodmansterne

DORKING PLU

Abinger, Capel, Dorking, Dorking Rural (1894–1930), Effingham, Mickleham, Newdigate, Ockley, Wotton

EPSOM PLU

Ashtead, Banstead, Great Bookham, Little Bookham, Carshalton, Cheam, Chessington, Cobham, Cuddington, Epsom, Ewell, Fetcham, Headley (1879–1930), Leatherhead, Stoke d'Abernon, Sutton

FARNHAM PLU (1846–1930) (Surrey, Hants)

Ash and Normandy, Dockenfield,[17] Farnham, Farnham Rural (1894–1930), Frensham, Frimley, Seale, Shottermill (1896–1930), Waverley (1858–94)

GODSTONE PLU

Bletchingley, Caterham, Chelsham, Crowhurst, Farleigh, Godstone, Horne, Limpsfield, Lingfield (1894–1930), Oxted, Tandridge, Tatsfield, Titsey, Warlingham, Woldingham

GUILDFORD PLU

Albury, Artington (1894–1930), Bowling Green (1858–83), East Clandon, West Clandon, Compton,

48

Godalming, Godalming Rural (1894–1930), Guildford (1908–30), Guildford Christchurch (1904–08), Guildford The Friary (1858–1908), Guildford Holy Trinity (1836–1908), Guildford St Mary (1836–1908), Guildford St Nicolas (1836–1908), East Horsley, West Horsley, Merrow, Ockham, Pirbright, Puttenham, Send and Ripley, Shere, Stoke (1836–94), Stoke (1904–08), Stoke next Guildford (1894–1904), Stoke Within (1894–1904), Wanborough, Wisley, Woking, Worplesdon

HAMBLEDON PLU
Alfold,[18] Bramley, Chiddingfold, Cranleigh, Dunsfold, Elstead, Ewhurst, Hambledon, Hascombe, Haslemere, Peper Harow, St Martha, Shalford, Thursley, Witley, Wonersh

KINGSTON PLU
Coombe (1894–1930), Long Ditton, Thames Ditton, Esher, Ham with Hatch, Hook, Kingston upon Thames, Malden, New Malden (1894–1930), East Molesey, West Molesey, Surbiton (1894–1930), Tolworth (1895–1930), Wimbledon

REIGATE PLU
Betchworth, Buckland, Burstow, Chaldon, Charlwood, Chipstead, Gatton, Headley (1836–79), Horley, Kingswood, Leigh, Mertsham, Nutfield, Reigate (1899–1930), Reigate Borough (1836–99), Reigate Foreign (1836–94), Walton on the Hill

RICHMOND PLU
Barnes, Kew, Mortlake, Petersham, Richmond, North Sheen (1894–1930)

In Other Poor Law Counties:
EAST GRINSTEAD PLU (Sussex, Surrey)
Lingfield (1836–97)
WINDSOR PLU (Berks, Surrey)
Egham, Thorpe (1835–94)
Surrey Poor Law County, in Metropolis (1855–89),
London Poor Law County thereafter:
BERMONDSEY PAR
Bermondsey
CAMBERWELL PAR
Camberwell
LAMBETH PAR
Lambeth
NEWINGTON ST MARY PAR
Newington
ROTHERHITHE PAR
Rotherhithe
ST OLAVE PLU
Southwark St John Horsleydown, Southwark St Olave, Southwark St Thomas
ST SAVIOUR'S PLU
Southwark Christchurch, Southwark St Saviour
SOUTHWARK ST GEORGE THE MARTYR PAR
Southwark St George the Martyr
WANDSWORTH AND CLAPHAM PLU
Battersea, Clapham, Putney, Streatham, Tooting Graveney, Wandsworth

SUSSEX

In Sussex Poor Law County:[27]
ARUNDEL INCORP (18th cent–1869)
Arundel
BATTLE PLU
Ashburnham, Battle, Bexhill, Brightling, Catsfield, Crowhurst, Dallington, Ewhurst, Hollington (1835–97), Hollington Rural (1897–1930), Hollington St John (1897–1925), Mountfield, Penhurst, Sedlescombe, Westfield, Whatlington
BRIGHTON INCORP (1810[28]–1930)
Brighton
CHAILEY PLU (1835–98)
Barcombe, Chailey, East Chiltington, Ditchling, Hamsey, Plumpton, Newick, Ringmer, Streat, Westmeston, Wivelsfield
CHICHESTER INCORP (1753–1930)
Chichester (1896–1930), Chichester All Saints (until 1896), Chichester The Close (until 1896), Chichester Newtown, or St John (until 1896), Chichester St Andrew (until 1896), Chichester St Bartholomew (until 1896), Chichester St James (until 1896), Chichester St Martin (until 1896), Chichester St Olave (until 1896), Chichester St Pancras (until 1896), Chichester St Peter the Great or Sub-Deanery (until 1896), Chichester St Peter the Less (until 1896), St Bartholomew Rural (1894–95), St Pancras Rural (1894–96), Sub-Deanery Rural (1894–96)
CUCKFIELD PLU
Albourne, Ardingly, Balcombe, Bolney, Clayton, Clayton Urban (1894–1930), Cowfold (1835–97), Cuckfield, Cuckfield Rural (1894–1930), Hayward's Heath (1894–1930), Horsted Keynes, Hurstpierpoint, Keymer, Keymer Urban (1894–1930), Lindfield, Newtimber, Pyecombe, Slaugham, Twineham
EASTBOURNE PLU
Alciston (1898–1930), Alfriston, Berwick (1898–1930), East Dean, West Dean, Eastbourne, Folkington, Friston, Hampden Park (1911–12), Jevington, Litlington, Lullington, Norway (1894–99), Pevensey, Seaford, Selmeston (1898–1930), Westham, Willingdon, Wilmington
WEST FIRLE PLU (1835–98)
Alciston, Beddingham, Berwick, Chalvington, West Firle, Glynde, Ripe, Selmeston
EAST GRINSTEAD PLU (Sussex, Surrey 1836–97, ent Sussex 1897–1930)
Crawley (1835–80), Forest Row (1894–1930), East Grinstead, Hartfield, West Hoathly, Withyham, Worth
HAILSHAM PLU
Arlington, Chalvington (1898–1930), Chiddingly, Hailsham, Heathfield, Hellingly, Herstmonceux, Hooe, Laughton, Ninfield, Ripe (1898–1930), Warbleton, Wartling

49

Sussex *continued*

HASTINGS PLU

Blacklands (1894–97), Fairlight, Guestling, Hastings (1909–30), Hastings All Saints (1835–1909), Hastings Holy Trinity (1835–1909), Hastings St Andrew (1835–1909), Hastings St Clement (1835–1909), Hastings St Leonards (1835–1909), Hastings St Mary Bulverhythe (1835–1909), Hastings St Mary in the Castle (1835–1909), Hastings St Mary Magdalen (1835–1909), Hastings St Michael (1835–1909), Ore, Pett

HORSHAM PLU

Lower Beeding, Billingshurst (1870–1930), Cowfold (1897–1930), Crawley (1880–1930), West Grinstead, Horsham, Horsham Rural (1894–1930), Ifield, Itchingfield, Nuthurst, Rudgwick (1869–1930), Rusper, Shipley, Slinfold, Warnham

LEWES PLU

Barcombe (1898–1930), Beddingham (1898–1930), Chailey (1898–1930), Chalvington, East Chiltington (1898–1930), Ditchling (1898–1930), West Firle (1898–1930), Glynde (1898–1930), Hamsey (1898–1930), Lewes (1913–30), Lewes All Saints (1835–1913), Lewes The Castle Precincts (1858[29]–1913), Lewes St Ann (1835–1913), Lewes St Ann Without (1894–1930), Lewes St John the Baptist, Southover (1835–1913), Lewes St John under the Castle (1835–1913), Lewes St John Without (1894–1930), Lewes St Michael (1835–1913), Lewes St Thomas a Becket, Cliffe (1835–1913), South Malling (1835–1913), South Malling Without (1894–1930), Newick (1898–1930), Plumpton (1898–1930), Ringmer (1898–1930), Southover Without (1894–1930), Streat (1898–1930), Westmeston (1898–1930), Wivelsfield (1898–1930)

MIDHURST PLU (Sussex, Hants until 1844, ent Sussex 1844–1930)

North Ambersham,[30] South Ambersham,[30] Bepton, North Chapel (1835–69), Chithurst, Cocking, Didling, Easebourne, Elsted, Fernhurst, Graffham (1869–1930), Harting, Heyshott, Iping, East Lavington, West Lavington (1866[29]–1930), Linch, Linchmere, Lodsworth, Lurgashall, Midhurst, Rogate,[31] Selham, Stedham, Terwick, Tillington, Treyford, Trotton, Woolbeding

NEWHAVEN PLU

Bishopstone, East Blatchington, Denton, Denton Urban (1894–1930), Falmer, South Heighton, Iford, Kingston (1835–94), Kingston near Lewes (1894–1930), Kingston Urban (1894–1930), Newhaven, Ovingdean, Peacehaven (1929–30), Piddinghoe, Rodmell, Rottingdean, Southease, Stanmer, Tarring Neville, Telscombe

PETWORTH PLU

Barlavington (1869–1930), Bignor (1869–1930), Billingshurst (1835–70), Burton (1869–1930), Bury (1869–1930), North Chapel (1869–1930), Coates (1869–1930), Duncton, Egdean (1869–

1930), Fittleworth (1869–1930), Kirdford, Petworth, Rudgwick (1835–69), Stopham (1869–1930), Sutton, Wisborough Green

EAST PRESTON INCORP (1791–1869), PLU (1869–1930)

Amberley (1791–1869), Angmering (1806–1930), Arundel (1869–1930), Broadwater (1799–1902), Burpham, Clapham (1869–1930), Climping (1799–1930), Durrington (1803–1929), Ferring, Ford (1799–1930), Goring by Sea (1791–1929), Heene (1869–1902), Houghton (1803–1930), Kingston (1869–1930), Lancing (1869–1869), Littlehampton, Lyminster, Patching (1869–1930), Poling (1806–1930), East Preston, Rustington (1806–1930), South Stoke (1869–1930), West Tarring (1803–1930), Tortington (1799–1930), Warningcamp (1869–1930), Wick (1901–30), Wigginholt (1803–69), Worthing (1894–1930)

RYE PLU (Sussex, Kent until 1895, ent Sussex 1895–1930)

Breckley, Brede, Broomhill,[32] East Guldeford, Icklesham, Iden, Northiam, Peasmarsh, Playden, Rye, Rye Foreign (1894–1930), Udimore; St Thomas the Apostle, Winchelsea

STEYNING PLU

Aldrington, Ashurst, Upper Beeding, West Blatchington, Botolphs, Bramber, Coombes, Edburton, Fulking (1894–1930), Hangleton, Henfield, Hove, Kingston by Sea, Lancing (1869–1930), Patching (1835–1928), Portslade (1835–1928), Portslade by Sea (1898–1930), Poynings, Preston (1835–1928), Preston Rural (1894–1928), Shermanbury, New Shoreham, Old Shoreham, Shoreham-by-Sea (1910–30), Sompting, Southwick, Steyning, Woodmancote

SUTTON INCORP (1791–1869)

Barlavington (1804–69), Bersted (1792–1869), Bignor, Burton, Bury, Clapham, Coates, Coldwaltham (1804–35), Duncton, Egdean (1792–1869), Fittleworth (1804–69), Greatham (1804–69), Heyshott (date of inclusion uncertain), Patching, Slindon (1792–1858), Sutton, Warningcamp (1866[29]–69)

THAKENHAM PLU

Amberley (1869–1930), Ashington, West Chiltington, Coldwaltham, Findon, Greatham (1869–1930), Hardham, Parham, Pulborough, Rackham (1848–1930), North Stoke (1869–1930), Storrington, Stopham (1835–69), Sullington, Thakenham, Warminghurst, Washington, Wigginholt (1869–1930), Wiston

TICEHURST PLU (Sussex, Kent)

Bodiam, Burwash, Etchingham, Frant,[33] Lamberhurst,[34] Salehurst, Ticehurst, Wadhurst

UCKFIELD PLU

Buxted, Crowborough (1905–30), Danehill (1898–1930), Fletching, Framfield, Hadlow Down (1905–30), East Hoathly, Little Horsted, Isfield, Maresfield, Mayfield, Rotherfield, Uckfield, Waldron

Sussex continued

WESTBOURNE PLU
Bosham, Chidham, Compton, West Dean, Funtington, East Marden, North Marden, Up Marden, Racton, Stoughton, West Thorney, Westbourne

WESTHAMPNETT PLU
Aldingbourne, Appledram, Barnham, Bersted (1869–1930), Binderton, Binsted, Birdham, Bognor (1894–1930 [called Bognor Regis from 1929]), Boxgrove, East Dean, Donnington, Earnley, Eartham, Eastergate, Felpham, New Fishbourne, Hunston, West Itchenor, Lavant (1872–1930), East Lavant (1835–72), Mid Lavant (1835–72), Madehurst, Merston, Middleton, North Mundham, Oving, Pagham, Portfield (1894–96), Rumboldswyke (1835–96), Selsey, Sidlesham, Singleton, Slindon (1858–1930), West Stoke, Tangmere, Walberton, Up Waltham, Westhampnett, East Wittering, West Wittering, Yapton

In Other Poor Law Counties:
CRANBROOK PLU (Kent, Sussex)
Hawkhurst[35]
HAMBLEDON PLU (Surrey, Sussex)
Alfold[36]
HEADLEY INCORP (Hants, Sussex)
Bramshott[37] (18th cent–1869)
PETERSFIELD PLU (Hants, Sussex)
Bramshott[37] (1869–1930)
TONBRIDGE PLU
Horsmonden[34]

WARWICKSHIRE

In Warws Poor Law County:[33]
ALCESTER PLU (Warws, Worcs)
Alcester, Great Alne, Arrow, Aston Cantlow, Bidford on Avon, Coughton, Exhall, Haselor, Ipsley,[34] Kinwarton, Morton Bagot, Oldberrow,[35] Oversley, Salford Priors, Sambourn, Spernall, Studley, Weethley, Wixford

ASTON PLU (1836–1911)
Aston, Aston Manor (1894–1911), Castle Bromwich (1894–1911), Curdworth, Erdington (1894–1911), Minworth, Sutton Coldfield, Water Orton (1894–1911), Wishaw

ATHERSTONE PLU (Warws, Leics)
Ansley, Atherstone, Baddesley Ensor, Baxterley, Bentley, Grendon, Hartshill, Mancetter, Merevale,[36] Oldbury, Polesworth

Warwickshire continued

BIRMINGHAM INCORP/PLU (1783–1930)
Aston (1911–12), Aston Manor (1911–12), Balsall Heath (1911–12), Birmingham, Edgbaston (1911–12), Erdington (1911–12), Handsworth (1911–30), Harborne (1911–12), Perry Barr (1928–30), Quinton (1911–12), Yardley (1911–12)

COVENTRY INCORP/PLU
Coventry (1900–30), Coventry Holy Trinity (until 1894), Coventry Holy Trinity Within (1894–1900), Coventry Holy Trinity Without (1894–1928), Coventry St Michael (until 1894), Coventry St Michael Within (1894–1900), Coventry St Michael Without (1894–1928)

FOLESHILL PLU (Warws, Coventry Co of Itself [1836–42])
Ansty, Bedworth, Binley, Exhall, Foleshill, Keresley, Shilton, Stoke (1836–1928), Stoke Heath (1920–28), Walsgrave on Sowe, Willenhall, Withybrook, Wyken

MERIDEN PLU
Allesley, Berkswell, Bickenhill, Castle Bromwich (1911–30), Coleshill, Corley, Coundon, Curdworth (1911–30), Fillongley, Hampton in Arden, Kinwalsey (1836–95), Lea Marston, Maxstoke, Meriden, Minworth (1911–30), Great Packington, Little Packington, Sheldon, Shustoke, Sutton Coldfield (1911–30), Water Orton (1911–30), Nether Whitacre, Over Whitacre, Wishaw (1911–30)

NUNEATON PLU
Arley, Astley, Bulkington, Burton Hastings (between 1896/1900–1930), Caldecote, Chilvers Coton (1836–1920), Nuneaton, Stretton Baskerville (between 1896/1900–1930), Weddington, Wolvey (between 1896/1900–1930)

RUGBY PLU (Warws, Northants, Leics)
Bilton, Birdingbury, Bourton on Dunsmore, Brandon and Bretford, Brinklow (soon after 1836[37]–1930), Brownsover, Churchover, Clifton upon Dunsmore, Combe Fields, Cosford, Dunchurch, Easenhall (soon after 1836[37]–1930), Frankton, Grandborough, Harborough Magna, Hillmorton, Church Lawford, Little Lawford, Long Lawford, Leamington Hastings, Marton, Monks Riding (1862–85), Newbold on Avon, Kings Newnham, Newton and Biggin, Princethorpe, Rugby, Ryton on Dunsmore, Stretton on Dunsmore, Thurlaston, Willoughby, Wolfhampcote, Wolston

SOLIHULL PLU (Warws, Worcs [1836–1911])
Baddesley Clinton, Balsall, Barston, Bushwood, Elmdon, Knowle, Lapworth, Nuthurst, Packwood, Solihull, Tanworth, Yardley[38] (1836–1912)

SOUTHAM PLU
Chadshunt, Chapel Ascote, Chesterton, Fenny Compton, Burton Dassett, Gaydon, Harbury, Hodnell (1858–1930), Bishop's Itchington, Long Itchington, Ladbroke, Lighthorne, Napton on the Hill, Priors Hardwick, Priors Marston, Lower Radbourn (1858–1930), Upper Radbourn (1858–1930), Lower Shuckburgh, Upper Shuckburgh, Southam, Stockton, Stoneton[39] (1858–1930), Ufton, Watergall (1858–1930), Wills Pastures (1858–1930), Wormleighton

Warwickshire *continued*

STRATFORD ON AVON PLU (Warws, Glos, Worcs)
Alveston, Atherstone on Stour, Bearley, Beaudesert, Bickmarsh (1894—1930), Billesley, Binton, Charlecote, Claverdon, Combrook, Compton Verney, Eatington, Fulbrook, Hampton Lucy, Kineton, Langley, Luddington, Loxley, Milcote (1894—1930), Moreton Morrell, Newbold Pacey, Preston Bagot, Snitterfield, Old Stratford (1836—94), Old Stratford and Drayton (1894—1930), Old Stratford Within (1894—1930), Stratford on Avon, Temple Grafton, Welford,[40] Wellesbourne Hastings and Walton, Wellesbourne Mountford, Weston on Avon,[40] Whitchurch, Wolverton, Wootton Wawen

WARWICK PLU
Ashow, Baginton, Barford, Beausale, Blackdown (1894—1930), Bubbenhall, Budbrooke, Cubbington, Eathorpe, Guy's Cliffe (1862—1930), Haseley, Hatton, Honiley, Hunningham, Kenilworth, Leamington (1902—30), Leamington Priors (1836—1902), Leek Wootton, Lillington (1836—1902), Milverton (1836—94), New Milverton (1894—1902), Old Milverton, Norton Lindsey, Offchurch, Pinley (1836—86), Radford Semele, Rowington, Sherbourne, Shrewley, Stivichall, Stoneleigh, Bishops Tackbrook, Wappenbury, Warwick (1921—30), Warwick St Mary (1836—1921), Warwick St Nicholas (1836—1921), Wasperton, Weston under Wetherley, Whitnash, Wroxall

In Other Poor Law Counties:

BANBURY PLU (Oxon, Warws)
Avon Dassett (1836—1930), Farnborough (1836—1930), Mollington[41] (1836—89), Mollington[41] (1889—95), Radway (1836—1930), Ratley and Upton (1836—1930), Shotteswell, Warmington (1836—1930)

CHIPPING NORTON PLU (Oxon, Warws, Glos)
Barton on the Heath, Little Compton,[42] Long Compton

HINCKLEY PLU (Leics, Warws [1836—80s])
Burton Hastings (1836—between 1896/1900), Hinckley,[43] Stretton Baskerville (1836—between 1896/1900), Wolvey (between 1896/1900—1930)

KINGS NORTON PLU (Worcs, Warws [1836—1911], Birm CB [1889—1911])
Balsall Heath[44] (1894—1911), Edgbaston, Harborne[45]

LUTTERWORTH PLU (Leics, Warws, Northants [1835—94])
Copston Magna, Monks Kirby, Pailton, Stretton under Fosse, Wibtoft, Willey

SHIPSTON ON STOUR PLU (Worcs, Warws, Glos)
Barcheston, Batsford,[46] Brailes, Burmington, Cherington, Compton Wynyates, Halford, Honington, Idlicote, Ilmington,[47] Butlers Marston, Oxhill, Pillerton Hersey, Pillerton Priors, Stourton, Stretton on Fosse, Sutton under Brailes,[42] Tysoe, Whatcote, Whichford, Great Wolford, Little Wolford

TAMWORTH PLU (Staffs, Warws)
Amington and Stonydelph, Austrey, Bolehall and Glascote, Drayton Bassett,[48] Kingsbury, Middleton, Newton Regis, No Man's Heath (1861—87), Seckington, Shuttington, Tamworth, Tamworth Castle (1836—94), Wilnecote and Castle Liberty

WESTMORLAND

In Westm Poor Law County:[7]

EAST WARD PLU
Appleby (1894—1930), Appleby St Laurence (1836—94), Appleby St Michael or Bongate (1836—94), Ashby, Bongate (1894—1908), Brough, Colby (1894—1930), Crackenthorpe (1894—1930), Crosby Garrett, Dufton, Hartley, Hillbeck, Hoff (1894—1930), Kaber, Kirkby Stephen, Kirkby Thore, Mallerstang, Long Marton, Milburn, Murton (1894—1930), Musgrave (1894—1930), Great Musgrave (1836—94), Little Musgrave (1836—94), Nateby, Newbiggin, Ormside, Orton, Ravenstonedale, Smardale (1836—94), Soulby, Brough Sowerby, Temple Sowerby, Stainmore, Tebay (1897—1930), Waitby, Warcop, Wharton, Winton

KENDAL PLU (Westm, Lancs [1836—95])
Ambleside, Arnside (1897—1930), Applethwaite (1836—94), Barbon, Beetham, Bowness on Windermere (1894—1930), Burton, Casterton, Crook, Crosthwaite and Lyth, Dalton,[8] Dillicar, Docker, Farleton, Fawcett Forest, Firbank, Grasmere, Nether Graveship (1836—1908), Grayrigg, Haverbrack, Helsington, Heversham (1896—1930), Heversham with Milnthorpe (1836—96), Hincaster, Holme, Hugill, New Hutton, Old Hutton and Holmescales, Hutton Roof, Kendal, Kentmere, Killington, Kirkby Lonsdale, Kirkland (1836—1908), Lambrigg, Langdales, Levens, Longsleddale, Lupton, Mansergh, Meathop and Ulpha, Middleton, Milnthorpe (1896—1930), Natland, Patton, Preston Patrick, Preston Richard, Rydal and Loughrigg, Scalthwaiterigg (1897—1930); Scalthwaiterigg, Hay and Hutton in the Hay (1836—97); Sedgwick, Skelsmergh, Stainton, Nether Staveley, Over Staveley, Strickland Ketel, Strickland Roger, Troutbeck, Underbarrow and Bradleyfield, Undermillbeck, Whinfell, Whitwell and Selside, Witherslack, Windermere (1894—1930)

WEST WARD PLU
Askham, Bampton, Barton (1894—1930), High Barton (1836—94), Bolton, Brougham, Cliburn, Clifton, Crosby Ravensworth, Lowther, Martindale, King's Meaburn, Morland, Newby, Patterdale, Shap (1896—1905), Shap Rural (1905—30), Shap Urban (1905—30), Sleagill, Sockbridge, Great Strickland, Little Strickland, Thrimby, Low Winder (1836—94), Yanwath and Eamont Bridge

WILTSHIRE

In Wilts Poor Law Co.[12]

ALDERBURY PLU (1836-95), renamed 28 May 1895 SALISBURY PLU (1895-1930)
Alderbury, Alderton, Britford, Clarendon Park, Coombe Bissett, West Dean (1883-1930), Downton, Earldoms (1836-96), Fisherton Anger (1836-94), Fisherton Anger Within (1894-1905), Fisherton Anger Without (1894-1905), East Grimstead, West Grimstead, Harnham (1904-05), East Harnham (1896-1904), West Harnham, Homington, Landford, Langley Wood (1836-94), Laverstock and Ford, Milford (1836-94), Milford Within (1894-1905), Milford Without (1894-1904), Morgans's Vale and Woodfalls (1923-30), No Man's Land, Nunton and Bodenham, Odstock, Pitton and Farley, Redlynch (1896-1930), Salisbury The Close of the Canons of the Cathedral Church (1836-1905), Salisbury St Edmund (1869-1905), Salisbury St Martin (1869-1905), Salisbury St Thomas (1869-1905), New Sarum (1905-30), Old Sarum (1836-94), Standlynch (1836-97), Standlynch with Charlton All Saints (1894-1930), Stratford sub Castle, Stratford Tony, Whiteparish, Winterslow

AMESBURY PLU
Allington, Amesbury, Boscombe, Bulford, Cholderton, Durnford, Durrington, Figheldean, Idmiston, Maddington, Milston, Newton Tony, Orcheston St George, Orcheston St Mary, Rollestone, Shrewton, Tilshead, Wilsford cum Lake, Winterbourne Dauntsey, Winterbourne Earls, Winterbourne Gunner, Winterbourne Stoke, Woodford

BRADFORD PLU (1835-95), renamed 5 July 1895 BRADFORD-ON-AVON PLU (1895-1930) (Wilts, Somerset until 1882, ent Wilts 1882-1930)
Atworth (1885-1930), Bradford-on-Avon, Bradford Without (1894-1930), Broughton Gifford, Great Chalfield (1835-85), Little Chalfield (1835-85), Cottles (1835-85), Holt (1894-1930), Limpley Stoke (1894-1930), Monkton Farleigh, Westwood (1894-1930), Wingfield, Winsley (1894-1930), South Wraxall (1894-1930)

BRADFORD-ON-AVON PLU–See BRADFORD

CALNE PLU
Blackland (1835-90), Bowood (1835-90), Bremhill, Calne (1835-90), Calne Within (1890-1930), Calne Without (1890-1930), Calstone Wellington (1835-90), Cherhill, Compton Bassett, Heddington, Highway (1835-90), Hilmarton, Yatesbury

CHIPPENHAM PLU
Avon (1835-95), Biddestone (1885-1930), Biddestone St Nicholas (1835-85), Biddestone St Peter (1835-95), Box, Castle Combe, Chippenham (1835-94), Chippenham Within (1894-1930), Chippenham Without (1894-1930), Christian Malford, Colerne, Corsham, Ditteridge (1835-84), Draycot Cerne, Grittleton, Hardenhuish, Kellaways (1895-1930), West Kington,

Kington Langley, Kington St Michael, Lacock, Langley Burrell (1835-94), Langley Burrell Within (1894-1930), Langley Burrell Without (1894-1930), Leigh Delamere, Littleton Drew, Nettleton, Pewsham, Seagry, Slaughterford, Stanton St Quintin, Sutton Benger, Tytherton Kellaways (1835-95), North Wraxall, Yatton Keynell

CRICKLADE AND WOOTTON BASSETT PLU
Ashton Keynes, Braydon, Broad Town, Clyffe Pypard, Cricklade (1899-1930), Cricklade St Mary (1835-99), Cricklade St Sampson (1835-99), Eisey (1835-96), Latton, Leigh, Lydiard Millicent, Lydiard Tregoze, Lyneham, Marston Meysey (1881-1930), Purton, Tockenham, Wootton Bassett

DEVIZES PLU
Allington, Alton Barnes, Beechingstone, Bromham, All Cannings, Bishops Cannings, Cheverell Magna, Cheverell Parva, Chirton, Chittoe, Devizes St James, Devizes St John the Baptist, Devizes St Mary the Virgin, Easterton, Erlestoke, Etchilhampton, Fullaway (1835-94), Market Lavington, West Lavington, Marden, Marston, Patney, Potterne, Poulshot, Roundway (1894-1930), Rowde, Rowde Within (1894-1930), Stanton St Bernard, Stert, Urchfont, Worton

HIGHWORTH AND SWINDON PLU (1835-98), renamed 24 Mar 1889 SWINDON AND HIGHWORTH PLU (1899-1930)
Bishopstone, Blunsdon St Andrew, Castle Eaton, Chiseldon, Draycot Foliat (1835-94), Hannington, Haydon Wick (1928-30), Highworth, Little Hinton, Inglesham,[13] Liddington, South Marston (1894-1930), Rodbourne Cheney (1835-1928), Stanton Fitzwarren, Stratton St Margaret, Swindon, Wanborough, Wroughton

MALMESBURY PLU (Wilts, Glos until 1844, ent Wilts 1844-1930)
Brinkworth, Brokenborough (1835-94), Brokenborough (1897-1930), Brokenborough Within (1894-97), Brokenborough Without (1894-97), Charlton, Crudwell, Dauntsey, Easton Grey, Foxley, Garsdon, Hankerton, Hullavington, Lea and Cleverton, Luckington, Malmesbury The Abbey, Malmesbury St Paul (1835-94), Malmesbury St Paul Within (1894-1930), Malmesbury St Paul Without (1894-96), Minety,[14] Norton, Oaksey, Sherston (1896-1930), Sherston Magna (1835-96), Sherston Pinkney (1835-96), Great Somerford, Little Somerford, Sopworth, Westport St Mary (1835-94), Westport St Mary Within (1894-1930), Westport St Mary Without (1894-1930)

MARLBOROUGH PLU
Avebury, Berwick Bassett, Clatford Park (1858[15]-96), Broad Hinton, Fyfield, East Kennett, Marlborough (1925-30), Marlborough St Mary the Virgin (1835-1925), Marlborough St Peter and St Paul (1835-1925), Mildenhall, Ogbourne St Andrew, Ogbourne St George, West Overton, Overton Heath (1835-95), Preshute (1835-1901), Preshute

(1925–30), Preshute Within (1901–25), Preshute Without (1901–25), North Savernake, South Savernake with Brimslade and Cadley, Winterbourne Bassett, Winterbourne Monkton
MELKSHAM PLU (1835–98), renamed 16 Sept 1898 TROWBRIDGE AND MELKSHAM PLU (1898–1930)
Hilperton, Melksham (1835–94), Melksham Within (1894–1930), Melksham Without (1894–1930), Seend, Semington, Staverton (1894–1930), Trowbridge, Whaddon (1935– 94)
MERE PLU (Wilts, Somerset, Dorset until 1896, ent Wilts 1896–1930)
Maiden Bradley with Yarnfield,[16] Kingston Devetill, Monkton Deverill, Kilmington,[17] East Knoyle, West Knoyle, Mere, Upper Pertwood (1835–85), Sedgehill, Stourton with Gasper,[16] Zeals (1896–1930)
PEWSEY PLU
Alton Priors, Burbage, Chute (1879–1930), Chute Forest (1879–1930), Collingbourne Ducis, Collingbourne Kingston, Easton, Enford, Everleigh, Fittleton, Huish, Ludgershall (1879–1930), Manningford Abbots, Manningford Bohune, Manningford Bruce, Milton Lilbourne, Netheravon, North Newnton, Pewsey, Rushall, North Tidworth (1879–1930), Upavon, Wilcot, Wilsford, Woodborough, Wootton Rivers
SALISBURY INCORPORATION (1770–1869)
Salisbury St Edmund, pt Salisbury St Martin, Salisbury St Thomas
SALISBURY PLU–See ALDERBURY PLU
SWINDON AND HIGHWORTH PLU–See HIGHWORTH AND SWINDON PLU
TISBURY PLU (Wilts, Dorset until 1880s, ent Wilts thereafter)
Alvediston, Ansty, Berwick St John, Berwick St Leonard, Chicklade, Chilmark, Donhead St Andrew, Donhead St Mary, Fonthill Bishop, Fonthill Gifford, Hindon, Semley, Sutton Mandeville, Swallowcliffe, Teffont Evias, Teffont Magna, Tisbury (1927–30), East Tisbury (1835–1927), West Tisbury, Tollard Royal,[18] Wardour (1835–1927)
TROWBRIDGE AND MELKSHAM PLU–See MELKSHAM PLU
WARMINSTER PLU
Bishopstrow, Boyton, Chitterne (1907–30), Chitterne All Saints (1835–1907), Chitterne St Mary (1835–1907), Codford St Mary, Codford St Peter, Corsley, Brixton Deverill, Hill Deverill, Longbridge Deverill, Heytesbury, Horningsham, Imber, Knook, Norton Bavant, Sherrington, Stockton, Sutton Veney, Tytherington, Upton Lovell, Upton Scudamore, Warminster
WESTBURY AND WHORWELLSDOWN PLU
Steeple Ashton, West Ashton, North Bradley, Bratton (1894–1930), Bulkington, East Coulston, Dilton Marsh (1894–1930), Edington, Heywood (1894–1930), Great Hinton, Keevil, Southwick, Westbury

WILTON PLU
Barford St Martin, Baverstock, Bemerton (1894–1930), Berwick St James, Bishopstone, Burcombe (1835–94), Burcombe Without (1894–1930), Bower Chalke, Broad Chalke, Compton Chamberlayne, Dinton, Ebbesbourne Wake, Fifield Bavant (1835–94), Fisherton de la Mere, Fovant, Fugglestone St Peter (1835–94), Groveley Wood, Little Langford, Steeple Langford, Netherhampton, South Newton (1835–94), South Newton (1894–1930), Stapleford, Wilton, Great Wishford, Wylye

In Other Poor Law Counties:
ANDOVER PLU (Hants)
Chute (1835–79), Chute Forest (1835–79), Ludgershall (1835–79), North Tidworth (1835–79)
CIRENCESTER PLU (Glos)
Kemble,[19] Poole Keynes,[19] Somerford Keynes,[19] Marston Meysey (1835–81), Poulton,[20] Shorncott (1835–94)
DURSLEY PLU (Glos)
Kingswood[20]
FARINGDON PLU (Berks)
Coleshill[21]
FORDINGBRIDGE PLU (Hants)
Damerham,[22] Martin,[22] Toyd Farm with Allenford[22] (from 1858), Whitsbury[22]
NEW FOREST (Hants)
Bramshaw[25]
HUNGERFORD PLU (Berks) (1835–96), renamed 4 June 1896 HUNGERFORD AND RAMSBURY PLU (1896–1930)
Aldbourne, Baydon, Great Bedwyn, Little Bedwyn, Buttermere, Chilton Foliat,[23] Froxfield, Grafton, Ham, Hippenscombe, Hungerford,[24] Ramsbury, Shalbourne,[23] Tidcombe and Fosbury
ROMSEY PLU (Hants)
Melchet Park,[22] Plaitford,[22] West Wellow[22]
STOCKBRIDGE (Hants)
West Dean (1835–83)
TETBURY PLU (Glos)
Ashley, Long Newnton
WOKINGHAM PLU (Berks)
Hurst,[26] Shinfield,[26] Swallowfield,[26] Wokingham[26]

WORCESTERSHIRE

In Worcs Poor Law County:[28]

BROMSGROVE PLU (Worcs, Warws, Salop, Staffs [1836—44])

Alvechurch, Belbroughton, Bentley Pauncefoot (soon after 1836[29]—1930), Bromsgrove, North Bromsgrove (1894—1930), Beoley (1911—30), Clent,[14] Cofton Hackett, Frankley, Grafton Manor (1863—1930), Hagley, Hunnington,[15] Pedmore, Redditch (soon after 1836[29]—1930), North Redditch (1894—1930), Romsley,[15] Stoke in Bromsgrove (1894—1930), Stoke Prior, Tardebigge (until soon after 1836[30]), Tutnall and Cobley (soon after 1836[29]—1930), Webheath (soon after 1836[29]—1930), Wythall (1911—30)

DROITWICH PLU

Claines (1836—85), North Claines (1885—1930), South Claines (1894—98), Crowle, Crutch (1858—1930), Dodderhill, Dodderhill In Liberties (1836—84), Doverdale, Droitwich (1920—30), Droitwich St Andrew (1836—1920), Droitwich St Nicholas (1836—1920), Droitwich St Peter (1836—1920), Elmbridge, Elmley Lovett, Hadzor, Hampton Lovett, Hanbury, Hartlebury, Himbleton, Hindlip, Huddington, Marlborough in the Vines (1858—80), Martin Hussingtree, Upper Mitton (1894—1928), Oddingley, Ombersley, Paper Mills (1858[31]—84), Salwarpe, Shell (1858—84), Stock and Bradley, Tibberton, Unnamed (1894—1930), Upton Warren, Warndon, Westwood Park (1858—1930)

EVESHAM PLU (Worcs, Glos)

Aldington, Badsey, Bengeworth (1836—1924), Bretforton, Broadway, Cleeve Prior, Evesham (1924—30), Evesham All Saints (1836—1924), Evesham St Lawrence (1836—1924), Great and Little Hampton, Harvington, Church Honeybourne, Ab Lench, Church Lench, Rous Lench, North and Middle Littleton, South Littleton, Norton and Lenchwick, Offenham, Sedgeberrow, Wickhamford

KIDDERMINSTER PLU (Worcs, Staffs, Salop [1836—95])

Upper Arley,[32] Bedwley, Broom,[14] Chaddesley Corbett, Churchill, Dowles,[32] Kidderminster Borough, Kidderminster Foreign, Lower Mitton (1836—1928), Ribbesford, Rushock, Stone, Stourport (1928—30), Wolverley, Wribbenhall (1901—30)

KINGS NORTON PLU (1836—1912) (Worcs, Warws [1836—89], Birm CB [1889—1912], Staffs [1836—94])

Beoley, Kings Norton, Northfield, Unnamed (1894—1911)

MARTLEY PLU

Abberley, Alfrick, Areley Kings, Astley, Bransford, Broadwas, Clifton upon Teme,[11] Cotheridge, Doddenham, Grimley, Hallow (1836—85), North Hallow (1885—1930), South Hallow (1885—98), Hillhmapton, Holt, Kenswick (1861—1930), Knightwick, Leigh, Lulsley, Martley, Pensax, Lower Sapey (*ca* 1894—1930), Shelsley Beauchamp, Shelsley Kings, Shelsley Walsh, Shrawley, Stanford on Teme, Stockton on Teme, Suckley, Wichenford, Great Witley, Little Witley

PERSHORE PLU

Abberton, Besford, Birlingham, Bishampton, Bredicot, Bricklehampton, Broughton Hackett, Charlton, Churchill, Great Comberton, Little Comberton, Cropthorne, Defford, Dormston, Eckington, Elmley Castle, Fladbury, Grafton Flyford, Flyford Flevell, Hill and Moor, Kington, Naunton Beauchamp, Netherton, Norton juxta Kempsey, Peopleton, Pershore Holy Cross, Pershore St Andrew, North Piddle, Pinvin, Pirton, Spetchley, Stoulton, Strensham, Throckmorton, Upton Snodbury, White Ladies Aston, Whittington, Wick, Wyre Piddle

STOURBRIDGE PLU (Worcs, Staffs, Salop [1836—44], Birm CB [1901—11])

Cakemore[15] (1836—1919), Cradley, Halesowen, Hasbury,[15] Hawne,[15] Hill[15] (1836—1911), Hill and Cakemore (1911—30), Illey,[15] Lapal,[15] Lutley, Lye (soon after 1836[29]—1930), Oldswinford (until soon after 1836[30]), Quinton[33] (between 1891/1901—1911), Ridgacre[15] (1836—between 1891/1901), Stourbridge, Upper Swinford (soon after 1836[29]—1930), Wollaston (soon after 1836[29]—1930), Wollaston (soon after 1836[29]—1930), Wollescote

TENBURY PLU (Worcs, Salop, Heref)

Bockleton, Eastham, Hanley Child, Hanley William, Knighton on Teme, Kyre Magna, Kyre Parva, Lindridge, Orleton, Rochford,[12] Stoke Bliss,[13] Tenbury[11]

UPTON UPON SEVERN PLU

Berrow, Birtsmorton, Bushley, Castlemorton, Earls Croome, Hill Croome, Croome d'Abitot, Eldersfield, Guarlford (1894—1930), Hanley Castle, Holdfast, Kempsey, Longdon, Madresfield, Great Malvern, Little Malvern, South Malvern (1894—96), Malvern Link (1894—1930), Malvern Wells (1896—1930), Newland, Powick, Queenhill, Ripple, Severn Stoke, Upton upon Severn, Welland

WORCESTER PLU

Bedwardine St John (1836—94), Bedwardine St Michael (1836—98), Whistones (1836—98), Worcester (1898—1930), Worcester All Saints (1836—98), Worcester Blockhouse (1858—98), Worcester College Precincts (1858—98), Worcester St Alban (1836—98), Worcester St Andrew (1836—98), Worcester St Clement (1836—98), Worcester St Helen (1836—98), Worcester St John Bedwardine City (1894—98), Worcester St John Bedwardine County (1894—1930), Worcester St Martin (1836—94), Worcester St Martin City (1894—98), Worcester St Martin County (1894—1930), Worcester St Nicholas (1836—98), Worcester St Peter the Great (1836—94), Worcester St Peter the Great City (1894—98), Worcester St Peter the Great County (1894—1930), Worcester St Swithin (1836—98)

In Other Poor Law Counties:

ALCESTER PLU (Warws, Worcs)

Abbots Morton, Feckenham, Feckenham Urban (1894—1930), Inkberrow, Ipsley,[16] Upper Ipsley (1894—1930), Oldberrow[34]

WEST BROMWICH PLU (Staffs, Worcs, Salop [1836—44])
Oldbury,[15] Warley (1844—1908), Warley Salop[15] (1836—44), Warley Wigorn (1836—84)
BROMYARD PLU (Heref, Worcs [1836—*ca* 1894])
Acton Beauchamp,[35] Edvin Loach,[12] Lower Sapey (1836—*ca* 1894)
CLEOBURY MORTIMER PLU (Salop, Worcs)
Bayton, Mamble, Rock
DUDLEY PLU (Staffs, Worcs)
Dudley
LEDBURY PLU (Heref, Worcs)
West Malvern (1897—1930), Mathon (1836—94), Mathon Rural[36] (1894—97), Mathon Urban (1894—97)
NEWENT PLU (Glos, Worcs, Heref)
Redmarley d'Abitot, Staunton
SHIPSTON ON STOUR PLU (Warws, Glos, Worcs)
Batsford,[37] Blockley, Shipston on Stour, Tidmington, Tredington
SOLIHULL PLU (Warws, Worcs [1836—1911])
Yardley (1836—1911)[38]
STOW ON THE WOLD PLU (Glos, Worcs)
Daylesford, Evenlode
STRATFORD ON AVON PLU (Warws, Glos, Worcs)
Alderminster
TEWKESBURY PLU (Glos, Worcs)
Bredon, Bredon's Norton, Chaceley, Conderton, Overbury, Pendock, Teddington
WINCHCOMB PLU (Glos, Worcs)
Cutsdean

YORKSHIRE

In Yorks Poor Law County:[107] (Riding/Adm Co as indicated)
AYSGARTH PLU (1869—1930) [N Riding]
High Abbotside, Low Abbotside, Askrigg, Aysgarth, Bainbridge, Bishopdale, Burton cum Walden, Carperby cum Thoresby, Hawes, Newbiggin, Thoralby, Thornton Rust
BAINBRIDGE GILBERT UNION (until 1869) [N Riding]
High Abbotside, Low Abbotside, Askrigg, Aysgarth, Bainbridge, Burton cum Walden, Hawes, Thoralby
BARNSLEY PLU (1850—1930) [W Riding]
Ardsley (1850—1921), Barnsley, Barugh, Billingley, Carlton, Cudworth, Darfield, Darton, Dodworth, Hoyland Nether, Monk Bretton (1850—1921), Notton, Royston, Stainbrough, Wombwell, Woolley, Worsbrough
BARWICK GILBERT UNION (until 1869) [W Riding]
Acaster Selby, Ackton, Alwoodley (until 1861), Appleton Roebuck, Askham Bryan, Barkston, Barwick in Elmet, Bilbrough, Bilton, Bolton Percy, Bramham cum Oglethorpe, Cattal, Catterton, Clifford with Boston, Kirk Deighton, Featherstone, Church Fenton,

Ferry Fryston, Hunsingore, Hutton Wandesley, East Keswick (until 1861), Long Marston, Newton Kyme cum Toulston, Normanton, Pontefract Park, Purston Jaglin, Great Ribston with Walshford, Ryther cum Ossendyke, Seacroft, Shadwell, Steeton, Tadcaster East, Thorp Arch, Thornville, Tockwith, Ulleskelf, Walton, Whitwood, Wigton, Wilstrop, Wyke
BEDALE PLU (1839—1920) [N Riding]
Ainderby Miers with Holtby, Aiskew, Bedale, Burneston, Burrill with Cowling, Burton upon Ure, Carthorpe, Clifton upon Ure, Crakehall; Exelby, Leeming and Newton; Firby, Gatenby, Hackforth, Killerby, Kirkby Fleetham, Kirklington cum Upsland, Langthorne, Masham, Rand Grange, Rootwith, Scruton, Snape, Swainby with Allerthorpe, Swinton with Watermarske, Theakston, Thirn, Thornton Walass, Well
BEVERLEY PLU (1836—1930) [E Riding]
Aike, Beverley St Martin, Beverley St Mary, Beverley St Nicholas, Beswick, Brantingham, Bishop Burton, Cherry Burton, South Cave, South Dalton, Ellerker, Elloughton with Brough, Eske, Etton, Holme on the Wolds, Kilnwick, Leconfield and Arram, Leven, Lockington, Lockington in Kilnwick (1836—94), Lund, Meaux, Molescroft, North Newbald, South Newbald, Routh, Rowley, Scorborough, Skidby, Storkhill and Sandholme, Thearne, Tickton and Hull Bridge, Walkington, Wawne, Weel, Woodmansey and Beverley Parks
NORTH BIERLEY PLU (1848—1930) [W Riding]
Allerton (1848—98), North Bierley, Bolton (1848—98), Calverley (1894—1930), Calverley with Farsley (1848—94), Clayton, Cleckheaton, Denholme (1894—. 1930), Drighlington, Eccleshill (1869—1930), Farsley (1894—1930), Heaton (1848—98), Hunsworth, Idle, Pudsey, Shipley, Thornbury (1894—98), Thornton, Tong, Tyersall (1894—98), Wilsden, Wyke
BRADFORD PLU (1837—98), PAR (1898—1930) [W Riding]
Allerton (1837—48), North Bierley (1837—48), Bolton (1837—48), Bowling (1837—98), Bradford, Calverley with Farsley (1837—48), Clayton (1837—48), Cleckheaton (1837—48), Drighlington (1837—48), Heaton (1837—48), Horton (1837—98), Hunsworth (1837—48), Idle (1837—48), Manningham (1837—98), Pudsey (1837—48), Shipley (1837—48), Thornton (1837—48), Tong (1837—48), Wilsden (1837—48), Wyke (1837—48)
BRAMLEY PLU (1862—1930) [W Riding]
Armley (1869—1904), Armley and Bramley (1904—25), Bramley (1862—1904), Farnley (1869—1904), Gildersome, Wortley (1869—1904)
BRIDLINGTON PLU (1836—1930) [E Riding]
Argam, Auburn (1836—94), Barnston, Bempton, Bessingby, Boynton, Bridlington, Buckton, Burton Agnes, Burton Fleming, Carnaby; Dringhoe, Upton and Brough; Easton, Flamborough, Fordon, Fraisthorpe (1836—96), Fraisthorpe with Auburn and Wilsthorp (1896—1930), Gransmoor, Grindale, Haisthorpe

Hilderthorpe (1836—1923), Hunmanby, Lissett, Reighton, Rudston, Sewerby cum Marton, Skipsea, Speeton, Thornholme, Thwing, Ulrome, Wilsthorpe (1836—96), Wold Newton

CARLTON GILBERT UNION (until 1869) [W Riding]
Adel cum Eccup, Chapel Allerton, Armley, Arthington, Askwith, Baildon, Beamsley in Addingham, Beamsley in Skipton, Beeston, Bramhope (until 1861), Burley in Wharfedale, Carlton, Churwell, Collingham, Denton, Dunkeswick, Eccleshill, Farnley, Harewood, Hawksworth, Headingley cum Burley, Horsforth (until 1861), Ilkley, Kirkby Overblow (until 1861), Leathley (until 1861), Menston, Middleton, Nesfield with Langbar, Otley, Pool (until 1861), Potter Newton, Rawdon, Rigton (until 1861), Rothwell, Silsden, Templenewsham, Thorner, Weeton, Wortley

DEWSBURY PLU (1837—1930) [W Riding]
Batley, Birkenshaw (1894—1930), Birstall (1894—1930), Dewsbury, Gomersal, Heckmondwike, Liversedge, Mirfield, Morley, Ossett (1890—1930), Ossett cum Gawthorpe (1837—90), Ravensthorpe (1894—1925), Soothill (1837—94), Soothill Nether (1894—1925), Soothill Upper (1894—1910), Thornhill (1837—1925), Whitley Lower (1837—96)

DONCASTER PLU (1837—1930) [W Riding, N Riding (1837—95), Notts (1837—95)]
Adwick le Street, Adwick upon Dearne, Armthorpe, Askern, Auckley,[108] Austerfield, Balby with Hexthorpe (1837—1914), Barnbrough, Barnby Dun with Kirk Sandall (1921—30), Barnby upon Don (1837—1921), Bawtry, Bentley with Arksey, Bilham (1837—1920), Blaxton, Bolton upon Dearne, Braithwell, Brodsworth, Burghwallis, Cadeby, Campsall, Cantley, Carr House and Elm Field (1862—1914), Clayton with Frickley, Conisbrough, Denaby, Doncaster, Edlington, Finningley,[109] Hampole, Hickleton, Hooton Pagnell, Kirk Bramwith, Langthwaite with Tilts (1837—83), Loversall, Marr, High Melton, Mexborough, Moss, Norton, Owston, Rossington, Kirk Sandall (1837—1921), Long Sandall (1837—86), Skellow (1837—1915), Spotbrough, Stainton, Stainton Urban (1924—30), Stancill with Wellingley and Wilseck (1837—86), Stotfold (1837—1920), Sutton, Thorpe in Balne, Thurnscoe, Tickhill, Tickhill Outer (1894—95), Wadworth, Warmsworth, Whealtey (1837—1914)

DRIFFIELD PLU (1836—1930) [E Riding]
Bainton, Beeford, Bracken, Brigham, Butterwick, Cottam, Cowlam, North Dalton, Great Driffield, Little Driffield (1836—85), Eastburn, Emswell with Little Driffield (1885—1930), Emswell with Kellythorpe (1836—85), Fimber, Foston on the Wolds, Foxholes with Boythorpe, North Frodingham, Garton on the Wolds, Gembling, Harpham, Helperthorpe, Hutton Cranswick, Great Kelk, Little Kelk, Kilham, Kirkburn and Battleburn, Langtoft, Lowthorpe, Luttons Ambo, Middleton on the Wolds, Nafferton, Neswick, Rotsea, Ruston Parva, Skerne, Sledmere, Southburn, Sunderlandwick, Tibthorpe, Towthorpe, Wansford, Watton, Weaverthorpe, Wetwang

EASINGWOLD PLU (1837—1930) [N Riding, Durham (1837—44)]
Aldwark, Alne, Angram Grange, Brafferton, Brandsby cum Stearsby, Carlton Husthwaite, Coxwold, Crayke,[110] Dalby cum Skewsby, Easingwold, Farlington, Flawith, Huby, Husthwaite, Linton upon Ouse, Marton cum Moxby, Myton on Swale, Newburgh,· Newton upon Ouse (soon after 1837[111]—1930), Oulston, Raskelf, Stillington, Sutton on the Forest, Tholthorpe, Thormanby, Thornton on the Hill, Whenby, Wildon Grange, Yearsley

ECCLESALL BIERLOW PLU (1837—1930) [W Riding (1837—1904), Derbys]
Ecclesall Bierlow (1837—1904), Nether Hallam (1837—1904), Upper Hallam (1837—1904), Heeley (1880—1904)

GOOLE PLU (1837—1930) [W Riding, Lincs Pts Lind]
Adlingfleet, Airmyn, Eastoft, Fockerby, Goole, Goole Fields (1894—1930), Gowdall, Haldenby, Hook, Ousefleet, Pollington, Rawcliffe, Reedness (1837—48), Reedness (1894—1930), Snaith and Cowick,[112] Swinefleet (1837—84), Swinefleet (1894—1930), Swinefleet and Reedness (1884—94), Whitgift

GUISBOROUGH PLU (1837—1930) [N Riding]
Brotton, Coatham (1899—1921), Commondale, Danby, Easington, Eston (1837—75), Guisborough, Hutton Lowcross, Kilton, Kirkleatham, Liverton, Loftus, Marske, Moorsholm, Morton, Newton, Normanby (1837—75), Ormesby (1837—75), Pinchinthorpe, Redcar, Skelton, Skinningrove, Stanghow, Tocketts, Upleatham, Upsall, Westerdale, Wilton

HALIFAX PLU (1837—1930) [W Riding]
Barkisland, Brighouse (1894—1930), Clifton,[113] Elland (1894—1930), Elland with Greetland (1837—94), Fixby, Greetland (1894—1930), Upper Greetland (1894—1930), Halifax, Hartshead,[113] Hipperholme (1894—1930), Hipperholme with Brighouse (1837—94), Luddenden Foot (1894—1930), Midgley, Norland, Northowram (1837—1930 Norwood Green and Coley (1894—1930), Ovenden (1837—94), Queensbury (1894—1930), Rastrick (1837—1915), Rishworth, Shelf, Skircoat (1837—99), Southowram, Sowerby, Sowerby Bridge (1894—1926), Soyland, Stainland with Old Lindley, Warley (1837—1900)

HELMSLEY PLU (orig, 'HELMSLEY BLACKMOOR') (1837—1930) [N Riding]
Ampleforth (1887—1930), Ampleforth Birdforth (1837—87), Ampleforth Oswaldkirk (1837—87), Ampleforth St Peter (1837—87), Arden, Beadlam, Bilsdale Midcable (1837—48); Bilsdale, West Side; Bransdale, West Side (1837—48); Old Byland, Byland Abbey (1837—87), Byland with Wass (1887—1930), Cawton, Cold Kirby, Coulton, Dale Town (soon after 1837[111]—1930), Great Edstone (1837—48), Little Edstone (1837—48), Fadmoor (1837—48); Farndale, East Side (1837—48); Farndale, West Side (1837—48); Farndale, Low Quarter (1837—48); Gillamoor (1837—48); Gilling East, Grimston, Harome, Hawnby, Helmsley, North Holme (1837—48), Hutton le Hole (1837—48), Kirkby Moorside (1837—48), Laskill

Pasture, Murton (soon after 1837[111]—1930), Muscoates (1837—48), Nawton (1837—48), East Newton and Laysthorp, Nunnington (1837—48), Oldstead, Oswaldkirk, Pockley, Rievaulx, Scawton, Skiplam (1837—48), Snilesworth (soon after 1837[111]—1930), Sproxton, Stonegrave, Thorpe le Willows, Wass (1837—87), Welburn (1837—48), Wombleton (1837—48)

HEMSWORTH PLU (1850—1930) [W Riding]
Ackworth, Badsworth, Brierley, North Elmsall, South Elmsall, Hamphall Stubbs (soon after 1850[111]—1930), West Hardwick, Havercroft with Cold Hiendley, Hemsworth, Hessle (1850—88), Hessle and Hill Top (1888—1930), South Hiendley, Hill Top (1850—88), Great Houghton, Little Houghton, Huntwick with Foulby and Nostell (soon after 1850[111]—1930), South Kirkby, Ryhill, Shafton, Skelbrooke, Kirk Smeaton, Little Smeaton, Thorpe Audlin, Upton, Walden Stubbs, Wintersett

HOLBECK TP/PAR (1862—69), PLU (1869—1904), PAR (1904—25) [W Riding]
Beeston (1869—1904), Churwell (1869—1904), Holbeck

HOWDEN PLU (1837—1930) [E Riding]
Asselby, Aughton, Barkholme, Barmby on the Marsh, Belby, Bellasize, Bishopsoil (1880—1930), Blacktoft, Brackenholme with Woodhall, Breighton and Gunby, Broomfleet, Bubwith, North Cave with Everthorpe and Drewton, Cheapsides (1858—92), Cotness, Eastrington, Ellerton Priory, Faxfleet, Foggathorpe, Gilberdike, Gribthorpe, Harlthorpe, Hemingbrough, Holme upon Spalding Moor, Hotham, Howden, Kilpin, Knedlington, Laxton, Laytham, Menthorpe cum Bowthorpe, Metham, New Village[114] (1837—81), Portington and Cavil, Saltmarshe, Scalby, Skelton, Spaldington, Thorpe, Wallingfen (1881—1930), Willitoft, Wressell (soon after 1837[111]—1930), Yokefleet

HUDDERSFIELD PLU (1837—1930) [W Riding]
Almondbury (1837—1924), Austonley (1837—1921), Cartworth (1837—1921), South Crosland, Cumberworth, Cumberworth Half (1837—76), Dalton (1837—1924), Farnley Tyas (1837—1925), Fulstone, Golcar, Hepworth, Holme, South Holme (1894—95), Honley, Huddersfield, Kirkburton, Kirkheaton, Lepton, Lindley cum Quarmby (1837—1924), Lingards (1837—96), Linthwaite, Lockwood (1837—1924), Longwood (1837—1924), Marsden (1898—1930), Marsden in Almondbury (1837—98), Marsden in Huddersfield (1837—98), Meltham, Netherthong (1837—1921), Scammonden, Scholes (1894—1930), Shelley, Shepley, Skelmanthorpe (1876—1930), Slaithwaite, Thurstonland (1837—1925), Thurstonland and Farnley Tyas (1925—30), Upperthong (1837—1921), Whitley Upper, Wooldale (1837—1921)

HULL INCORP [E Riding]
Kingston upon Hull Holy Trinity and St Mary

HUNSLET TP/PAR (1862—69), PLU (1869—1930) [W Riding]
Hunslet (1862—1925), Middleton (1869—1920),

Oulton with Woodlesforth (1869—1930), Rothwell (1869—1930), Templenewsham (1869—1927), Thorpe Stapleton (1869—1925)

KEIGHLEY PLU (1837—1930) [W Riding]
Bingley, Bingley Outer (1894—98), Haworth, Keighley, Morton, Oakworth (1894—1930), Oxenhope (1894—1930), Stanbury (1894—1930), Steeton with Eastburn, Sutton

KIRKBY MOORSIDE PLU (1848—1930) [N Riding]
Appleton le Moors (soon after 1848[111]—1930); Bransdale, West Side; Great Edstone, Little Edstone, Fadmoor; Farndale, East Side; Farndale, Low Quarter; Farndale, West Side; Gillamoor, North Holme, Hutton le Hole, Kirkby Moorside, Muscoates, Nawton, Ness (1887—1930), East Ness (soon after 1848[111]—87), West Ness (soon after 1848[111]—87), Normanby (soon after 1848[111]—1930), Nunnington, Salton (soon after 1848[111]—1930), Skiplam, Thornton Riseborough (soon after 1848[111]—1930), Welburn, Wombleton

KNARESBOROUGH PLU (1854—1930) [W Riding]
Bilton (1894—1930), Bilton and Harrogate (1854—94), Brearton, Burton Leonard, Farnham, Felliscliffe, Ferrensby, Flaxby, Follifoot, Goldsborough, Hampsthwaite, Harrogate (1894—1930), Haverah Park, Killinghall, Knaresborough, Knaresborough Outer (1894—1930), Nidd, Pannal, Plompton, Ripley, Scotton, Scriven (1894—1930), Scriven with Tentergate (1854—94), South Stainley with Cayton, Starbeck (1894—1930), Tentergate (1894—95), Walkingham Hill with Occaney

LEEDS GUARDIANS (1844—69), PLU (1869—1912), PAR (1912—30) [W Riding]
Chapel Allerton (1869—1904), Headingley cum Burley (1869—1904), Holbeck (1844—62), Hunslet (1844—62), Leeds, Potter Newton (1869—1904), Roundhay (1869—1912), Seacroft (1869—1912)

LEYBURN PLU (1837—1930) [N Riding]
Agglethorpe with Coverham, Akebar, Arrathorne, Barden, Bellerby, Burrill with Cowling (1837—39), Burton upon Ure (1837—39), Cadbergh with East Scrafton, Carlton Highdale, Carlton Town, Castle Bolton, Clifton upon Ure (1837—39), Colsterdale (1894—1930), Constable Burton, Ellingstring, Ellingtons, Fearby, Finghall, Garriston, Harmby, East Huxwell, West Huxwell, Healy with Sutton, Hornby, Hunton, Hutton Hang, Ilton cum Pott (soon after 1837[111]—1930), Leyburn, Melmerby, Middleham, Newton le Willows, Patrick Brompton, Preston, Redmire, Rookwith (1837—39), West Scrafton, Spennithorne, Thornton Steward, Thirn (1837—39), Wensley, East Witton Within, East Witton Without, West Witton

MALTON PLU (1837—1930) [N Riding, E Riding]
Acklam with Barthorpe, Airyholme with Howthorpe and Baxton Howe, Amotherby, Appleton le Street, Barton le Street, Barton le Willows, Birdsall, Brawby, Broughton, Bulmer, Burythorpe, Butterwick, Coneysthorpe, Crambe, Duggleby, Eddlethorpe, Firby, Foston, Fryton, Ganthorpe, North Grimston, Great Habton, Little Habton, Henderskelf, East Heslerton, West Heslerton, Hildenley, South Holme, Hovingham

Yorkshire: Malton *continued*

Howsham, Huttons Ambo, Kennythorpe, Kirby Grindalythe, Kirkham, Knapton, Langton, Leavening, Leppington, Malton (1896—1930), New Malton (1837—96), Old Malton (1837—96), Menethorpe, Norton, Raisthorpe and Burdale, Rillington, Ryton, Scagglethorpe, Scackleton, Scampston, Settrington, Sheriff Hutton with Cornbrough, Slingsby, Stittenham, Swinton, Terrington with Wigganthorpe, Thirkleby, Thornton le Clay, Thorpe Bassett, Wath, Welburn, Westow, Wharram le Street, Wharram Percy, Whitwell on the Hill, Wintringham, Yedingham

MIDDLESBROUGH PLU (1875—1930) [N Riding]
West Acklam, Eston, Hemlington, Ingleby Barwick, Linthorpe (1875—1913), Maltby, Marton, Middlesbrough, Normanby (1875—1915), Ormesby, Stainton, Thornaby

NORTHALLERTON PLU (1837—1930) [N Riding]
Ainderby Miers with Holtby (1837—39), Ainderby Steeple, Aiskew (1837—39), Appleton Wiske, Bedale (1837—39), Birkby, Borrowby, Brompton, Cotcliffe (1858—1930), East Cowton, South Cowton, Crakenhall (1837—39), Crosby, Danby Wiske, Deighton, Ellerbeck, Firby (1837—39), Gueldable (1837—88), Hackforth (1837—39), East Harlsey, West Harlsey, Hornby, Hutton Bonville, Killerby (1837—39), Kiplin, Kirby Sigston, Kirkby Fleetham (1837—39), Landmoth cum Catto, Langthorne (1837—39), Great Langton, Little Langton, Lazenby (1858—1930), Leake (1858—1930), Morton upon Swale, Northallerton, Osmotherley, North Otterington, Rand Grange (1837—39), Romanby, West Rounton, Scruton (1837—39), Nether Silton, Over Silton, Great Smeaton, Little Smeaton, Sowerby under Cotcliffe, Thimbleby, Thornton le Beans, Thornton Watlass (1837—39), Thrintoft, Warlaby, Welbury, Whitwell, Winton, Yafforth

GREAT OUSEBURN GILBERT UNION (until 1854), PLU (1854—1930) [W Riding, N Riding]
Acomb (1854—1930), Aldborough[115] (1854—1930), Allerton Mauleverer with Hopperton (1854—1930), Arkendale, Baldersby (until 1854), Bickerton (until 1854), Boroughbridge (1854—1930), Burton Leonard (until 1854), Cattal (1869—1930), Clareton[116] (until 1888), Coneythorpe (until 1888), Coneythorpe and Clareton (1888—1930), Copgrove (1854—1930), Dishforth (until 1854), Lower Dunsforth,[117] Upper Dunsforth with Branton Green,[117] Farnham (1854—1930), Farnham (until 1854), Goldsborough (until 1854), Green Hammerton, Kirk Hammerton, Helperby, Hessay, Humberton[118] (1854—95), Hunsingore (1869—1930), Hutton Conyers (until 1854), Kirby Hall, Kirby Hill, Knapton, Langthorpe, Markington with Wallerthwaite (until 1854), Marton cum Gratton, Milby[118] (1854—95), Minskip, Morton le Moor (until 1854), Bishop Monkton (until 1854), Moor Monkton (1854—1930), Norton le Clay, Great Ouseburn, Little Ouseburn, Nether Poppleton (1854—1930), Upper Poppleton (1854—1930), Rainton with Newby (until 1854), Great Ribston with Walshford (1869—1930), Little Ribston (until 1854), Roecliffe (1854—1930), Rufforth, Shipton, Sickinghall (until

1854), Skelton (until 1854), Staveley (1854—1930), Thornton Bridge (1854—1930), Thornville (1869—1930), Thorpe Underwoods (1854—1930), Tollerton, Westwick (1854—1930), Whixley, Widdington, Youlton

PATELEY BRIDGE PLU (1837—1930) [W Riding]
Bewerley, Birstwith (soon after 1837[111]—1930), Bishop Thornton, High and Low Bishopside, Clint, Dacre, Fountains Earth, Hartwith cum Winsley, Menwith with Darley, Down Stonebeck, Upper Stonebeck, Thornthwaite with Padside, Thruscross, Warsill

PATRINGTON PLU (1836—1930) [E Riding]
Burstwick with Skeckling (soon after 1836[111]—1930), Burton Pidsea (soon after 1836[111]—1930), Easington, South Frodingham, Halsham, Hilston, Hollym, Holmpton, Keyingham, Kilnsea, Ottringham, Out Newton, Owstwick, Owthorne, Patrington, Paull, Rimswell, Roos, Ryhill and Camerton, Skeffling, Sunk Island, Thorgumbald, Tunstall, Waxholme, Welwick, Winestead, Withernsea

PENISTONE PLU (1849—1930) [W Riding]
Cawthorne, Clayton West, Denby, Gunthwaite, High Hoyland, Hoyland Swaine, Hunshelf, Ingbirchworth, Kexborough, Langsett, Oxspring, Penistone, Silkstone, Thurgoland, Thurlstone

PICKERING PLU (1837—1930) [N Riding]
Aislaby, Allerston, Appleton le Moors (1837—soon after 1848[111]), Barughs Ambo, Cawthorn, Cropton, Ebberston, Farmanby (1837—87), Hartoft, Kingthorpe, Kirby Misperton, Lastingham, Levisham, Lockton, Marishes, Marton, Middleton, Newton, Normanby (1837—soon after 1848[111]), Pickering; Rosedale, East Side; Rosedale, West Side; Sinnington, Spaunton, Thornton Dale, Thornton Risebrough (1837—soon after 1848[111]), Thurnhill,[119] Wilton, Wrelton

POCKLINGTON PLU (1836—1930) [E Riding]
Alethorpe, Barmby on the Moor, Bielby, Bishop Wilton with Belthorpe, Bolton, Bugthorpe, Burnby, High Catton, Low Catton, North Cliffe, South Cliffe, East Cottingwith, Everingham, Fangfoss, Fridaythorpe, Full Sutton, Great Givendale with Grimthorpe, Goodmanham, Harswell, Hayton, Huggate, Kilnwick Percy, Kirby Underdale, Londesborough with Easthorpe, Market Weighton and Arras, Melbourne, Millington with Little Givendale, Newton upon Derwent, Nunburnholme, Ousethorpe, Pocklington, Sancton and Houghton, Scrayingham, Seaton Ross, Shipton Thorpe, Skirpenbeck, East Stamford Bridge, Storwood, Sutton upon Derwent, Thixendale, Thorpe le Street, Thornton, Waplington, Warter, Wilberfoss, Yapham cum Meltonby, Youlthorpe with Gowthorpe

PONTEFRACT PLU (1862—1930) [W Riding]
Ackton (1869—1930), Balne, Beal or Beaghall (1869—1930), Birkin, Brotherton (1869—1930), Burton Salmon (1869—1930), Byram cum Poole (1862—91), Byram cum Sutton (1891—1930), Carleton (1869—1930), Castleford (1869—1930), Cridling Stubbs, Darrington (1869—1930), Eggborough, Fairburn (1869—1930), Featherstone (1869—1930), Ferry

59

Fryston (1869—1930), Monk Fryston, Glass Houghton (1869—1930), East Hardwick, Heck, Hensall, Hillam, Kellington, Knottingley, Ledston (1869 and only brief time later), Methley (1869—1930), Monkhill (1862—92), Pontefract, Pontefract Park (1869—1920), Purston Jaglin (1869—1930), Snydale, Stapleton, Sutton (1869—91), Tanshelf (1862—1920), Whitley, Whitwood (1869—1930), Womersley

GREAT PRESTON GILBERT UNION (until 1869) [W Riding]

Allerton Bywater, Altofts, Austhorpe (until 1862), Bardsey cum Righton (until 1861), Beal or Beaghall, Birkin (until 1862), Brotherton, Burton Salmon, Byram cum Poole (until 1862), Carleton, Castleford, Crofton, Darrington, Fairburn, Monk Fryston (until 1862), Garforth, Glass Houghton, West Haddesley, Hambleton, Hillam (until 1862), Kippax, Kirkby Wharfe and North Milford (until 1862), Ledsham, Ledston, Lotherton cum Allerford (until 1862), Methley, Micklefield, Middleton, South Milford, Great and Little Preston, Roundhay, Saxton with Scarthingwell, Sherburn in Elmet, Syndale (until 1862), Stapleton (until 1862), Swillington, Tanshelf (until 1862), Weardley (until 1861), Womersley (until 1862)

REETH PLU (1840—1930) [N Riding]

Arkengarthdale, Ellerton Abbey, Grinton, Marrick, Melbecks, Muker, Reeth

RICHMOND PLU (1837—1930) [N Riding]

Aldbrough, Appleton, Arkengarthdale (1837—40), Aske, Bolton upon Swale, Brompton on Swale, Brough, Calbourn, Caldwell, Catterick, North Cowton, Downholme, Easby, Ellerton Abbey (1837—40), Ellerton upon Swale, Eppleby, Forcett with Carkin, Gayles, Gilling, Grinton (1837—40), Hipswell, Hudswell, Kirby Hill, East Layton, West Layton, Marrick (1837—40), Marske, Melsonby, Middleton Tyas, Moulton, New Forest, Newsham, Ravensworth, Reeth (1837—40), Richmond, St Martin,[120] Scorton, Scotton, Skeeby, Stainton, Stanwick St John, Tunstall, Uckerby, Walburn, Whashton

RIPON PLU (1852—1930) [W Riding, N Riding]

Aismunderby with Bongate (1852—94), Aldfield, Asenby (soon after 1852[111]—1930), Azerley, Baldersby, Bishopton (1852—1900), Clotherholme, Cundall with Leckby (soon after 1852[111]—1930), Dishforth, Eavestone, Givendale, Grantley, Grewelthorpe, Bridge Hewick, Copt Hewick, Howgrave, Hutton Conyers, Ingerthorpe, Kirkby Malzeard, Laverton, Lindrick with Studley Royal Fountains, Littlethorpe (1894—1930), Markingfield Hall (1866—1930), Markington with Wallerthwaite (1854—1930), Marton le Moor, Melmerby, Middleton Quernhow, Bishop Monkton (1854—1930), Newby with Mulwith, Norton Conyers, Nunwick cum Howgrave,[117] Rainton with Newby, Ripon, Sawley, Sharow, Skedling, Skelton, North Stainley with Sleningford, Studley Roger, Sutton Grange, Sutton Howgrave, East Tanfield, West Tanfield, Wath, Whitcliffe with Thorpe (1852—94), Winksley

ROTHERHAM PLU (1837—1930) [W Riding, Derbys (1837—94)]

Aston cum Aughton, Bramley, Brampton (1894—97), Brampton Bierlow (1837—94), Brampton Bierlow (1897—1930), Brampton en le Morthen (1837—1923), Brinsworth, Catcliffe, Dalton, Greasbrough, Hooton Levitt, Hooton Roberts, Kimberworth (1837—94), Laughton en le Morthen (1837—1923), Maltby, West Melton (1894—1923), Orgreave, Ravenfield, Rawmarsh, Rotherham, Swinton, Thrybergh, Thurcroft (1923—30), Tinsley, Treeton, Ulley, Wath upon Dearne, Wentworth, Whiston, Wickersley

SADDLEWORTH GILBERT UNION (until 1853), PAR (1853—94), PLU (1894—1930) [W Riding]

Saddleworth, Springhead (1894—1930), Upper Mill (1894—1900)

SCARBOROUGH PLU (1837—1930) [N Riding, E Riding]

East Ayton, West Ayton, Brompton, Broxa, Burniston, Cayton, Cloughton, Falsgrave (1837—90), Filey, Folkton, Ganton, Gristhorpe, Hackness, Harwood Dale, Hutton Buscel, Irton, Lebberston, Muston, Newby (1837—86), Osgodby (1837—86), Sawdon (1837—56), Scalby (1837—1902), Scarborough, Seamer, Sherburn, Silpho, Snainton, Staintondale, Suffield cum Everley, Throxenby (1837—1909), Troutsdale, Willerby, Wykeham

SCULCOATES PLU (1837—1930) [E Riding]

Anlaby, Cottingham (1837—94), Cottingham (1898—1930), Cottingham Within (1894—98), Cottingham Without (1894—98), Drypool (1837—98), Kirk Ella, West Ella, North Ferriby, Garrison Side (1858—98), Haltemprice (1862—1930), Hedon, Hessle (1837—94), Hessle (1899—1930), Hessle Within (1894—98), Hessle Without (1894—99), Marfleet (1837—98), Melton, Newington (1877—98), Preston, Sculcoates, Southcoates (1837—98), Sutton and Stoneferry (1837—98), Sutton on Hill (1894—1930), Sutton Within (1894—98), Swanland, Wauldby, Welton, Willerby

From 1898 many places incorporated in Hull civil parish.

SEDBERGH PLU (1840—1930) [W Riding]

Dent, Garsdale, Sedbergh

SELBY PLU (1837—1930) [W Riding, E Riding]

Barlby, Barlow, Biggin (soon after 1837[111]—1930), Brayton, Burn, Camblesforth, Carlton, Cawood, Cliffe cum Lund, Drax, Long Drax, North Duffield, South Duffield, Little Fenton (soon after 1837[111]—1930), Gateforth, Chapel Haddlesey, West Haddlesey (1869—1930), Hambleton (1869—1930), Temple Hirst, Hirst Courtney, Kelfield, Newland, Osgodby, Riccall, Selby, Skipwith, Thorpe Willoughby, Wistow

SETTLE PLU (1837—1930) [W Riding]

Airton, Arncliffe, Austwick, Bentham, Burton in Lonsdale, Clapham cum Newby, Giggleswick, West Halton, Halton Gill, Hanlith, Hawkswick, Hellifield, Horton in Ribblesdale, Ingleton, Kirkby Malham, Langcliffe, Lawkland, Litton, Malham, Malham Moor, Nappa, Otterburn, Long Preston, Rathmell, Scosthrop, Settle, Stainforth, Swinden, Thornton in Lonsdale, Tosside, Wigglesworth

SHEFFIELD PLU (1837—1930) [W Riding]
Attercliffe cum Darnall (1837—1902), Brightside
Bierlow (1837—1902), Bradfield Urban (1914—30),
Ecclesall (1904—30), Ecclesfield Urban (1921—30),
Handsworth (soon after 1837[111]—1930), Sheffield
SKIPTON PLU (1837—1930) [W Riding]
Addingham, Appletreewick, Bank Newton, Barden,
Barnoldswick, Beamsley (1886—1930), Beamsley in
Addingham (1869—86), Beamsley in Skipton (1869—
86), Bolton Abbey, Bordley (soon after 1837[111]—
1930), Bracewell, Bradley's Both, Brogden,
Broughton, Buckden, Burnsall (soon after 1837[111]—
1930), Calton, Carleton, Coates (1837—1923), Con-
iston Cold, Conistone with Kilnsey, Cononley (soon
after 1837[111]—1930), Cowling (soon after 1837[111]—
1930), Cracoe, Draughton, Earby (1909—30), Elslack
(soon after 1837[111]—1930), Embsay with Eastby,
Eshton, Farnhill, Flasby with Winterburn, Gargrave,
Glusburn, Grassington, Halton East, Hartlington,
Hazlewood with Storiths, Hebden, Hetton, Kettlewell
with Starbottom, Kildwick, Linton, Lothersdale
(1894—1930), Martons Both, Rylstone, Salterforth,
Silsden (1869—1930), Skipton, Stirton with Thorlby,
Thornton in Craven, Thorpe, Thresfield
SKIRLAUGH PLU (1837—1930) [E Riding]
Aldborough, Atwick, Benningholme and Grange,
Bewholme and Nunkeeling, Bilton, Bonwick,
Brandesburton, Catfoss, Catwick, Coniston, Great and
Little Cowdens, Danthorpe, Dunnington, Ellerby,
Elstronwick, Filing, Flinton, Ganstead, Garton with
Grimston, Goxhill, Great Hatfield, Little Hatfield,
Hempholme, Hornsea, Humbleton, Lelley, Mappleton
and Rowlston, Marton, Moor Town, East Newton,
West Newton with Burton Constable, Rise, Long
Riston, Seaton and Wassand, Sigglesthorne; North
Skirlaugh, Rowton and Arnold; South Skirlaugh,
Sproatley, Swine, Thirtleby, Withernwick, Wyton
STOKESLEY PLU (1837—1930) [N Riding]
Great Ayton, Little Ayton, Bilsdale Midcable (1848—
1930), Broughton, Great Busby, Little Busby, Carlton,
Crathorne, Easby, Faceby, Hemlington (1837—75),
Hilton, Hutton Rudby, Ingleby Arncliffe, Ingleby
Greenhow, Kildale, Kirby in Cleveland, Castle Leav-
ington (1875—1930), Kirk Leavington (1875—1930),
Marton (1837—75), Middleton upon Leven, Newby,
Nunthorpe, Picton (1875—1930), Potto, East Rounton,
Rudby in Cleveland, Seamer, Sexhow, Skutterskelf,
Stokesley, Whorlton, High Worsall (1875—1930), Low
Worsall (1875—1930), Yarm (1875—1930)
TADCASTER PLU (1862—1930) [W Riding]
Aberford, Acaster Selby (1869—1930), Allerton Byw-
ater (1869—1930), Appleton Roebuck (1869—1930),
Askham Bryan (1869—1930), Austhorpe, Barkston
(1869—1930), Barwick in Elmet (1869—1930), Bil-
brough (1869—1930), Bolton Percy (1869—1930),
Catterton (1869—1930), Colton, Church Fenton
(1869—1930), Garforth (1869—1930), Grimston,
Healaugh (1864—1930), Huddleston cum Lumby,
Kippax (1869—1930), Kirkby Wharfe and North
Milford, Lead, Ledsham (1869—1930), Ledston

(1869—1930), Lotherton cum Aberford, Micklefield
(1869—1930), South Milford (1869—1930), New-
thorpe, Newton Kyme cum Toulston (1869—1930),
Oxton, Parlington, Great and Little Preston (1869—
1930), Ryther cum Ossendyke (1869—1930), Saxton
with Scarthingwell (1869—1930), Sherburn in Elmet
(1869—1930), Steeton (1869—1930), Sturton Grange,
Stutton with Hazlewood, Swillington (1869—1930),
Tadcaster East (1869—1930), Tadcaster West, Towton,
Ulleskelf (1869—1930)
THIRSK PLU (1837—1930) [N Riding]
Ainderby Quernhow, Bagby (soon after 1837[111]—
1930), Balk, Birdforth (1837[111]—1930), Boltby,
Carlton Miniott, Catton, Cowesby, Dalton, Eldmire
with Crakenhill, Fawdington (soon after 1837[111]—
1930), Felixkirk, Holme, Hood Grange (1858—1930),
Howe, Humberton (1895—1930), Hutton Sessay,
Kepwick, Kilburn, North Kilvington, South Kilvington,
Kirby Knowle, Kirby Wiske, Knayton with Brawith,
Maunby, Milby (1895—1930), Newby Wiske, New-
sham with Breckenbrough, South Otterington, Pickhill
with Roxby, Sand Hutton, Sessay, Sinderby, Skipton
on Swale, Sowerby, Sutton under Whitstone Cliffe,
Thirkleby, Thirlby, Thirsk, Thornborough, Thornton le
Moor, Thornton le Street, Topcliffe, Upsall
THORNE PLU (1837—1930) [W Riding, Lincs Pts Lind]
Crowle,[59] Fishlake, Hatfield, Stainforth, Sykehouse,
Thorne
TODMORDEN PLU (1837—1930) [W Riding, Lancs
(1837—97]
Blackshaw (1894—1930), Erringden, Hebden Bridge
(1894—1930), Heptonstall, Langfield (1837—97),
Mytholmroyd (1894—1930), Stansfield (1837—97),
Todmorden (1897—1930), Wadsworth
WAKEFIELD PLU (1837—1930) [W Riding]
Altofts (1869—1930), Alverthorpe (1894—1916),
Alverthorpe with Thornes (1837—94), Ardsley East,
Ardsley West, West Bretton, Chevet (soon after
1837[111]—1930), Crigglestone, Crofton (1869—1930),
Emley, Flockton, Horbury, Kirkhamgate (1916—30),
Lofthouse with Carleton (soon after 1837[111]—1930),
Lupset (1902—25), Newland with Woodhouse Moor
(1858—1930), Normanton (1869—1930), Norton
Within (1901—04), Oulton with Woodlesford (1837—
69), Outwood (1894—1930), Sandal Magna (1837—
1925), Sharlston, Stanley (1894—1930), Stanley cum
Wrenthorpe (1837—94), Shitlington, Thorpe, Wak-
efield, Walton, Warmfield cum Heath
WETHERBY PLU (1861—1930) [W Riding]
Angram, Bardsey cum Rigton, Bickerton, Bilton
(1869—1930), Boston Spa (1896—1930), Bramham
cum Oglethorpe (1869—1930), Clifford (1869—1930),
Clifford with Boston (1869—96), Collingham (1869—
1930), Cowthorpe, Kirk Deighton (1869—1930), North
Deighton, Dunkeswick (1869—1930), Harewood
(1869—1930), Healaugh (1861—64), Hutton
Wandesley (1869—1930), Kearby with Netherby, East
Keswick (1861—1930), Kirkby Overblow (1861—
1930), Linton, Long Marston (1869—1930),
Micklethwaite, Little Ribston, Rigton (1861—1930),
Scarcroft, Shadwell (1869—1912), Sicklinghall,

Yorkshire: Wetherby *continued*

Spofforth with Stockeld, Thorner (1869—1930), Thorp Arch (1869—1930), Tockwith (1869—1930), Walton (1869—1930), Weardley, Weeton (1869—1930), Wetherby, Wighill, Wigton (1869—1930), Wilstrop (1869—1930), Wothersome, Wyke (1869—1930)

WHARFEDALE PLU (1861—1930) [W Riding]
Adel cum Eccup (1869—1928), Alwoodley (1861—1928), Arthington (1869—1930), Askwith, Baildon, Blubberhouses, Bramhope, Burley in Wharfedale, Carlton, Castley, Clifton with Norwood, Denton, Esholt, Farnley, Fewston, Guiseley, Hawksworth, Horsforth, Ilkley, Leathley, Lindley, Menston, Middleton, Nesfield with Langbar, Newall with Clifton, Otley, Pool, Rawdon, Stainburn, Great Timble, Little Timble, Weston (soon after 1861[111]—1930), Yeadon

WHITBY PLU (1837—1930) [N Riding]
Aislaby, Barnby, Borrowby, Egton, Eskdaleside (1837—85), Eskdaleside cum Ugglebarnby (1885—1930), Ellerby, Fylingdales, Glaisdale, Goathland, Hawsker with Stainsacre, Helredale (1894—1925), Hinderwell, Hutton Mulgrave, Lythe, Mickleby, Newholm with Dunsley, Newton Mulgrave, Roxby, Ruswarp (1837—1925), Sneaton, Ugglebarnby (1837—85), Ugthorpe, Whitby

WORTLEY PLU (1838—1930) [W Riding]
Bradfield, Ecclesfield, Hoyland Swaine (1838—49), Hunshelf (1838—49), Ingbirchworth (1838—49), Langsett (1838—49), Oxspring (1838—49), Penistone (1838—49), Stocksbridge (1849—1930), Tankersley, Thurgoland (1838—49), Thurlstone (1838—49), Wortley

YORK PLU (1838—1930) [all 3 Ridings]
Acaster Malbis,[121] Acomb (1837—54), Askham Richard, Beningbrough, Bishopthorpe, Bossall with Buttercrambe, Claxton, Clifton (1837—94), Clifton Within (1894—1900), Clifton Without (1894—1930), Copmanthorpe, Deighton, Dringhouses (1837—94), Dringhouses Within (1894—1900), Dringhouses Without (1894—1930), Dunnington, Earswick, Elvington, Escrick, Flaxton, Gate Fulford (1837—1900), Water Fulford, Grimston, Harton, Haxby, Gate Helmsley, Upper Helmsley, Heslington (1885—1930), Heslington St Lawrence (1837—85), Heslington St Paul (1837—85), Heworth (1837—94), Heworth Within (1894—1900), Heworth Without (1894—1930), Holgate (1837—1900), Holtby, Huntington, Kexby, Langwith, Lillings Ambo, Middlethorpe (1837—94), Middlethorpe Within (1894—1900), Middlethorpe Without (1894—1930), Murton, Naburn, Osbaldwick, Overton, Upper Poppleton (1837—54), Rawcliffe, Sand Hutton, Shipton, Skelton, West Stamford Bridge with Scoreby, Stillingfleet with Moreby, Stockton on the Forest, Strensall, Thorganby with West Cottingwith, Towthorpe, Warthill (1925—30), Warthill Copyhold (soon after 1837[111]—1930), Warthill Freehold (soon after 1837[111]—1930), Wheldrake, Wiggington, York (1900—30), York All Saints North Street (1837—

1900), York All Saints Pavement (1837—1900), York Castle, York Davy Hill (1861—1900), York Minster Hall with Bedern (1837—1900), York Mint Hall (1837—1900), York Holy Trinity Goodramgate (1837—1900); York Holy Trinity, King's Court (1837—1900); York Holy Trinity Micklegate (1837—1900), York St Andrew (1837—1900), York St Crux (1837—1900), York St Cuthbert (1837—1900), York St Dennis (1837—1900), York St George (1837—1900), York St Giles in the Suburbs (1837—1900); York St Helen, Stonegate (1837—1900); York St John Delpike (1837—1900); York St John, Micklegate (1837—1900); York St Lawrence (1837—1900), York St Margaret (1837—1900), York St Martin le Grand (1837—1900), York St Martin Micklegate with St Gregory (1837—1900), York St Mary Bishophill Junior (1837—1900), York St Mary Bishophill Senior (1837—1900); York St Mary, Castlegate (1837—1900); York St Maurice (1837—1900), York St Michael le Belfrey (1837—1900); York St Michael, Spurriergate (1837—1900); York St Nicholas (1837—1900); York St Olave, Marygate (1837—1900); York St Peter le Willows (1837—1900), York St Peter the Little (1837—1900), York St Sampson (1837—1900), York St Saviour (1837—1900), York St Wilfrid (1837—1900)

In Other Poor Law Counties:

BURNLEY PLU (1837—1930) [Lancs, W Riding (1837—95)]
Cliviger[122]

CLITHEROE PLU (1837—1930), [Lancs, W Riding]
Bashall Eaves, Bolton by Bowland, Bowland Forest High, Bowland Forest Low, West Bradford, Easington, Gisburn, Gisburn Forest, Grindleton, Horton, Middop, Great Mitton, Newsholme, Newton, Paythorne, Rimington, Sawley, Slaidbur, Waddington

DARLINGTON PLU (1837—1930) [Durham, N Riding]
Barton, Cleasby, Cliffe, Croft, Dalton upon Tees, Over Dinsdale, Eryholme, Girsby, Manfield, Newton Morrell, Stapleton

STOCKTON PLU (1837—1930) [Durham, N Riding (1837—75)]
West Acklam, Ingleby Barwick, Castle Leavington, Kirk Leavington, Linthorpe, Maltby, Middlesbrough Picton (soon after 1837[111]—1930), Stainton, Thornaby High Worsall, Low Worsall, Yarm

TEESDALE PLU (1837—1930) [Durham, N Riding]
Barforth, Barningham, Boldron, Bowes, Brignall Cotherstone, Egglestone Abbey, Gilmonby, Holwick Hope, Hunderthwaite, Hutton Magna, Lartington, Lunedale, Mickleton, Ovington, Rokeby, Romandkirk Scargill, Startforth, Wycliffe with Thorpe

WORKSOP PLU (1836—1930) [Notts, Derbys, W Riding]
North and South Anston, Dinnington, Firbeck, Gildingwells, Harthill with Woodall, Letwell, St John with Throapham, Thorpe Salvin, Todwick, Wales Wallingwells[123] (1862—1930), Woodsetts

WALES

This section is based upon the 1851 *Census Population Tables*. It has been retyped by Catherine Camfield from the photocopy of these which appeared in the first edition. Sheila Rowlands, who proof-read, comments: 'Revision of this section is a long term matter. Attempts to adapt the lists of places to the English counties' pattern just don't work. However close this list of registration districts and sub-districts is to the PLUs, they still remain RDs *etc*. This section is therefore at an interim stage of revision. Re-typing and correction of some of the major errors should make the whole thing clearer to the user. It is hoped that some further work will be done in co-operation with CROs before the next edition.'

This Guide is intended for those using records generated between 1834 and 1930. Spelling is generally the Anglicized version that will be met by researchers into records of that period, rather than that which is favoured today. Much progress has been made in providing correct Welsh spelling of placenames in recent decades, but to use these late twentieth-century accepted versions when earlier administrators used others would not help the users of this Guide.

ANGLESEY

623 ANGLESEY

LLANGEFNI
Tregayan; Llangwyllog; **Llangefni**; Llangristiolus; Heneglwys; Cerrig-Ceinwen; Tref-draeth; Llangadwaladr or Eglwysael; Aberffraw
BRYNGWRAN
Llangwyfan; Llanfaelog; Llechylched; Ceirchiog; Llanbeulan; Trewalchmai; Bodwrog; Llandrygarn with Gwyndu; Llanllibio; Llantrisaint; Llechcynfarwydd; Rhodogeidio or Ceidio; Llanerchymedd; Gwredog
LLANDYFRYDOG
Llandyfrydog; Coedana; Llanfihangel Tre-'r-Beirdd; Llanfair-Mathafarn-Eithaf; Llanddyfnan; Pentraeth; Llanbedr-Goch; Llaneugrad; Llanallgo; Penrhoslligwy
AMLWCH
Llaneilian; Llanwenllwyfo; **Amlwch**
LLANDDAUSAINT
Rhosbeirio; Bodewryd; Llanbadrig: Cemmaes, Clygyrog; Llanfechell; Llanrhwydrys; Llanfairynghornwy; Llanrhyddlad; Llanfflewyn; Llanbabo; Llanddausaint; Llanfaethly; Llanfwrog; Llanfachreth; Llanfigael
HOLYHEAD
Bodedern; Llanynghenedl; Llanfair-yn-eubwll; Llanfihangel-yn-Howyn; Rhoscolyn; **Holyhead**

In CAERNARVONSHIRE Districts:
620 CAERNARVON: Llangeinwen; St Peter Newborough; Llangaffo; Llanidan; Llanfairynycwmmwd
621 BANGOR: Llanedwen; Llanddaniel-Fab; Llanfihangel Esceifiog; Llanffinan; Penmynydd; Llansadwrn; Llaniestyn; Llanddona; Llanfihangel-Tyn-Sylwy; Penmon; Llangoed; Llanfaes; Beaumaris; Llandegfan; Llandysilio; Llanfair-Pwllgwyngyll

BRECONSHIRE

599 BUILTH

ABERGWESSIN
Llanddewi-Abergwessin; Llanfihangel-Abergwessin; Llangammarch: Treflis, Penbuallt; Llanlleonvel: Gwarafog; Llanafan-fechan or Llanfechan; Llanafan-fawr (part of): Llanfihangel (part of Llanfihangel-Bryn-Pabuan)
COLWYN *(all places in Radnorshire)*
Disserth: Trecoed; Llandrindod; Bettws-Disserth; Llansaintfraed-in-Elvel; Cregrina; Rhulen; Llanbadarn-y-Garreg; Aberedw; Llanvareth
BUILTH
Llanelwedd *(Radnor)*; Builth otherwise Llanfair-in-Buallt; Llanganten; Llysdinam (part of Llanafan-fawr); Rhosferig (part of Llanfihangel-Bryn-Pabuan); Llanynys; Maes-Mynis; Llan-ddewi'r-Cwm; Alltmawr; Llangynog; Gwen-ddwr [all except Trawsgoed]; Crickadarn

600 BRECKNOCK

MERTHYR-CYNOG
Merthyr Cynog: Lower Dyffrin Honddu, Upper Dyffrin Honddu, Yscir-Vawr, Yscir-Vechan; Garthbrengy; Llanfihangel-fechan (part of Llandefailog-fach); Llanfihangel-nant-brane
DEVYNNOCK
Llandilovane; Llywell: Traian-Glas, Traian-Mawr with Trecastle Ward, Ysclydach; Trallong; Devynnock: Glyntawe, Cray, Glynn, Maescar, Senny
BRECKNOCK
Llanspyddid: Modrydd, Pen-Pont; Aberyscir; Battle; Llandefailog-fach (part of); Llanthew; **Brecknock** - St John the Evangelist: Upper Division with Venny-Vach, Lower Division or St Mary, Military in the Barracks; Christ's College; Castle Inn; St David or Llanfaes; Cantreff: Nantddu

Breconshire: Brecknock *continued*

PENKELLY
Llanvrynach; Llanvigan: Glynn Collwn, Penkelly;
Llanthetty: Dyffrin, Vro
LLANGORSE
Llansaintfraed; Llanhamlach; Llanywern;
Talachddu; Trawsgoed (part of Gwen-ddwr);
Llandefally; Llanvillo; Llandefailog-Tre-Graig;
Llanfihangel-Tal-y-llyn; Llangorse; Llangasty-Tal-
y-llyn; Cathedine

601 CRICKHOWELL
CWMDU
Llanfihangel Cwmdu: Blayney, Cenol, Cilwych,
Tretower
LLANGUNIDER
Llangunider: Blainey with Duffryn, Vro
LLANGATTOCK
Llangattock: Penallt, Prisk and Killey
LLANELLY
Llanelly
CRICKHOWELL
Crickhowell; Llangenny; Llanbedr; Partrishow;
Talgarth (part of): Grwyne-fawr, Grwyne-fechan

602 HAY
TALGARTH
Talgarth (part of): Talgarth Borough, Forest, Pwll-
y-wrach, Trefecca; Llanelieu; Bronllys; Llyswen;
Aberllunvey; Glasbury (part of): Tregoyd and
Velindre, Pipton
CLYRO
Glasbury (part of; part in *Radnor*; part formerly in
Radnor); Boughrood *(Radnor)*; Llanstephan
(Radnor); Llandilo-Graban *(Radnor)*; Llanbedr-
Painscastle *(Radnor)*; Llandewyfach *(Radnor)*;
Bryngwyn *(Radnor)*; Clyro *(Radnor)*; Clyro;
Bettws-Clyro; Llowes *(Radnor)*
HAY
Llanigon: Glynfach; **Hay**; Cusop *(Herefs.)*;
Dorstone *(Herefs.)*; Bredwardine *(Herefs.)*; Clifford
(Herefs.); Whitney *(Herefs.)*

In GLAMORGANSHIRE Districts:
582 MERTHYR TYDFIL: Vainor; Penderyn
584 NEATH: Ystradvelltey; Ystradgunlais
In CARMARTHENSHIRE Districts:
587 LLANDOVERY: Llandulas-in-Tyr Abbot;
Llanwrtyd
In RADNORSHIRE Districts:
605 RHAYADER: Llanwrthwl
602 HAY: Glasbury (part of *Radnor*)

CAERNARVONSHIRE
619 PWLLHELI
CRICCIETH
Criccieth; Llanystymdwy; Abererch; Llanarmon;
Llangybi; Llanaelhaiarn; Carngiwch
PWLLHELI
Llannor; Denio: **Pwllheli;** Penrhos; Llanfihangel-
Bachellaeth; Llanbedrog; Llangian; Llanengan;
Llandegwning
ABERDARON
Rhiw; Llanfaelrhys; Aberdaron; Bardsey Isle;
Bryncroes; Bodferin; Llangwnadle; Penllech;
Meyllteyrn; Bottwnog
NEVIN
Llaniestyn; Tudweiliog; Edeyrn; Llandudwen;
Bodvean; Ceidio; **Nevin;** Pistyll

620 CAERNARVON
LLANDWROG
Clynnog; Llanllyfni; Llandwrog; Llanwnda
LLANRUG
Bettws Garmon; Llanberis; Llanrug;
Llanddeiniolen; Llanfair-is-Gaer
CARNARVON
Llanbeblig: **Carnarvon;** Llanfaglan
LLANIDAN *(all places in Anglesey)*
Llangeinwen; St Peter Newborough; Llangaffo;
Llanidan; Llanfairynycwmmwd

621 BANGOR
BEAUMARIS *(all places in Anglesey)*
Llanedwen; Llanddaniel-Fab; Llanfihangel-
Esceifiog; Llanffinan; Penmynydd; Llansadwrn;
Llaniestyn; Llanddona; Llanfihangel Tyn Sylwy;
Pemnon; Llangoed; Llanfaes; **Beaumaris;**
Llandegfan; Llandysilio; Llanfair-Pwllgwyngyll
BANGOR
Bangor; Llandegai
LLANLLECHID
Llanllechid; Aber; Llanfair-fechan

622 CONWAY
CONWAY
Dwygyfylchi; **Conway;** Gyffin
CREUDDYN
Eglwys-Rhos; Llandudno; Llandrillo-yn-Rhos
(Denbigh): Eirias; Llangwstennin; Llysfaen;
Llanelian *(Denbigh)*; Llansantffraid-Glan-Conway
(Denbigh)
LLECHWEDD-ISAF
Llangelynin; Caerhun; Llanbedr-y-Cennin:
Dolgarrog

Caernarvonshire *continued*

In DENBIGHSHIRE Districts:
614: LLANRWST: Maenan; The Abbey; Gwydir;
Trefriw; Llanrhychwyn; Bettws-y-coed; Dol-
wyddelan; Penmachno; Eidda
In MERIONETHSHIRE Districts:
618: FESTINIOG: Beddgelert (part of);
Llanfihangel-y-Pennant; Dolben-maen; Penmorfa;
Ynys-cynhaiarn; Tref-llys

CARDIGANSHIRE

593 CARDIGAN
NEWPORT *(all places in Pembrokeshire)*
Llanychlwydog; Dinas; Newport; Nevern; Bayvil;
Meline; Eglwyswrw; Whitechurch; Llanfair-Nant-
Gwyn
CARDIGAN
Llantood *(Pembroke)*; Bridell *(Pembroke)*;
Cilgerran *(Pembroke)*; Monington *(Pembroke)*;
Moylgrove *(Pembroke)*; St Dogmells *(Pembroke)*;
Cardigan: St Mary, Military in Barracks;
Llangoedmore; Verwick; Mount
LLANDYGWIDD
Aberporth; Blaenporth; Tremain; Llechryd;
Llandygwidd; Manerdivy *(Pembroke)*;
Llanfihangel-Penbedw *(Pembroke)*

594 NEWCASTLE-IN-EMLYN
CENARTH
Chapel Colman *(Pembroke)*; Penrhydd *(Pembroke)*,
Castellan *(Pembroke)*; Llanfyrnach *(Pembroke)*;
Kilrhedin (part in *Pembroke*; part in *Carmarthen*);
Clydey *(Pembroke)*; Cenarth including the town of
Newcastle *(Carmarthen)*; Penboyr *(Carmarthen)*;
Llangeler *(Carmarthen)*
PENBRYN
Llanfair-Tref-Helygen; Llandyfriog; Brongwyn;
Troedyraur; Bettws-Evan; Penbryn; Llangranog
LLANDYSSIL
Llangunllo; Henllan; Llanfair-Orllwyn; Bangor;
Llandyssil; Llanfihangel-ar-arth *(Carmarthen)*

595 LAMPETER
LLANYBYTHER *(all in Carmarthenshire)*
Llanllwni; Llanfihangel-Rhos-y-Corn; Llanybyther
PENCARREG
Pencarreg *(Carmarthen)*; Llanycrwys: Fforest
(Carmarthen), Mynachty *(Carmarthen)*; Cellan;
Llanfair-clydogau
LAMPETER
Bettws-Bledrws; Llangybi; Trefilan; Silian;
Lampeter-Pont-Stephen: **Lampeter**, Tref-y-coed
LLANWENOG
Llanwenog; Llanwnen

Cardiganshire *continued*

596 ABERAYRON
LLANDISILIO
Dihewid; Llanarth; Llandisilio-Gogo;
Llanllwchaiarn; Llanina
LLANSAINTFFRAID
Llanfihangel-Ystrad; Cilcennin; Cilie-Aeron;
Llanerch-ayron; Henfynyw; Llanddewi-Aberarth;
Llanbadarn-Tref-Eglwys; Llansaintffraid

597 ABERYSTWITH
LLANRHYSTYD
Llanrhystyd: Haminiog, Mefenydd; Llanddeinol;
Llangrwyddon or Llanygwyryfon; Llanilar; Rhostie
ABERYSTWITH
Llanychaiarn; Llanbadarn-Fawr (part of):
Aberystwith, Ucha-yn-dre, Issa-yn-dre, Vainor,
Broncastellan, Clarach, Lower Llanbadarn-y-
Croyddin
GENEUR-GLYNN
Elerch (part of Llanbadarn-Fawr); Llanfihangel-
Geneur-Glyn (part of): Henllys, Cynnill-Mawr,
Ceulan-y-Maes-Mawr, Cyfoeth-y-Brenin, Tyr-y-
Mynach; Llancynfelin
RHEIDOL
Llanbadarn-Fawr (part of): Upper Llanbadarn-y-
Croyddin, Cwmrheidol, Melindwr, Parcel Canol,
Trefeirig; Llanafan; Llanfihangel-y-Croyddin:
Lower Llanfihangel-y-Croyddin, Upper
Llanfihangel-y-Croyddin or Eglwys Newydd

598 TREGARON
GWNNWS
Llanfihangel Lledrod: Lledrod; Gwnnws; Yspytty-
Ystwyth; Yspytty-Ystrad-Meiric
LLANGEITHO
Llanbadarn-Odwyn; Llangeitho; Nantecwnlle;
Llanddewi-brefi (part of): Gartheli, Gwynfil,
Blaenpenal; Bettws-Leiki
TREGARON
Llanddewi-brefi (part of): Llanio, Gogoyan, Garth
and Ystrad, Prisk and Carfan, Gorwydd, Dothie-
Camddwr, Dothie-Piscottwr; Caron-ys-Clawdd:
Argoed and Ystrad, Tref-Lynn, Blaen-Caron, Croes
and Berwyn, Tre-Cefel, Blaen-Aeron, Caron-Uwch-
Clawdd or Strata Florida

In MONTGOMERYSHIRE Districts:
606 MACHYNLLETH:
Llanfihangel-Geneur-Glyn (part of); Scybor-y-Coed

65

CARMARTHENSHIRE

586 LLANELLY
LOUGHOR
Loughor *(Glamorgan)*; Llangennech; Berwick (part of Llanelly)
LLANELLY
Llanelly (part of); **Llanelly** Borough; Hengoed; Westfa
PEMBREY
Pembrey; **Kidwelly**: St Mary Within, St Mary Without
LLANNON
Glyn (part of Llanelly); Llannon; Llanedy

587 LLANDOVERY
LLANDDAUSAINT
Llanddausaint
LLANGADOCK
Llangadock: Above Sawthe, Dyffrun Cidrich, Gwynfe Quarter-Bach
LLANSADWRN
Llansadwrn; Llanwrda
MYDDFAI
Myddfai
LLANDINGAT
Llandingat: **Llandovery**, Telych, Forest, Ystrad
LLANFAIR-AR-Y-BRYN
Llanfair-ar-y-bryn: Rhandir-Isaf, Rhandir-Canol, Rhandir-Uchaf, Rhandir-Abbot
LLANWRTYD
Llandulas in Tyr Abbot *(Brecon)*; Llanwrtyd *(Brecon)*: Clawdd-madog, Llechweddor
CILYCWM
Cilycwm
CONWIL-CAYO
Conwil-Cayo

588 LLANDILOFAWR
TALLEY
Llansawel; Talley
LLANFYNYDD
Brechfa; Llanfynydd; Llanfihangel-Cilfargen
LLANGATHEN
Llanegwad; Llangathen
LLANDILO
Llandyfeisant; Llandilofawr (including **Llandilo Town**) (part of)
LLANDEBIE
Llandilofawr (part of); Llanfihangel-Aberbythych; Llandebie; Bettws

589 CARMARTHEN
LLANGENDEIRNE
Llanddarog; Llanarthney; Llangunnor; Llangendeirne; Llandefeilog; St Ishmaels
ST CLEARS
Llanstephan; Laugharne; Laugharne with Laugharne township; Llansadurnen; Llandawke; Llandowror; Llanginning; St Clears; Llanfihangel-abercowin; Llandilo-abercowin; Llangunnock
CARMARTHEN
Llangain; **Carmarthen**: St Peter, Military in Barracks, Castle Green; Abergwili
CONWIL
Llanllawddog; Llanpumpsaint; Newchurch; Merthyr; Abernant; Conwil-in-Elfet; Treleach-ar-Bettws; Mydrim; Llanwinio

In PEMBROKESHIRE Districts:
590 NARBERTH: Llanboidy; Henllan-Amgoed; Llanglydwen;Cilymaenllwyd (part of); Llanfallteg (part of); Llandissilio (part of); Egremont; Llangan (part of); Cyffic; Eglwys-cymmin; Pendine; Marros
In CARDIGANSHIRE Districts:
594 NEWCASTLE-IN-EMLYN: Cilrhedin (part of); Cenarth; Penboyr; Llangeler; Llanfihangel-Ar-Arth
595 LAMPETER: Llanllwni; Llanfihangel-Rhos-y-Corn; Llanybyther; Pencarreg; Llanycrwys

DENBIGHSHIRE

611 WREXHAM
HOPE
Tryddyn *(Flint)* (part of Mold); Hope *(Flint)*; Gresford (part of): Merford and Hoseley *(Flint)*, Llay, Burton, Allington, Gresford, Gwersyllt; Brymbo (part of Wrexham)
MALPAS
Shocklach *(Chester)* (part of): Church Shocklach, Oviatt Shocklach; Malpas *(Chester)* (part of): Overton, Chorlton, Malpas, Newton-juxta-Malpas, Bradley, Chidlow, Agden, Wigland, Stockton, Wichaugh, Oldcastle, Cuddington; Worthenbury *(Flint)*; Threapwood (part in *Flint*; part in *Chester*); Bangor: Eyton, Royton, Pickhill, Sesswick, Bangor *(Flint)*; Holt: Dutton Diffeth, Dutton Cacca, Dutton-y-Bran, **Holt**, Ridley, Sutton; Marchwiel: Sontley
RUABON
Erbistock (part in *Flint*; part in *Denbigh*); Ruabon
WREXHAM
Gresford (part of): Erthig, Borras-Riffre, Erlas; Wrexham (part of): **Wrexham** Regis, **Wrexham** Abbott, Esclusham Below, Bersham, Esclusham Above, Minera, Broughton, Stansty, Acton, Borras-Hovah, Gourton, Bieston, Abenbury-Fawr, Abenbury-Fechan *(Flint)*

Denbighshire *continued*

612 RUTHIN

LLANARMON
Llandegla; Llanarmon; Llanferras
RUTHIN
Llanbedr-Dyffryn-Clwyd; Llanychan; Llanfwrog;
Ruthin; Llanrhydd; Efenechtyd
LLANELIDAN
Llanfair-Dyffryn-Clwyd; Llanelidan; Derwen
GYFFYLLIOG
Clocaenog: Isa, Ucha; Gyffylliog; Nantglyn
LLANRHAIADR
Llanrhaiadr-in-Kinmerch; Llanynys
LLANDYRNOG
Llanganhafal; Llandyrnog; Llangwyfan;
Aberwheeler (part of Bodfari)

613 ST ASAPH

ST ASAPH
Bodfari (part of) *(Flint)*; Tremeirchion *(Flint)*;
Cwm *(Flint)*; Dyserth *(Flint)*; Meliden *(Flint)*;
Rhuddlan *(Flint)*; St Asaph: **St Asaph** *(Flint)*,
Meriadog, Wygfair
ABERGELE
St George; Abergele; Llanddulas; Bettws-yn-Rhos
or Bettws-Abergele; Llanfair-Talhaiarn
DENBIGH
Llannefydd; Henllan; Denbigh; Llansannan

614 LLANRWST

LLANRWST
Gwytherin; Llangerniew; Eglwys-fach: Maenan
(Caernarvon); The Abbey *(Caernarvon)*;
Llanddoget; Llanrwst (all except Gwydir)
BETTWS-Y-COED *(all in Caernarvonshire)*
Gwydir (part of Llanrwst); Trefriw; Llanrhychwyn;
Bettws-y-coed; Dol-wyddelan
YSPYTTY
Penmachno *(Caerns.)*; Yspytty: Eidda *(Caerns.)*,
Tir-Ifan, Trebrys; Pentrevoelas; Gwern-Howel

In SHROPSHIRE Districts:
361 OSWESTRY: Llansillin (part of); Chirk
In MONTGOMERYSHIRE Districts:
309 MACHYNLLETH: Carreghova (in
Denbighshire to Oct 1844); Llangedwyn;
Llancadwalladr; Llanarmon-Mynydd-Mawr;
Llanrhaiadr-yn-Mochnant (part of)
In FLINTSHIRE Districts:
10 HOLYWELL: Penbedw
In MERIONETHSHIRE Districts:
15 CORWEN: Cerrig-y-Druidion; Llanfihangel-
Glyn-Myfyr (part of); Llangwm; Bryn-Eglwys;
Llantysilio; Llangollen; Llanarmon-Dyffryn-
Ceiriog; Llansaintffraid-Glan-Ceiriog

In CAERNARVONSHIRE Districts:
622 CONWAY: Llandrillio-yn-Rhos; Llanelian;
Llansaintffraid-Glan-Conway

***DENBIGHSHIRE** prior to the Act of 7 and 8 Vict,
c 61* Severed from *Denbighshire* by the above
Statute:
609 LLANFYLLIN: Carreghova (annexed to
Montgomery)

FLINTSHIRE

610 HOLYWELL

WHITFORD
Gwaenysgor; Newmarket; Llanasa; Whitford;
Caerwys
HOLYWELL
Holywell; Ysceifiog; Nannerch: Penbedw *(Denbigh)*
FLINT
Halkin; **Flint**; Caer-fallwch; Northop: Golftyn,
Wepre, Leadbrook Major, Kelsterton, Leadbrook
Minor, Soughton
MOLD
Cilcen: Cefyn, Llan or Tre-Llan, Llysdan-hunedd,
Llys-y-coed, Maes-y-groes, Mechlas, Trellynian;
Mold (part of): Arddynwent, Argoed, Bistree,
Broncoed, Gwernafield, Gwsaney, Hartsheath,
Hendrebiffa, Leeswood, Llwynegrin, Mold, Nerquis

In SHROPSHIRE Districts:
362 ELLESMERE: Overton; Penley; Iscoyd;
Hanmer
In CHESHIRE Districts:
459 GREAT BOUGHTON: Higher Kinnerton (in
Doddleston); Hawarden
In DENBIGHSHIRE Districts:
611 WREXHAM: Tryddyn; Hope; Merford and
Hoseley; Worthenbury; Treapwood (part of);
Bangor; Erbistock (part of); Abenbury-Fechan
613 ST. ASAPH: Bodfari (part of); Tremeirchion;
Cwm; Dyserth; Meliden; Rhuddlan; St Asaph (part of)

GLAMORGAN

581 CARDIFF

CAERPHILLY
Eglwysilan: Energlyn, Park, Hendredenny,
Glyntaff, Rhydyboithan; Ruddry; Van (part of
Bedwas); Lisvane; Llanedarn; Llanishen;
Whitchurch
CARDIFF
St Mellons *(Monmouth)*; Rumney *(Monmouth)*;
Roath: Military in Barracks; **Cardiff** St John and
St Mary; Llandaff; Radyr; St Fagan; Cairau;
Leckwith; Michaelstone-le-Pit; Llandough-juxta-
Penarth; Penarth; Cogan; Lavernock

Glamorgan: Cardiff *continued*

ST NICHOLAS
Sully; Cadoxton-juxta-Barry; Merthyr Dovan;
Highlight; Barry; Porthkerry; Penmark; Llancarvan;
Llantrithyd; Welsh St Donats; Bonvilston;
Llanvithin; St Nicholas; St Lythans; Wenvoe;
St Andrew; Michaelston-super-Ely; St George
LLANTRISAINT
St Bride-super-Ely; Peterstone-super-Ely;
Pendoylan; Llanillterne; Pentyrch; **Llantrisaint;**
Llantwit Vairdre

582 MERTHYR TYDFIL
GELLIGAER
Llanwonno; Llanfabon; Gelligaer: Brithdir,
Ysgwyddgwyn, Garth-gynyd; Cefn, Hengoed
LOWER MERTHYR TYDFIL
Merthyr Tydfil (part of)
UPPER MERTHYR TYDFIL
Merthyr Tydfil (part of); Vainor *(Brecon)*
ABERDARE
Penderyn *(Brecon)*; Aberdare; Ystradyfodwg:
Rhigos, Middle, Home, Clydach

583 BRIDGEND
MAESTEG
Llangynwyd (part of): Middle Llangynwyd, Lower
Llangynwyd, Cwmdu; Bettws; Llangeinor;
Llandyfodog; Llanharan; Llanilid; Coychurch:
Higher Coychurch, Pencoed, Lower Coychurch,
Peterstone; St Brides Minor: Ynysawdre
COWBRIDGE
Llangan or Llanganua; St Mary Hill; Llanharry;
Ystradowen; Llansannor; Penlline; **Cowbridge;**
St Hilary; St Mary Church; Flemingston; Eglwys-
Brewis; St Athan; Gileston; Llanmaes; Llantwit
Major; Llandow; St Donats; Marcross; Monknash;
Llanmihangel; Llandough; Llanblethian;
Llysworney; Nash; Stembridge; Colwinstone
BRIDGEND
St Andrew Minor; Wick; St Brides Major: St
Brides, Lampha, Southerndown; Ewenny; Coyty:
Higher Coyty, Lower Coyty; Newcastle: Higher
Newcastle, Lower Newcastle; Laleston: Higher
Laleston, Lower Laleston; Merthyr Mawr;
Tythegston; Newton; Nottage; Pyle; **Kenfig**

584 NEATH
MARGAM
Margam; Higher Llangynwyd (part of
Llangynwyd); Aberavon; Michaelstone-super-
Avon: Michaelstone; Baglan; Briton Ferry; **Neath;**
Llantwit-juxta-Neath: Resolven, Clyne, Lower
Llantwit

Glamorgan: Neath *continued*

YSTRADVELLTE
Cadoxton (part of): Lower Neath, Middle Neath,
Upper Neath; Glyn-corrwg: Blaengwrach;
Ystradvellte *(Brecon)*
YSTRADGUNLAIS
Ystradgunlais *(Brecon)*; Llanguick
CADOXTON
Cadoxton (part of): Blaenhonddau, Dyffryn-
Clydach, Coedfrank, Ynis-y-mond, Upper Dylais,
Lower Dylais; Cillybebill
LLANSAMLET
Llansamlet

585 SWANSEA
LLANDILO-TALYBONT
Llangyfelach (part of): Rhyndwy-Clydach, Mawr,
Penderry; Llandilo-Talybont
LLANGYFELACH
Clase (part of Llangyfelach); Llanrhidian Higher
(part of Llanrhidian); St John near Swansea;
Swansea (part of): Swansea Higher, **Swansea,**
Military in Barracks, Swansea Lower, St Thomas
GOWER
Oystermouth; Bishopston; Pennard; Ilston;
Penmaen; Nicholaston; Penrice; Oxwich; Port-
Eynon; Knelston; Reynoldston; Llandewy; Rhosilli;
Llangennith; Llanmadock; Cheriton; Llanrhidian
Lower (part of Llanrhidian)

In MONMOUTHSHIRE Districts:
580 NEWPORT: Michaelstone-y-Vedw (part of); viz
Llanvedw; Machen (part of); viz Rhydgwern
In CARMARTHENSHIRE Districts:
586 LLANELLY: Loughor

MERIONETH

615 CORWEN
GWYDDELWERN
Cerrig-y-Druidion *(Denbigh)*; Llanfihangel-Glyn-
Myfyr *(Denbigh)*; Cefnpost; Llangwm *(Denbigh)*;
Bettws-Gwerfil-Goch; Bottegir-bach;
Gwyddelwern; Llangar; Llandrillo
CORWEN
Corwen; Llansaintffraid-Glyn-Dyfrdwy; Bryn-
Eglwys *(Denbigh)*; Llantysilio (Denbigh);
Llangollen *(Denbigh)*: Glyn-Traian, Llangollen
Traian; Llansaintffraid-Glyn-Ceiriog *(Denbigh)*;
Llanarmon-Dyffryn-Ceiriog *(Denbigh)*

616 BALA
BALA
Llandderfel; Llanfor; Llanycil; Llanuwchyllyn;
Llangower

68

Merioneth *continued*

617 **DOLGELLY**

TALYLLYN

Llanymawddwy; Mallwyd: Caereinion-fechan *(Montgomery)*; Talyllyn; Llanfihangel-y-Pennant; Llanegryn; Llangelynin

BARMOUTH

Dolgelly; Llanfachreth; Llanelltyd; Llanaber (including Barmouth); Llanddwywe: Is-Graig, Uwch-Graig; Llanenddwyn

618 **FESTINIOG**

LLANFIHANGEL-Y-TRAETHAU

Llanbedr; Llanfair-juxta-Harlech; Llandanwg; Llanfihangel-y-Traethau; Llandecwyn

FESTINIOG

Trawsfynydd; Festiniog; Maentwrog; Llanfrothen

TREMADOC

Beddgelert *(Caernarvon)*: Nantmor; Llanfihangel-y-Pennant *(Caernarvon)*; Dolben-maen *(Caernarvon)*; Penmorfa *(Caernarvon)*; Ynys-cynhaiarn *(Caernarvon)*; Tref-llys *(Caernarvon)*

In MONTGOMERYSHIRE Districts:
606 MACHYNLLETH: Pennal; Towyn

MONMOUTHSHIRE

576 **CHEPSTOW**

SHIRE-NEWTON

Portskewett; Caldicott; Ifton; Roggiett; Llanvihangel near Roggiett; Undy; St Bride Netherwent (all except Llandevenny); Caerwent: Crick; Llanvair Discoed: Dinham; Shire-Newton; Itton: Howick; Newchurch; Kilgwrrwg; Wolves-Newton; Llangwm; Llansoy; Llanvihangel-Tor-y-Mynydd

CHEPSTOW

Trelleck Grange (part of Trelleck); Little Tintern; Chapel Hill; Penterry; St Arvans; **Chepstow**; Mounton; Matherne; St Pierre and Runstone; Tidenham *(Glos.)*

LYDNEY *(all in Gloucestershire)*

Woollaston; Alvington; Lydney: Aylburton; Hewelsfield; St Briavels

577 **MONMOUTH**

COLEFORD

Newland (part of) *(Glos.)*: Bream, Clearwell, Newland, Coleford; West Dean *(Glos.)*: Worcester Walk, York or Park-End Walk, Denby Walk (part of), Speech House Walk (part of); Staunton *(Glos.)*; English Bicknor *(Glos.)*

Monmouthshire: Monmouth *continued*

DINGESTOW

Welsh-Bicknor *(Herefs.* formerly in *Monmouth)*; Whitchurch *(Herefs.)*; Ganarew *(Herefs.)*; Welsh Newton *(Herefs.)*; Llanrothall *(Herefs.)*; Garway *(Herefs.)*; Skenfrith; St Maughans; Llangattock-Vibon-Avel; Llanvihangel-ystern-Llewern; Llantillio-Crossenny; Penrose; Tregare; Dingestow; Grace Dieu Park; Rockfield

MONMOUTH

Dixton Newton; **Monmouth**

TRELLECK

Wonastow; Mitchel-Troy; Penalt; Llandogo; Trelleck (all except Trelleck Grange); Llanishen; Llangoven; Cwmcarvan; Pen-y-Clawdd; Ragland; Llandenny

578 **ABERGAVENNY**

LLANARTH

Bettws-Newydd; Bryngwyn; Llanarth: Clytha; Llanvair-Kilgidin; Llanvihangel-nigh-Usk; Llansaintfraed; Llanthewy-Rhytherch

LLANVIHANGEL

Llanvapley; Llanthewy Skirrid; Llanvetherine; Llangattock Llingoed; Llanvihangel Crucorney: Penbiddle; Cwmyoy: Fwthog *(Herefs.)*, Bwlch Trewyn (formerly in *Herefs.)*; Oldcastle

ABERGAVENNY

Llantillio Pertholey; **Abergavenny:** Lloyndu, Hardwicke; Llangattock-nigh-Usk; Llanover Lower (part of Llanover); Llanellen; Llanwenarth (part of Llanwenarth); Llanfoist (part of)

BLAENAVON

Llanfoist (part of); Llanwenarth (part of Llanwenarth); Llanover Upper (part of Llanover)

ABERYSTRUTH

Aberystruth

TREDEGAR

Bedwelty (part of): Manmoel, Ushlawrcoed

ROCK BEDWELTY

Bedwelty (part of): Ishlawrcoed

579 **PONTYPOOL**

PONTYPOOL

Llanhilleth; Trevethin with **Pontypool**; Mamhilad; Llanvihangel-Pont-y-Moile; Panteague

LLANGIBBY

Llanvrechva; Llanthewy-Vach; Llandegveth; Llangibby; Usk (part of); Glascoed

USK

Usk (part of): **Usk,** Gwehellog; Llanbaddock; Monkswood; Goytrey; Kemeys Commander; Trostrey; Gwernesney; Llangeview; Llanllowell; Llantrissent

Monmouthshire *continued*

580 NEWPORT

CAERLEON
Llanvaches; Penhow; Llanmartin with Llandevaud;
Llanwern; Bishton; Wilcrick; Llandevenny (part of
St Bride Netherwent); Magor: Redwick; Witson or
Whitson; Goldcliff; Nash; Christchurch: Caerleon-
ultra-Pontem; Llangstone; Kemeys Inferior;
Tredunnock; Llanhennock; Llangattock: **Caerleon**
NEWPORT
St Woollos: **Newport**, Military in Barracks
ST WOOLLOS
St Bride Wentllooge; Peterstone; Marshfield;
Coedkernew; Bassaleg: Duffryn, Graig, Rogerstone;
Michaelstone-y-vedw, Llanvedw *(Glamorgan)*;
Risca; Henllis; Bettws; Malpas; Llanvihangel
Llantarnam
MYNYDDYSLWYN
Mynyddyslwyn: Clawrplwyf, Mynyddmaen,
Penmain; Bedwas (part of): Lower Bedwas, Upper
Bedwas; Machen: Lower Machen, Upper Machen,
Rhydgwern *(Glamorgan)*

In HEREFORDSHIRE Districts:
348 DORE: Grosmont; Llangua
In GLAMORGANSHIRE Districts:
581 CARDIFF: St Mellons; Rumney

MONTGOMERYSHIRE

606 MACHYNLLETH

MACHYNLLETH
Scybor-y-Coed *(Cardigan)* (part of Llanfihangel-
Geneur-Glyn); **Machynlleth:** Isygarreg,
Uchygarreg; Penegos
PENNAL
Pennal *(Merioneth)*; Towyn *(Merioneth)*; Llanwrin
DAROWEN
Cemmes: Brynuchel with Tafolog, Gwernybwlch;
Darowen: Caerseddfan, Noddfa; Llanbrynmair

607 NEWTOWN

UPPER LLANIDLOES
Llangirrig; **Llanidloes** (part of Llanidloes)
LOWER LLANIDLOES
Llanidloes (part of Llanidloes); Tref-Eglwys
LLANWNOG
Carno; Llanwnog; Llandinam; Penstrowed;
Aberhafesp
KERRY
Mochdre; Kerry
NEWTOWN
Newtown; Llanllwchaiarn

Montgomeryshire: Newtown *continued*

TREGYNON
Bettws; Tregynon; Llanwyddelan; Llanllugan;
Manafon

608 MONTGOMERY

MONTGOMERY
Berriew; **Montgomery**; Llandysil; Llanmerewig;
Castlewright (part of Mainstone); Aston (part of
Lydham); Churchstoke (part *Montgomery*; part
Salop)
CHIRBURY
Chirbury *(Salop)*; Worthin (part of): Worthin
(Salop), Rhosgoch, Trelystan; Forden
(WELSH)POOL
Leighton (part of Worthin); Buttington:
Cletterwood, Hope, Trewern; Alberbury (part of):
Middleton, Uppington; Guilsfield; Pool or
Welshpool: Cyfronydd, **Pool**; Castle Caereinion

609 LLANFYLLIN

LLANFAIR
Llangyniew; Llanfair-Caereinon; Llanerful;
Llangadfan; Garthbeibio; Llanfihangel
LLANSAINTFFRAID
Meifod; **Llanfyllin**; Llanfechan; Llansaintffraid:
Collfryn, Llanerchila, Tredderwenfawr, Trewylan;
Cefnlenyd; Llandrinio; Llandysilio; Carreghova
(formerly *Denbigh*) (part of Llan-y-Mynech)
LLANRHAIADR
Llangedwyn *(Denbigh)*; Llancadwalladr *(Denbigh)*
Llanarmon-Mynydd-Mawr *(Denbigh)*; Llanrhaiadr
yn-Mochnant *(Denbigh; Montgomery)*; Hirnant;
Llanwddyn; Pennant; Llangynog

In SHROPSHIRE Districts:
Snead; Hyssington (part of); Alberbury (part of)
In MERIONETHSHIRE Districts:
617 DOLGELLY: Caereinion-fechan

MONTGOMERYSHIRE prior to the Act of 7 and
Vict. c. 61. Annexed to Montgomeryshire by the
above Statute; viz -
609 LLANFYLLIN: Carreghova (part of *Denbigh*
Oct 1844)

PEMBROKESHIRE

590 NARBERTH

LLANBOIDY
Llanboidy *(Carmarthen)*; Eglwys Fair a Churig
(Carmarthen) (part of Henllan-Amgoed);
Llanglydwen *(Carmarthen)*; Cilymaenllwyd
(Carmarthen) (part of); Llanfallteg *(Carmarthen*
Pembroke); Monachlogddu

Pembrokeshire: Narberth *continued*

LLANDISSILO
Llangolman; Llandilo; Maenclochog: Maenclochog
with Vorlan; New-Moat; Llys-y-fran; Clarbeston;
Bletherston; Llanycefn; Llandissilio *(Pembroke;*
Carmarthen); Egremont *(Carmarthen)*; Grondre
(part of Cilymaenllwyd)
AMROTH
Henllan-Amgoed *(Carmarthen)* (part of); Llangan:
Llangan *(Carmarthen)*, Llangan *(Pembroke)*; Cyffic
(Carmarthen); Eglwys-cymmin *(Carmarthen)*;
Pendine *(Carmarthen)*; Marros *(Carmarthen)*;
Amroth; Crunwear; Ludchurch
NARBERTH
Crinow; Lampeter-Velfrey; Llandewy Velfrey:
Henllan; Castle Dyrran *(Carmarthen)* (part of
Cilymaenllwyd); **Narberth** North (part of Narberth)
SLEBECH
Narberth South (part of Narberth); Robeston
Wathen; Llawhaden; North Newton; Slebech;
Mounton; Minwere; Martletwy; Coedcanlas
BEGELLY
Yerbeston; Loveston; Reynoldston; Jeffreston;
Begelly: Williamston; St Issells

591 PEMBROKE
TENBY
Redberth; Gumfreston; **Tenby**: St Mary Out-
Liberty, St Mary In-Liberty; Caldy Island; St
Margaret's Island; Penally; Manorbier; Hodgeston;
Lamphey; St Florence; Carew; Lawrenny; Nash:
Upton; Cosheston; **Pembroke** St Michael
PEMBROKE
St Mary; Military in Barracks, Monkton Within,
Monkton Without; St Petrox; Stackpole Elidor;
Bosherston; St Twinells; Warren; Castlemartin;
Angle; Rhoscrowther; Pwllcrochan
ROOSE
Burton; Rosemarket; Llanstadwell

592 HAVERFORDWEST
MILFORD
Steynton (including **Milford**); Hubberston;
Herbrandston; St Ishmaels; Dale; Marloes; St
Bridcs; Hasguard; Talbenny; West Walton;
Walwins Castle; West Robeston; Johnston;
Llangwm; Freystrop
HAVERFORDWEST
Haroldston St Issells; **Haverfordwest**: St Thomas,
St Thomas, Furzy Park and Portfield, St Mary,
St Martin; Prendergast; Uzmaston; Boulston;
Wiston; Rudbaxton; Camrose; Lambston; West
Haroldston; Nolton; Roch; Treffgarne

Haverfordwest *continued*

ST DAVIDS
St Lawrence; Hayscastle; St Edrens; Llanreithan;
Llandeloy; Brawdy; St Elvis; Whitchurch; St
Davids: Cylch-Bychan, Cylch-Gwylod y-Wlad,
Cylch-Mawr, Cylch-y-Dre, Ramsey; Cathedral
Close; Llanhowell; Llanrian; Mathry; Granston
FISHGUARD
St Nicholas; Manorowen; Llanwnda; **Fishguard**;
Llanllawer; Llanychaer; Llanstinan; Jordanston;
Llanfair-Nant-y-Gof; Letterston; Little Newcastle;
St Dogwells; Ambleston; Spittal; East Walton;
Henry's Moat; Castlebythe; Puncheston; Morvil;
Pontfaen

In CARDIGANSHIRE Districts:
593 CARDIGAN: Llanychlwydog; Dinas; Newport;
Nevern; Bayvil; Meline; Eglwyswrw; Whitechurch;
Llanfair-Nant-Gwyn; Llantood; Bridell; Kilgerran;
Monington; Moylgrove; St Dogmells; Manerdivy;
Llanfihangel-Penbedw
594 NEWCASTLE-IN-EMLYN: Chapel Colman;
Penrhydd; Llanfyrnach; Cilrhedin (part of); Clydey

RADNORSHIRE
603 PRESTEIGNE
BRILLEY
Winforton *(Herefs.)*; Willersley *(Herefs.)*; Eardisley
(Herefs.); Brilley *(Herefs.)*; Huntington *(Herefs.)*;
Michaelchurch-on-Arrow
RADNOR
Glascomb: Drewern, Vaynor-Glare; Colva;
Gladestry; **Radnor** - Llanvihangel-Nantmellan:
Trewern and Gwythla, Llanfihangel-Nantmelan
(part of); Llandegley: Llanfihangel-Nantmelan (part
of), Swydd, Graig and Tynlan; New Radnor; Old
Radnor: Old Radnor and Burlingjobb, Walton and
Womaston, Evenjobb, Newcastle, Barland and
Burfa, Kinnerton, Salford and Badland, Ednol,
Upper Harpton (part of), Lower Harpton *(Herefs.)*
PRESTEIGNE
Knill *(Herefs.)*; Presteigne: High-street and
St David-street, Broad-street and Hereford-street,
Discoed or Discoyd, Rodd, Nash and Little
Brampton *(Herefs.)*, Combe *(Herefs.)*, Lower
Kinsham *(Herefs.)*; Willey *(Herefs.)*, Stapleton
(Herefs.), Litton and Cascob (formerly in *Herefs.*);
Cascob: Cascob, Litton and Cascob (formerly in
Herefs.); Pilleth; Whitton; Norton; Upper Kinsham
(Herefs.); Byton *(Herefs.)*; Lingen *(Herefs.)*

71

KINGTON

Kington *(Herefs.)*: Old and New Kington, Both Hergests, Lilwall, Pembers Oak and Chickward, Barton, Bradnor and Rushock; Lyonshall *(Herefs.)*; Pembridge *(Herefs.)*; Stanton-upon-Arrow *(Herefs.)*; Titley *(Herefs.)*

604 **KNIGHTON**

KNIGHTON

Brampton-Bryan: Boresford and Pedwardine *(Herefs.)*, Brampton-Bryan *(Herefs.)*, Stanage; Leintwardine *(Herefs.)* (part of): Walford, Letton and Newton, Adforton, Stanway, Paytoe and Grange; Bedstone *(Salop)*; Bucknell *(Salop)*: Buckton and Coxall *(Herefs.*; Stowe *(Salop)*; Knighton; Heyop (part of); Llanvair-Waterdine *(Salop)*; Bettws or Bettws-y-Crwyn *(Salop)*; Llanfihangel Beguildy (part of)

LLANBISTER

Llanfihangel Beguildy (part of); Llangynllo: Lower Llangynllo, Upper Llangynllo, Heyop (part of); Bleddfa; Llanfihangel-Rhydithon (part of); Llandewy-Ystradenny: Llanfihangel-Rhydithon (part of), Mystyrrhoes-llowdy, Church; Llanbister; Llananno; Llanbadarn-Fynydd

605 **RHAYADER**

RHAYADER

Abbey-cwm-hir: Cefnpawl, Golon; St Harmon: Cenarth, Clase, Rhiwrhiad; **Rhayader** - Cwmtoyddwr: Dyffryn-Gwy, Dyffryn-Elan; Llanwrthwl *(Brecon)*

NANTMEL

Nantmel: Gwastedin, Maesgwyn, Coedlasson, Vainor; Llanfihangel-Helygen; Llanyre; **Cefnllys**; Llanbadarn-fawr

In BRECONSHIRE Districts:

599 BUILTH: Disserth; Llandrindod; Bettws-Disserth; Llansaintfraed-in-Elvel; Cregrina; Rhulen; Llanbadarn-y-Gareg; Aberedw; Llanvareth; Llanelwedd

602 HAY: Glasbury (part of); Boughrood; Llanstephan; Llandilo-Graban; Llanbedr-Painscastle; Llandewyfach; Bryngwyn; Clyro; Llowes

RADNORSHIRE prior to the act of 7 and 8 Vict c 61. Annexed to Radnorshire by the above named Act; viz:-
603 PRESTEIGNE: Litton and Cascob (in *Herefordshire* down to Oct 1844)
Detached from RADNOR by the same Statute; viz:-
602 HAY: Glasbury (part of) (annexed to *Brecon*)

ALPHABETICAL LISTING OF UNIONS
Note. This includes Welsh Unions formed after 1851.

Aberaeron, *Cards.*
Abergavenny, *Mon.*
Aberystwyth, *Cards.*
Abingdon, *Berks.*
Albans, St., *Herts.*
Alcester, *Warw.*
Alderbury, *Wilts.*
Alstonfield, *Staffs.*
Alnwick, *Nhmbd.*
Alresford, *Hants.*
Alston, *Cumbs.*
Alton, *Hants.*
Altrincham, *Ches.*
Alverstoke, *Hants.*
Amersham, *Bucks.*
Amesbury, *Wilts.*
Ampthill, *Beds.*
Andover, *Hants.*
Anglesey, *Ang.*
Arrington, *Cambs.*
Arundel, *Sussex*
Asaph, St., *Flints.*
Ash, *Surrey*
Ashbourne, *Dbys.*
Ashby de la Zouch,
  Leics.
Ashford, East, *Kent*
Ashford, West, *Kent*
Ashton, Long, *Som.*
Ashton under Lyne,
  Lancs.
Aston, *Warw.*
Atcham, *Salop.*
Atherstone, *Warw.*
Auckland (Bishop's),
  Durh.
Austell, St., *Corn.*
Axbridge, *Som.*
Axminster, *Devon*
Aylesbury, *Bucks.*
Aylesford, North, *Kent*
Aylsham, *Norf.*
Aysgarth, *Yorks. N.R.*

Bainbridge, *Yorks. N.R.*
Bakewell, *Dbys.*
Bala, *Merioneth*
Banbury, *Oxon.*
Bangor, *Caerns.*
Barnet, *Herts.*
Barnsley, *Yorks. W.R.*
Barnstaple, *Devon*
Barrow in Furness,
  Lancs.

Barrow on Soar, *Leics.*
Barton Regis, *Glos.*
Barton upon Irwell,
  Lancs.
Barwick(-in-Elmet),
  Yorks. W.R.
Basford, *Notts.*
Basingstoke, *Hants.*
Bath, *Som.*
Battle, *Sussex*
Beaminster, *Dorset*
Beaumaris, *Caerns.*
Bedale, *Yorks. N.R.*
Bedford, *Beds.*
Bedminster, *Som.*
Bedwelty, *Mon.*
Belford, *Nhmbd.*
Bellingham, *Nhmbd.*
Belper, *Dbys.*
Berkhampstead, *Herts.*
Bermondsey, *London:
  Surrey*
Berwick-on-Tweed,
  Nhmbd.
Bethnal Green, *London:
  Middx.*
Beverley, *Yorks. E.R.*
Bicester, *Oxon.*
Bideford, *Devon*
Bierley, North, *Yorks.
  W.R.*
Biggleswade, *Beds.*
Billericay, *Essex*
Billesden, *Leics.*
Bingham, *Notts.*
Birkenhead, *Ches.*
Birmingham, *Warw.*
Bishops Auckland, *Dur.*
Bishops Stortford,
  Herts.
Blaby, *Leics.*
Blackburn, *Lancs.*
Blandford, *Dorset*
Blean, *Kent*
Blofield, *Norf.*
Blything, *Suff.*
Bodmin, *Corn.*
Bolton, *Lancs.*
Bootle, *Cumbd.*
Bosmere, *Suff.*
Bosworth, Market,
  Leics.
Boston, *Lincs.*
Boughton, Great, *Ches.*

Bourne, *Lincs.*
Bournemouth, *Hants.*
Brackley, *N'hants.*
Bradfield, *Berks.*
Bradford(-on-Avon),
  Wilts.
Bradford, *Yorks. W.R.*
Braintree, *Essex*
Bramley, *Yorks. W.R.,*
Brampton, *Cumbd.*
Brecknock, *Brecons.*
Brentford, *Middx.*
Bridge, *Kent*
Bridgend, *Glam.*
Bridgewater, *Som.*
Bridgnorth, *Salop.*
Bridlington, *Yorks. E.R.*
Bridport, *Dorset*
Brighton, *Sussex,*
Brinton, *Norf.*
Bristol, *Glos.*
Brixworth, *N'hants.*
Bromley, *Kent*
Bromsgrove, *Worcs.*
Bromwich, West, *Staffs.*
Bromyard, *Heref.*
Buckingham, *Bucks.*
Bucklow, *Ches.*
Builth, *Brecons.*
Buntingford, *Herts.*
Burnley, *Lancs.*
Burslem, *Staffs.*
Burton-on-Trent, *Staffs.*
Bury, *Lancs.*
Bury St. Edmunds, *Suff.*

Caernarvon, *Caerns.*
Caistor, *Lincs.*
Calne, *Wilts.*
Camberwell, *London:
  Surrey*
Cambridge, *Cambs.*
Camelford, *Corn.*
Cannock, *Staffs.*
Canterbury, *Kent*
Cardiff, *Glam.*
Cardigan, *Cards.*
Carlisle, *Cumbd.,*
Carlton, *Yorks. W.R.*
Carmarthen, *Carms.*
Carnarvon, *Caerns.*
Castle Ward, *Nhmbd.*
Catherington, *Hants.*
Caton, *Lancs.*

Caxton, *Cambs.*
Cerne, *Dorset*
Chailey, *Sussex*
Chapel en le Frith,
  Dbys.
Chard, *Som.*
Cheadle, *Staffs.*
Chelmsford, *Essex*
Chelsea, *London:
  Middx.*
Cheltenham, *Glos.*
Chepstow, *Mon.*
Chertsey, *Surrey*
Chester, *Ches.*
Chesterfield, *Dbys.*
Chester-le-Street, *Dur.*
Chesterton, *Cambs.*
Chichester, *Sussex*
Chippenham, *Wilts.*
Chipping Norton, *Oxon.*
Chipping Sodbury,
  Glos.
Chorley, *Lancs.*
Chorlton, *Lancs.*
Christchurch, *Hants.*
Church Stretton, *Salop.*
Cirencester, *Glos.*
Clapham, *London:
  Surrey*
Clavering, *Norf.*
Claydon, *Suff.*
Cleobury Mortimer,
  Salop.
Clerkenwell, *London:
  Middx.*
Clifton, *Glos.*
Clitheroe, *Lancs.*
Clun, *Salop.*
Clutton, *Som.*
Cockermouth, *Cumbd.*
Colchester, *Essex*
Columb, St. Major,
  Corn.
Congleton, *Ches.*
Conway, *Caerns.*
Cookham, *Berks.*
Corwen, *Merioneth*
Cosford, *Suff.*
Coventry, *Warw.*
Cowbridge, *Glam.*
Cranborne, *Dorset*
Cranbrook, *Kent*
Crediton, *Devon*
Crickhowell, *Brecons.*

73

Sleaford, *Lincs.*
Smallburgh, *Norf.*
Solihull, *Warw.*
Southam, *Warw.*
Southampton, *Hants.*
South Manchester,
 Lancs.
South Molton, *Devon*
South Shields, *Dur.*
South Stoneham, *Hants.*
Southwark, *London:*
 Surrey
Southwell, *Notts.*
Spalding, *Lincs.*
Spilsby, *Lincs.*
Stafford, *Staffs.*
Staines, *Middx.*
Stamford, *Lincs.*
Stepney, *London:*
 Middx.
Steyning, *Sussex*
Stockbridge, *Hants.*
Stockport, *Ches.*
Stockton, *Dur.*
Stoke Damerel, *Devon*
Stokesley, *Yorks. N.R.*
Stoke on Trent, *Staffs.*
Stone, *Staffs.*
Stoneham, South,
 Hants.
Stonehouse, East,
 Devon
Stourbridge, *Worcs.*
Stow, *Suff.*
Stow on the Wold,
 Glos.
Strand, *London: Middx.*
Stratford on Avon,
 Warw.
Stratton, *Corn.*
Strood, *Kent*
Stroud, *Glos.*
Sturminster, *Dorset*
Sudbury, *Suff.*
Sunderland, *Dur.*
Sutton, *Sussex*

Swaffham, *Norf.*
Swansea, *Glam.*
Swindon, *Wilts.*

Tadcaster, *Yorks. W.R.*
Tamworth, *Staffs.*
Tarvin, *Ches.*
Taunton, *Som.*
Tavistock, *Devon*
Teesdale, *Dur.*
Tenbury, *Worcs.*
Tendring, *Essex*
Tenterden, *Kent*
Tetbury, *Glos.*
Tewkesbury, *Glos.*
Thakeham, *Sussex*
Thame, *Oxon.*
Thanet, Isle of, *Kent*
Thetford, *Norf.*
Thingoe, *Suff.*
Thirsk, *Yorks. N.R.*
Thomas, St., *Devon*
Thornbury, *Glos.*
Thorne, *Yorks. W.R.*
Thrapston, *N'hants.*
Ticehurst, *Sussex*
Tisbury, *Wilts.*
Tiverton, *Devon*
Todmorden, *Lancs.*
Tonbridge, *Kent*
Torrington, *Devon*
Totnes, *Devon*
Towcester, *N'hants.*
Toxteth Park, *Lancs.*
Tregaron, *Cards.*
Trowbridge, *Wilts.*
Truro, *Corn.*
Tunstead, *Norf.*
Tynemouth, *Nhmbd.*

Uckfield, *Sussex*
Ulverstone, *Lancs.*
Uppingham, *Rutland*
Upton on Severn,
 Worcs.
Uttoxeter, *Staffs.*

Uxbridge, *Middx.*

Wakefield, *Yorks. W.R.*
Wallingford, *Berks.*
Walsall, *Staffs.*
Walsingham, *Norf.*
Wandsworth, *London:*
 Surrey
Wangford, *Suff.*
Wantage, *Berks.*
Ward, East, *Westmd.*
Ward, West, *Westmd.*
Ware, *Herts.*
Wareham, *Dorset*
Warminster, *Wilts.*
Warrington, *Lancs.*
Warwick, *Warw.*
Watford, *Herts.*
Wayland, *Norf.*
Weardale, *Dur.*
Wellingborough,
 N'hants.
Wellington, *Salop.*
Wellington, *Som.*
Wells, *Som.*
Welshpool, *Mont.*
Welwyn, *Herts.*
Wem, *Salop.*
Weobley, *Heref.*
West Ashford, *Kent*
Westbourne, *Sussex*
West Bromwich, *Staffs.*
Westbury on Severn,
 Glos.
Westbury, *Wilts.*
West Derby, *Lancs.*
West Firle, *Sussex*
West Flegg, *Norf.*
West Ham, *Essex*
Westhampnett, *Sussex*
Westminster, *London:*
 Middx.
West Ward, *Westmd.*
Wetherby, *Yorks. W.R.*
Weymouth, *Dorset*
Wharfedale, *Yorks. W.R.*

Wheatenhurst, *Glos.*
Whitby, *Yorks. N.R.*
Whitchurch, *Hants.*
Whitchurch, *Salop.*
Whitechapel, *London:*
 Middx.
Whitehaven, *Cumbd.*
Whittlesey, *Cambs.*
Whorwelsdown, *Wilts.*
Wigan, *Lancs.*
Wight, Isle of, *Hants.*
Wigton or Wigtown,
 Cumbs.
Willesden, *Middx.*
Williton, *Som.*
Wilton, *Wilts.*
Wimborne, *Dorset*
Wincanton, *Som.*
Winchcombe, *Glos.*
Winchester, *Hants.*
Windsor, *Berks.*
Winslow, *Bucks.*
Winstree, *Essex*
Wirrall, *Ches.*
Wisbech, *Cambs.*
Witham, *Essex*
Witney, *Oxon.*
Woburn, *Beds.*
Wokingham, *Berks.*
Wolstanton, *Staffs.*
Wolverhampton, *Staffs.*
Woodbridge, *Suff.*
Woodstock, *Oxon.*
Woolwich, *London:*
 Kent
Wootton Bassett, *Wilts.*
Worcester, *Worcs.*
Worksop, *Notts.*
Wortley, *Yorks. W.R.*
Wrexham, *Denbs.*
Wycombe, *Bucks.*

Yarmouth, Great, *Norf.*
Yeovil, *Som.*
York, *Yorks. E.R.*